BUILDING WEALTH ON A DIME

BUILDING
WEALTH
ON A DIME

Finding your Financial Freedom

KIMBERLY HAMILTON

WILEY

For general information on our other products and services or for technical support, please contact our Customer Care Department within the United States at (800) 762-2974, outside the United States at (317) 572-3993 or fax (317) 572-4002.

Wiley also publishes its books in a variety of electronic formats. Some content that appears in print may not be available in electronic formats. For more information about Wiley products, visit our web site at www.wiley.com.

Library of Congress Cataloging-in-Publication Data:

Names: Hamilton, Kimberly, author.
Title: Building wealth on a dime : finding your financial freedom /
    Kimberly Hamilton.
Description: Hoboken, New Jersey : Wiley, [2023] | Includes index.
Identifiers: LCCN 2022039049 (print) | LCCN 2022039050 (ebook) | ISBN
    9781119900009 (cloth) | ISBN 9781119900016 (adobe pdf) | ISBN
    9781119900023 (epub)
Subjects: LCSH: Finance, Personal. | Wealth.
Classification: LCC HG179 .H2537 2023 (print) | LCC HG179 (ebook) | DDC
    332.024—dc23/eng/20220923
LC record available at https://lccn.loc.gov/2022039049
LC ebook record available at https://lccn.loc.gov/2022039050

Cover Image: © Zouls/Shutterstock
Cover Design: Ross Fishkind

SKY10037632_102822

Contents

Contents

Contents

Contents

Preface

It's 2012, and I'm 23 years old, sitting at a kitchen table I share with three roommates. We live in a row house in an up-and-coming area of Washington, DC, one of the most expensive cities in the United States.[1] I'm warned not to walk on the north side of the block, where my roommate got mugged earlier that year, but I love the neighborhood because it reminds me of New York City. There are plenty of families in the area, hole-in-the-wall restaurants, and a metro within walking distance. I had moved from New York just a few months earlier, and something about this place felt like home.

Most importantly, I could afford it.

My dinner isn't anything spectacular; some tomato zucchini stew I found on a random food blog. It sounded like a good idea because it was easy to make, and the ingredients were cheap. I cook most of my meals to try and save money, making exceptions on the weekends to go out with friends. We're all in our 20s and 30s, trying our best to make ends meet.

Most of us have significant debt – student loans and credit cards – but we don't talk about it. We do talk about almost everything else: our families, who we're dating, sex, politics, and so on. But money is hard to talk about when you don't have much of it, so the majority of us who *do* work hard but still feel like we need more . . . give us anything else to talk about. Ideally, something with the potential to make us feel good, because money is hard for a lot of Americans.

According to the New York Federal Reserve, as of 2022, Americans have over $890 billion in credit card debt, $1.59 trillion in student loans, and over $1.4 trillion in car payments.[2] Combined with almost $11 trillion in mortgage debt, we owe over $16.5 trillion. You could spend $1 million every single day for an entire year for 42,000 YEARS (!!) and *still* not reach that amount.

That's wild when you consider money touches almost every aspect of our lives. You'd think we'd all be better at it by now.

Unfortunately, despite all of our practice spending money, it's not something most of us are "good" at for a few reasons. For starters, personal finance isn't something most of us are taught at home or in school, in part because all of our teachers and families were likely trying to figure it out too. But that doesn't mean it's an impossible topic to learn.

In fact, it turns out, we all learn about money all the time – just not the strategic stuff.

Research by a group of psychologists at Purdue University found that children can grasp basic concepts about money at three years old and form habits about money by age seven.[3] This means that even kids can learn about money, but most don't . . . at least not in ways that are helpful. Even when adults talk about money, it's rarely about strategy or based on evidence because no one ever told us what we're supposed to do.

So none of my roommates and I, nor my family and I, ever had a conversation about how I was supposed to make it in this new city. It's almost December and I'm logging into my bank accounts because the grace period on my student loans is ending, and I have no idea how I'm going to pay them. I'm not even sure how much I owe – I think I blacked out once I learned it was higher than my salary.

Sometimes, the worst part about debt is stomaching the realization that you signed up for that credit card or that loan yourself. Even if you felt like it was your only option at the time, when hindsight is 20/20, it can be a little too easy to bring yourself down. I certainly spent a good chunk of time thinking that way.

I grew up in a middle-class neighborhood and my immediate family never struggled with money, but it wasn't something that was normalized or talked about either. I didn't have any debt during undergrad due to a combination of scholarships and family support.[4] It was my master's degree from an expensive private university that I willingly took on debt for, with zero concept of what it would mean to pay back.

Looking back, I had no idea what I signed up for; I thought I would magically pay it off. I had no experience working a full-time job and barely any credit history. I had no understanding of how interest works. As the first person on my mom's side to go to college (my dad had help from the military) there wasn't a lot of knowledge about student debt to be passed down. There was no warning or disclaimer. I just figured if everyone else did it, I could too.

Turns out it wasn't as easy as I had hoped.

My first job out of graduate school offered a $37,000 salary, and I negotiated up to $40,000 with the master's degree I was so proud of and indebted to. It was my dream field, but the salary was significantly lower than I had expected.

I owed about $44,000 in student loans, living in one of the most expensive cities in the country. The cost of living wasn't that much different from when I lived in New York, but that was during my debt-free glory days. Life with debt was a whole different story. Now, I can look back and realize my situation wasn't so bad – I was always able to pay bills on time and millions of other Americans have non-mortgage debt upwards of $100,000. But at the time, the idea that I had more debt than I would make in a year was soul-sucking.

Not my vibe.

So, I enter my password into Sallie Mae, a major student loan servicing company that would be my archnemesis for years to come. I try to remember the type of repayment plan I have, but there are too many options to recall anything specific. Given that over 35 million

Americans had student debt in 2012 (over 43 million in 2022), you'd think the process would be more straightforward.

It's not.

I have to go to a completely different website to find out what type of repayment plan I have.[5] Once I'm there, I check all seven: a "Pay as you earn" plan; a "Revised pay as you earn" plan; a "Graduated repayment plan" – still no – an "Extended repayment plan"; a "Income-contingent repayment plan" – again, no – and an "Income-based repayment plan."

That last one sounds right!

Except . . . $hit. I forgot to apply (I won't bore you with the details).

So, I'm left with the standard 10-year repayment plan. I *think*. I finally find a copy of my statement. I push my tomato zucchini stew away like I'm protecting it from something it's not supposed to see, and I take a deep breath.

I would owe $503.90 monthly for the next 10 years of my life. I'd pay the $41,000 I originally borrowed, plus over $3,000 worth of interest I incurred while I was still in school, and over $16,700 in additional interest over the 10 years – almost 50% the price of my original debt. That's an extra $19,700 in total I didn't sign up for.

(Or at least I didn't realize it.)

I think back to hearing the phrase "Do it on a dime" as a kid, meaning, do it on a budget. It always made sense to me. Why spend more when you can spend less? Even in my early 20s, I was never a big spender. I've always loved to travel, so I'd prioritize saving for that every year, but otherwise was pretty frugal.

Some friends and family might have called me "cheap."

In reality, I didn't have much of a choice. When over 25% of your income after rent is going toward debt, it forces you to be strategic.

I thought to myself, "How am I supposed to save for the future when I don't have anything left to build with?" This wasn't a DIY project, or a lemonade stand. This was my life.

Immediately, I panic. My minimum payments come out to $503.93 if I stick to the 10-year plan. It's about 20% of my take-home pay before I make rent or save anything (and my rent was cheap). Weren't your 20s supposed to be . . . glamorous? Or at least fun in a we're-all-scraping-by-together kind of way?

I didn't think I'd make a ton of money out of grad school, but I didn't think my life would be filled with financial anxiety either. I thought I'd be able to go out to dinner without feeling anxious about the bill. I thought I'd be able to go grocery shopping without trying to calculate how I could make a week's worth of lunch for under $20.

(The answer was a lot of rice and pasta. Good thing I'm Puerto Rican and Italian.)

So there I was: $503.93 a month and over $19,000 worth of interest to go. At that rate, I'd be 33 before I paid off my debt. I always thought I'd have a family by that time . . . "How the hell does anyone afford kids?" I think to myself.

Other thoughts that immediately follow:

"How will I ever buy a home?"
"How am I paying 50% more than what I took out?"
"I went to school for ECONOMICS, for Christ's sake!!!"

It was my first real taste of feeling like I had lost control of my own life, and it was my fault. I couldn't blame anyone else. I couldn't ask my family for help. I just had to sit with it.

It wouldn't hit me until a few years later, but eventually, I realized that just because your finances go off course doesn't mean you can't catch up. I knew very little about personal finance at the time, but I had one thing going for me: I was determined as hell. That attitude can be really helpful when you're up against a challenge and knocking out my debt would be my biggest hurdle yet. There's nothing like paying down a seemingly endless amount of debt when you're already broke to test your perseverance.

I wouldn't learn about debt payoff strategies until a few months later, but I decided that night that I would change. I was going to learn about money because I never wanted to be surprised like this again. And I was NOT going to eat tomato zucchini stew for the next 10 years, that's for damn sure.

It turns out the willingness to learn was all I needed to shift my financial trajectory on a dime. And how many dimes did I have to get started?

I owed almost 450,000.

■ ■ ■

Fast-forward just a few years and it's incredible how drastically your life can change when you decide to redirect it. When I first started paying off my student debt, I had a negative net worth of around −$42,000 and very little savings. I knew nothing about money or how to manage it, and I thought investing was only for the wealthy. But in a few short years, all of that would change.

In the next few months, I read and listened to anything and everything related to personal finance until my eyes glazed over. A lot of it was boring and filled with words I didn't understand . . . but from that education, I came up with a system to pay off my debt in three years and automated my finances to reduce financial stress. Looking back, I should have had other financial goals at the time, like building an emergency fund or investing for retirement, but I didn't. I just couldn't see past my student loans, so they became priority #1.

The thing about personal finance is you *really* don't know what you don't know. You learn things later – this still happens to me – and think to yourself, "I should have" or "I could have" . . . and it sucks. So, in reading this book and learning more about how money works, I hope you give yourself some grace to forget and forgive the past. You can always make changes from this point forward.

Ultimately, after three years of what seemed like an eternity, I successfully paid off my student loans and saved myself over $10,000 in interest. By negotiating my salary (multiple times) and learning to invest, I also doubled my income between 2013 and 2017, and put a down payment on my first home right before my 30th birthday. I had gone from more debt than I made in an entire year to buying a $345,000 home in just five years.

A funny thing happens when you become debt-free, particularly after paying down what feels like a mountain of it. While there are strategies in this book to pay down debt quicker and save hundreds, maybe thousands, of dollars in interest, implementing those strategies requires money – and I didn't have much of it back then. So the fact that I was able to pay down all of my debt? I thought there would be a big celebration. I thought everyone would congratulate me on this herculean effort. But in reality, it was incredibly anticlimactic.

I made my last payment, and nobody cared – but it was still a life-changing moment for me, and I want that same feeling of freedom for you.

The term *financial freedom* can mean different things to different people; it's up to you to define it. For some, retirement is the ultimate financial freedom. For others, being debt-free defines that moment. For me, it's when I finally felt like I was in control of my future. Coming up with a way to automate my finances got me 90% of the way there, but actually being debt-free took it to a new level. I no longer lived in a headspace where my debt framed every decision. Instead, I could let my own priorities make the call.

Before you keep reading, take a quick second to think about what financial freedom would mean to you. What's the first thing that comes to mind? How might you feel? Write it down to remember what you're working toward – use it as a bookmark, label it as an alarm on your phone, or stick a Post-it by the door. Your definition might even change as you read this book. But whatever it is, let it motivate you. It may be something that seems small to others, but that's okay. If you're up for it, email me your answer at hello@be-worthfinance.com. I'll be your biggest cheerleader.

As someone who now talks about money regularly, you probably think it's easy for me to forget the emotional toll of what life felt like when I was struggling to figure it out. In reality, it's like financial PTSD – and I don't say that lightly. I say that as someone who really believes your finances can have that much of an emotional impact. I say that as someone filled with empathy when someone tells me they feel helpless or frustrated because they don't know how to get themselves out of a bad financial situation. Today, my life is different – I'm debt-free (except for my mortgage), I have a higher income, and I'll likely have the option to retire early. But I remember what it's like to feel like I had no control at all.

I hope this book helps you take back the reins.

Building wealth doesn't happen overnight, but it is possible – even on a budget – with the right systems. In this book, I'll cover exactly what you need to do to gain confidence in your money – the mental shifts and financial strategies. As you read it, you'll meet characters like Claire, who is having trouble making ends meet in New York; Eric, who is thinking about starting a family in Portland; and Tanya, a first-generation college student in Chicago, hell-bent on setting a new financial bar for her family. All of them, like you, will have unique financial situations, incomes, and quirks. Throughout this book, you'll see how they apply different strategies to their own lives – and while your situation may be different, you'll learn to build wealth, too.

In Chapter 1, I break down six key habits I believe have accelerated my ability to build wealth more than anything else on my financial journey. You may be surprised to learn they have nothing to do with how much you make. I call them "million dollar habits."

Chapters 2 and 3 focus on identifying your money mindset and the changes you can make to improve your emotional relationship with money. These chapters will be particularly helpful for those who have negative emotions toward money or need help setting boundaries – for themselves or with others.

In Chapter 4, you'll learn to develop and implement an automated plan for your money, and set realistic goals. I call it the "Money Moves System" and hope it will do wonders in reducing your financial anxiety. Then, if it's applicable to you, I'll cover debt payoff strategies in Chapter 5.

Chapter 6 is where you'll learn to set a new financial baseline – the metrics you need to know and the mental blocks to look out for. This will help you track progress over time and evaluate any major financial decisions down the road.

In Chapters 7–9, you'll learn how to start investing and more importantly, how to be strategic – don't worry, I promise it's not as complicated as you think! America is filled with a ton of hardworking people; I want your money to work even harder for you.

Lastly, in Chapters 10–12, we'll cover homeownership, including as a potential wealth-building strategy. A lot of people see homeownership as an obvious step in their financial journey – I'm not one of those people. Instead, I think it's important to make an informed decision based on several factors you'll learn in detail, including the basic steps to homeownership and costs involved.

Ultimately, the money makers you'll read about in this book and the financial situations they experience are all very common – but they don't have to be complicated to solve. As you move through the chapters, you'll learn the small shifts in behavior that pack a big punch and combine them with the strategies you need to make the most of your money moves. Ultimately, what might seem like small changes your money now, will be transformational in the long run.

Let's start with a dime.

Notes

1. Jason MacCormick, "10 Most Expensive Places to Live in the U.S.," CBS News, April 5, 2013. https://www.cbsnews.com/media/10-most-expensive-places-to-live-in-the-us/.
2. Federal Reserve Bank of New York, Center for Microeconomic Data. (Original source: Federal Reserve Bank of New York Consumer Credit Panel/Equifax. https://www.newyorkfed.org/microeconomics/hhdc. Accessed September 4, 2022.
3. Beth Kobliner, "Money habits are set by age 7. Teach your kids the value of a dollar now," PBS, Making Sen$e, April 5, 2018. https://www.pbs.org/newshour/economy/making-sense/money-habits-are-set-by-age-7-teach-your-kids-the-value-of-a-dollar-now
4. I actually started at the University of Miami on a partial scholarship with Air Force ROTC but after two years and a medical discrepancy was deemed ineligible, and transferred back to the City University of New York (CUNY) City College for a fraction of the tuition. I saw no difference in the quality of education provided.
5. I had federal student loans, so I went to www.studentaid.gov, which is still the government's student loan website today, although you'll make payments through your student loan servicer.

Chapter 1

Million Dollar Habits

If you're anything like I used to be, the idea of having $1 million one day might seem impossible. My goal in writing this book is to reverse that way of thinking.

I titled this book *Building Wealth on a Dime* for a reason; because the power of starting small should not be underestimated. As you follow the strategies in this book, what might seem like small changes to your normal routine or way of thinking can make for million dollar habits later, setting you up for success long before you see it in your bank account. I hope to convince you that building wealth doesn't require an inheritance or starting a tech company, but instead can be a few pretty easy things that you do regularly over time.

Now, in the long run, you'll undoubtedly need to invest for your money to grow – there's no way around that. No one gets wealthy by paying off debt or saving their way to a million dollars; this also means you'll need to be strategic. Having money to invest is worthless if you don't have a system to allocate those investments or if you invest without any strategy. Want to set a bunch of money on fire? I didn't think so. Luckily, there are simple ways to reduce your risk and build wealth faster using the strategies you'll learn in this book – but none of that matters if you don't have the right mindset and system in place to get started.

In other words, laying the foundation is key, and that starts with habits and mental shifts you can implement right now, regardless of how much money you make, spend, or save. There's a common saying in personal finance that if you can't manage $100 or $1,000, you'll never be able to manage $1 million (or more). I firmly believe that. I also think it's why so many lottery winners go broke.

Don't be *that* lottery winner.

In this chapter, you'll learn the habits and mental shifts you need to lay the groundwork for your financial journey. Later in the book, you'll learn the specific strategies and systems you need to put it all together. Ultimately, I hope to convince you that your current situation is in no way predictive of your financial future – so long as you're willing to make a few key changes.

To guide you along the way, this chapter breaks down six million dollar habits – the six actions I believe have had more of an impact on the financial futures of myself and my clients than anything else (see Figure 1.1).

Figure 1.1   Million Dollar Habits

#1 Start small, dream big

#2 Don't compare yourself to others

#3 Automate and stay consistent

#4 Start with day 1

#5 Keep it real

#6 Invest early and often

I'll refer to these throughout the book and the stories of Claire, Julia, Eric, and others – but before we get there, here's a rundown on each habit.

No. 1: Start Small, Dream Big

If you're reading this book, you likely picked it up because (a) you want to improve your finances and (b) you're looking to start off small. You might not have an extra $1,000 lying around to invest or pay down your debt – most Americans don't. According to a 2022 survey by Bankrate, 56% of Americans couldn't cover a $1,000 emergency, but that shouldn't stop you from making progress where you can.[1]

Thanks to advancements in technology and financial policies it has never been easier to build wealth, starting with as little as $5 – I'll show you how in Chapter 7, Invest Early and Often. For example, instead of buying an entire share of a company that may be out of your budget, you could start with *fractional shares* now – meaning you can invest in just a portion of an individual share. This is something you *literally* couldn't do just a few years ago, so investing required a lot more money to get started. Advances in technology and finance industries have made the possibility of building wealth more accessible than ever before.

Now, as a proud New Yorker, I'll give it to you straight – will a $5 investment make you wealthy over time? No, it won't. But the habit of consistently investing that $5, accelerating your debt payoff, or automating your savings– those are game changers. That's why my top million dollar habit is to start small and dream big. You can start with low dollar amounts, build them into powerful habits, and become more aggressive as your income allows over time.

In other words, the ball is in your court in a way it's never been before – and starting small is one way to take advantage of the opportunity. While most of the other habits revolve around certain actions you can take, this first habit is a crucial mindset shift. You have to believe something is possible to truly be motivated by it.

So let's get into your wildest dreams scenario.

When I had close to $45,000 in student debt, all I could think of was paying it off. I was obsessive about it, I was anxious about it, and it became really hard to look past my debt. I didn't dream about the bigger picture; my brain wouldn't let me.

I want you to dream bigger than I did.

Once I did pay off all my debt, my universe expanded. Instead of thinking about my debt, I started thinking about my first $100,000 – then my next $100,000, then $500,000. Your life, too, can go from 0 to 60 once you get major obstacles out of the way – mental and financial.

The lesson here is don't wait until your next milestone to dream big. Instead, I want you to think 10 steps ahead of where you are today. This book isn't about paying off debt – it's about building wealth. Specifically, the knowledge and habits you need to build it. So focus on the possibilities and let them motivate you.

If paying off your debt gets you to 0, what would life at 100 be like? I want you to think outside the box. Go beyond your comfort zone. What is your wildest dream scenario, and what would that mean for your finances? And your life?

Get laser-focused on *that*.

Hello, future you!

Not sure if changing your habits will be enough to change your future? Let's find out! Visit www.futureme.org and write an email to your future self about how you hope to improve your relationship with money. You can schedule it to send it a year from now to compare how you feel now to actual progress. Include this reminder in that email to yourself: "P.S. send Kimberly an email at hello@beworthfinance.com to let her know how *Building Wealth on a Dime* changed my money habits." I'd love to hear from you!

No. 2: Don't Compare Yourself to Others

In a world filled with social media and a country fueled on credit, it can be a little too easy to compare yourself to others who seem to have it all together. It's human nature to look to others for clues about how we should act, and unfortunately, that extends to financial situations too. The truth is, a lot of people struggle or lack confidence when it comes to their money, even those who seem to have it all figured out. They can be homeowners but house poor and unable to afford much else. They can be doctors but owe $300,000 in student loans. Regardless of who they are, their financial situation is likely much different from yours, so don't waste time comparing yourself to others. Plus, it's very rare that you ever know the intricacies of someone's financial life.

As you work through this book, you'll determine what goals are possible for you and your unique situation – that will be your goal post. *That* is a money game you can win.

Focus on what makes sense for you. Forget all the noise.

No. 3: Automate and Stay Consistent

Automating my finances is hands down one of the smartest and most impactful money moves I've made. The biggest reason I recommend automating your finances is that it frees up a ridiculous amount of mental energy. Once you know your money is going to the right places, the rest comes down to math and time – and I'm not worried about that for you. Once you have the right systems in place, and you start to see results, you'll find a way to increase your savings and investments. Automating your finances will help put them to work.

The second reason I'm hell-bent on automating your finances is that it helps you be consistent and build wealth without even realizing it. In my experience, by automating my money in such a way that I was left with a weekly spending cap – you'll learn all about this in Chapter 4 – I quickly realized what I was comfortable spending and, therefore, what I could realistically and consistently contribute to my goals, month after month. As I paid off my debt and my income increased, what started as a 20% monthly transfer of my take-home pay toward my debt turned into a 40% investment contribution to build wealth. Not a single time did I manually write a check or initiate a transfer – I've simply updated the same system I set up almost 10 years ago.

Automating your finances will help you stay consistent. The confidence and discipline you'll develop simultaneously will help you build wealth.

No. 4: Start with Day 1

Maybe you've tried a budget before, but it failed.

Maybe you took on a good amount of debt before you knew what it was like to pay your own bills.

Maybe an emergency came along and knocked your finances off track.

It happens to the best of us. The important thing is that you're about to learn a whole new way of doing things, so forgive yourself for any past money mistakes and focus on what you can change from this point forward. Think of today as day 1 of learning to manage your money or day 1 of building wealth in a totally new way – one that isn't complicated and doesn't require a financial advisor. One that you own and control, day in, day out.

And as you do learn more on your financial journey, try to avoid feeling down because you didn't know some of this information earlier. It's an extremely normal response to wish you knew valuable information sooner. You may get angry or frustrated. Depending on your relationship with your family, it can be easy to wish that they had taught you more – but the truth is, they probably didn't have this information either. All you can do is learn as much as you can and do your best to implement those learnings now.

No one teaches this stuff and that's part of the problem, so don't focus on that. Focus on your trajectory. Focus on the financial life ahead of you. Focus on taking what you learn and knocking it out of the park.

Where was this stuff in school?

When I was in high school, even college, there was very little to any financial education formally provided in schools. I had one class where I vaguely remember learning how to manage a checkbook – in effect, how to spend money – with no memory of learning how credit worked, how to save, or invest. Luckily, the tide is changing. According to the Next Gen Personal Finance 2022 State of Financial Education Report, which surveyed 11,927 public high schools, passed legislation for guaranteed access to at least one semester's worth of personal finance courses increased from 5 states to 13 in 2022, with more states expected to add or improve legislation in the coming years.[2] That said, the study also found that outside those guaranteed states, access to personal finance education drops significantly in urban schools, schools with larger minority populations, and schools with lower income, where more students are eligible for free and reduced lunch programs. This further underscores the need for equitable access to financial education.

No. 5: Keep It Real

As a Latina woman working in the male-dominated fields of economics, finance, and tech, I've felt and can appreciate constraints, like the gender or minority pay gap, that keep people from making what would otherwise be considered fair, relative to their male, white counterparts. These are real issues that can and do limit the level of income some women and minorities are able to earn in their respective fields. That said, while I can empathize with those impacted by it, this issue is not the focus of this book. While I'll discuss some of these systematic problems in Chapter 2, ultimately, I'm here to help you make the most of what you *do* have and show you how to make it grow – which brings me to Habit No. 5, Keep it real.

When dealing with personal finance, most people have either one of two issues: (a) they're not making enough money to cover their expenses, or (b) they do make enough, but that money is allocated poorly, in the wrong order, or beyond their means. If income is the problem (issue a), then you have two options:

1. You can lower your expenses to increase the amount of money you have to go toward other needs or goals.

2. You can figure out a way to generate more income to keep the flexibility you have in your spending.

That said, most people in my experience suffer from issue b – which is really more of a management problem. This is where keeping it real, with yourself, is going to be important. While I'll teach you ways to save and be more strategic in how you manage your money, the system will fail if you're not being realistic about what you spend on a regular basis and how that compares to your income. This isn't to say you can't spend money on things you enjoy or like (or love), but rather, that you need to be aware and align your money to how you prioritize those things.

In reading this book, I encourage you to push any pride aside and take an honest look at your current money habits. Can you afford your current lifestyle? Are you a spender or a saver? Are you pretty disciplined, or might you want to build in a buffer to your checking account in case you overspend? The answers to these questions will help when structuring your budget and your money goals in Chapter 4. Remember that being realistic with yourself is crucial to a successful financial plan.

No. 6: Invest Early and Often

The last habit (and maybe the most important to building wealth) is to invest as early and as often as possible. As you move through your financial journey, you'll have to remember that building wealth takes time. While it won't happen overnight, the sooner you can start investing, the harder your money will work for you. This doesn't mean that it will take forever to see results – in fact, you may feel a lot closer to financial freedom simply by taking the actions in this book. But I also realize it's not the same as seeing a few extra commas in your bank account and I want you to have *all* the commas!

So let's talk about building wealth for a minute.

Like setting any goal, it's important to define what being wealthy would actually look like if you achieved it. Is it having a certain amount of money? If so, what's that specific amount? If you had it, how might you live life differently? And is the goal to be able to purchase something really extravagant or just the things that really make you happy? Maybe those two are related; maybe they're not.

In the 2021 Modern Wealth Survey, Charles Schwab surveyed 1,000 Americans and asked what dollar figure they would use to define someone as wealthy, what was needed for financial happiness, and what was needed to be financially comfortable.[3] Survey respondents were 9% Gen Z, 33% Millennials, 31% Gen X, and 27% Baby Boomers. On average, those surveyed reported "wealthy" to be around $1.9 million (see Figure 1.2).

How does that compare to what you had in mind?

Figure 1.2   Modern Wealth Survey

Average net worth...		2021
Needed to be wealthy		$1.9 M
Needed for financial happiness		$1.1 M
Needed to be financially comfortable		$624K

Adapted from: https://www.aboutschwab.com/modern-wealth-survey-2021

While your initial reaction might be – hell yeah, I'll take $1.9 million – the real answer is probably, it depends on who you ask.

Whether $1.9 million seems "wealthy" to you might depend on a few questions: When do you want access to those funds? How old are you? And what lifestyle do you want to live? If being wealthy means retiring at 60, living comfortably and being able to pass down some savings to family, then $1.9 million might do the job. On the other hand, if being wealthy to you requires owning a yacht – I'm totally guilty of this – and a high-rise apartment in New York City, then $1.9 million isn't going to cut it.

Regardless of how you define wealth, how soon you start is important. The is because compound growth helps you build wealth over time – the earlier you start, the more your wealth can grow (I'll cover this in detail in Chapter 7. Invest Early and Often). For now, using the $1.9 million example, Table 1.1 shows how much it would take at various timeframes to reach $1.9 million.

Table 1.1   How Much Does It Take to Get to $1.9 Million?

Years Till Retirement	Monthly Investment Required to Reach $1.9 Million	Years Till Retirement	Monthly Investment Required to Reach $1.9 Million
10	$10,887.28	40	$723.86
15	$5,994.40	45	$500.98
20	$3,647.35	50	$348.75
25	$2,345.47	55	$243.75
30	$1,557.41	60	$170.83
35	$1,054.94	65	$119.96

As you can see, the earlier you start, the less money you need to invest to reach the same amount. Now, some of you might look at Table 1.1 and think that you don't have enough time to build wealth. That's not necessarily true – depending on your target amount and time horizon, you may just have to invest more over time. You also don't have to start with $1,000 or $100 per month. You can start with $5 and increase the amount and frequency over time. This can be as simple as increasing contributions to your 401(k) or starting a taxable brokerage account – I'll cover both in Chapter 7.

Others might look at the chart and say, *this is crazy, no one has 65 years to build wealth in their lifetime.* The reason I put that in there is intentional – because families that are educated about money are setting up tax-advantaged investment accounts for their kids the day they're born, and sometimes even before they are born – so some people (not necessarily rich, but financially educated) have the benefit of those full 65 years, to use that money for their education, a home, or retirement. I'll talk about how to create generational wealth for your family in Chapter 9, but for now, I just want you to know that that possibility is very real if you understand the options available to you.

Bottom line: don't underestimate the possibilities or focus on how long it's going to take you – just get started as soon as you can. Building wealth takes time, and every day counts!

Summary

Way to go money maker, you've made it through the first chapter on million dollar habits! Here they are again at a quick glance:

1. **Start small, dream big:** Don't be afraid to dream bigger than your next milestone and chase after those dreams with whatever amounts you can handle toward your debt, savings, and/or investments. Every dollar counts.

2. **Don't compare yourself to others:** Forget the Joneses. Your financial journey is unique to yours; don't compare yourself to someone else's lifestyle or financial situation.

3. **Automate and stay consistent:** Automating your finances and staying consistent is key to building wealth. Don't worry, I'll teach you how to do this one!

4. **Start with day 1:** Forgive and forget any past money mistakes. Focus on what you can change and implement from this day forward.

5. **Keep it real:** It's important to be realistic when thinking about your income potential, spending habits, and goals. This will come into play in Chapter 4 when you build your budget and implement the Money Moves System.

6. **Invest early and often:** Building wealth takes time, so don't put it off. The sooner you invest, the harder your money will work, so invest as early and as often as possible.

In the next two chapters, you'll do some mental jiujitsu to reframe any negative mindsets you may have and hype yourself up for all the information you're going to learn later in the book. Remember, we're laying the groundwork first, and you'll execute it later. Each chapter from this point forward will have some work for you to do till you have a fully automated system to reach your goals by the very end.

Notes

1. Karen Bennet. "Survey: Less than half of Americans have savings to cover a $1,000 surprise expense," Bankrate, January 19, 2022, https://www.bankrate.com/banking/savings/financial-security-january-2022/.
2. Next Gen Personal Finance. "NGPF's 2022 State of Financial Education Report," https://www.ngpf.org/state-of-fin-ed-report-2021-2022/.
3. Charles Schwab Corporation. "Schwab Modern Wealth Survey reveals Americans' changing priorities around spending, saving and mental health," https://www.aboutschwab.com/modern-wealth-survey-2021.

Worksheet: Million Dollar Habits

Thinking a bit deeper about Habit No. 1, Start small, dream big, how do you currently define financial freedom? Is it a feeling or a number (or both) – and how would you describe it? Write your answer below so you can reflect on how your thought process may have changed at the end of the book.

How do you describe financial freedom?

_____

_____

_____

_____

_____

_____

_____

_____

_____

_____

_____

_____

_____

_____

_____

_____

Chapter 2

Plans Change – So Can Your Money

*M*eet Claire, a 28-year-old woman originally from Cleveland, Ohio, who moved to Brooklyn, New York, a few years ago to work for an environmental consulting firm. As a kid, she was always fascinated by the water, even if she'd only been to Lake Erie, and eventually went to school for marine biology. She wanted to conduct research on a tropical island but turns out those jobs are hard to come by. Never did she think she'd live in a city with 8 million people.

Claire's gotten used to the city's noise at night – it's actually hard for her to sleep without it now – and has become an expert in the subway over the years. She loves her job, indie films, and a solid rooftop bar. She feels like she's doing okay with her money, but also like she could be further along.

Claire makes $60,000 per year, takes home about $3,429 per month after taxes, contributes 2% of her annual income to her 401(k), and has $37,000 in student loans. She's responsible with her money but doesn't have a ton left after spending $1,550 per month for a small apartment she shares with a roommate. She makes the minimum student debt payment of $386 a month and has a few thousand dollars in credit card debt from an unexpected trip to the emergency room. She fell off a Citi bike and had health insurance, but the out-of-network ambulance cost $800, and she put part of the surgery for her collarbone on a credit card. She's been making the minimum payments for over a year, but it's taking forever. She can cover her monthly bills and go out every once in a while but wonders if she'll need to have a roommate for the rest of her life. She's given up on the *idea of saving for a home but would at least like to rent her own place one day – and NYC prices are no joke.*

Let's take a look at Claire's current expenses in Table 2.1. They're already in the budget format you'll learn in Chapter 4, which splits expenses into take-home pay, fixed expenses, goals, and variable expenses.

Table 2.1 Claire's Current Expenses

Claire, 28	Monthly Expenses
Brooklyn, NYC, $60,000 salary No emergency savings	2% to 401(k) (pre-tax) = $100 Employer match to 401(k) = $100
Take-home pay	$3,429
Fixed expenses: • Rent: $1,550 • Utilities: $75 • Phone bill: $50 • MetroCard: $127 • Subscriptions: $46	$1,848
Goals: • Minimum student loans: $386 • Minimum credit card payment: $102 • Vacation fund: $200	$688
$3,429 − $1,848 − $688 = $893 remaining for variable expenses	
Variable expenses: $893 • Groceries: $250 • Dining/drinks: $200 • Other transport: $50 • Entertainment: $125 • Fitness: $84 • Shopping: $84 • Personal care: $100	$893 = variable spending cap $893 ÷ 4.3 = $208 weekly
Total Budget:	$3,429

So, Claire's trying to tackle a few different goals here. She has some debt to pay off but doesn't want to give up things that are important to her (like her gym membership) and eventually would like to afford her own place – renting or otherwise. Claire knows she's not taking full advantage of the employer match to her 401(k) – she's only contributing half of what her employer is willing to contribute – but tells herself she has more time to catch up. Obviously, if she made more money then she could do it all, but she never planned to live in one of the most expensive cities in America, either.

In this chapter, I'll cover a few shifts Claire can make to speed up progress on her goals, even if life hasn't gone exactly as she planned. I'll also cover why this isn't an unusual experience for most money makers – particularly younger generations – who might feel like they should be further along with their money.

The Story No One Told You

Most of the time, when you ask someone whether, 10 years ago, they could have predicted how their life would turn out today, the answer is – not a chance.

We're often told a certain story about how our lives should go, ignoring all financial circumstances and obstacles along the way, and then when life doesn't go according to plan, we throw our hands up in the air.

Go to school, go to college, get a job (hopefully a good one), meet the right partner, get married, buy a home, have children . . .

Sound familiar?

In reality, not everyone follows this path, and the paths we do pave are rarely linear – they curve and branch out all over the place. People skip steps and do them out of order. Other people want an entirely different route – not everyone wants to get married or have kids. But regardless of where life leads you, money is involved every step of the way.

And yet, no one ever talks about money in that story.

For example, did anyone ever talk to you about what happens if you don't get the dream job? Or how you'll afford the home if you don't have a partner? What about how you'll pay for a medical emergency if you don't have insurance (or even if you do)? Did anyone tell you how expensive raising children would be? What happens to the white picket fence if someone loses their job?

On the flip side, I *wish* the story talked more about how people make their money! But I guess investing in low-cost index funds wouldn't make for a thrilling movie trailer – you'll learn all about investing in Chapter 8.

More often than not, the story we're told and the expectations we set for ourselves don't match up with reality. Instead, life has a way of surprising us – in good and bad ways. The good ways? Oh man, I love a good surprise! But the bad ways? They can be tough, emotionally and financially.

Sometimes, you end up in a city you never expected to live in. Sometimes, you graduate and don't get the high-paying job that's supposed to pay back your loans. It can be a lot harder to buy a home as a single person than it is with a partner. And even if life *does* go to plan, it's always a lot more expensive than it is in the movies.

Claire feels all of this (and you might, too) but she's not alone. Luckily, there are things you can do to make the most of what you have, even when life throws a curveball or two. Combined with the knowledge and systems you'll learn in this book, you'll learn to set and achieve new expectations of your own.

The Real Reasons Money Feels Tight

In the previous section, I discussed how the story we're told rarely talks about money, but expectations aren't the only reason money feels tight for Claire. Even though she has a steady job, Claire is up against stagnating wages, rising inflation, the student debt crisis, and skyrocketing home values – all very real reasons why "making it" may seem more difficult now than it did in previous generations, especially for millennials and Gen Z.

Now, full disclaimer, I am no economist – but I am a human being, and even at the risk of bringing you into the dark side of our current economy, I think these circumstances and challenges are worth mentioning before you learn what you can do to rise above them.

And there *are* things you can do to rise above them. Don't forget, as I mentioned in Chapter 1, it has never been easier than it is today to invest and make your money grow, so bear with me as I cover these circumstances and keep your eye on the prize.

In the meantime, before we dive into the strategies and information you can use to overcome these obstacles, let's dive a bit deeper into the circumstances that money makers, like Claire, are facing.

Inflation and Slowing Wages

You may have heard the term *stagnating wages* in the news or media before, but are you curious about what it really means?

Stagnating wages refers to when, even though incomes have increased over the years – for example, the federal minimum wage has increased from $3.10 per hour in 1980 to $7.25 in 2022 – that when adjusted for *inflation* or the fact that prices for everything else have gone up, those same wages haven't increased much at all.

Inflation is when the purchasing power of your money goes down, measured by what's called the *Consumer Price Index* (CPI), which accounts for certain consumer goods like the price of food, energy, clothing, rent, and transportation. Notably, CPI does not include the cost of owning a home or a mortgage, although it does estimate what an owner would have to pay to rent a similar home in the same area.

For example, what might have cost you $4.73 in June 1982 would be worth $10 today, 30 years later (in June 2022) – so in theory, you'd need to spend more to buy the same thing. To be clear, it's normal for inflation to go up 2 to 3% every year in the United States, but it's been on a tear lately – increasing in 2022 over 9% from the previous year alone. The issue isn't so much inflation in and of itself so much as it is when inflation rises steadily and we can't keep up because our incomes don't adjust at the same pace. Claire's definitely felt it in the price of groceries lately.

So, using CPI, economists can adjust wages to determine what they've actually been worth over time – and it's not a good look. According to the Economic Policy Institute, the federal minimum wage is now worth 27% less than it was in 2009, and 40% less than it was in 1968 when adjusted for inflation (see Figure 2.1).[1]

Yikes.

Figure 2.1   Minimum Wage Adjusted for Inflation, 1968–2022

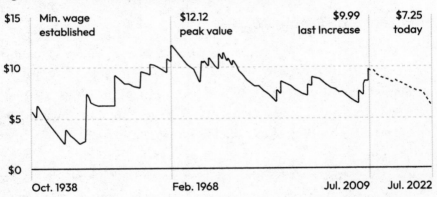

1968 Peak value of minumum wage

$12.12/hr ($25,210/yr)

2009 Last minimum wage increase

$9.99/hr ($20,779/yr)

2022 Today

$7.25/hr ($15,080/yr)

Source: Economic Policy Institute, https://www.epi.org/blog/ the-value-of-the-federal-minimum-wage-is-at-its-lowest-point-in-66-years/.

But what about money makers who make more than the federal minimum wage? Turns out, the situation isn't much better.

Figure 2.2 shows the (1) average, (2) median, and (3) real median personal income of Americans, annually, from 1980 to 2021. As opposed to the average personal income, which can be skewed by a bunch of high or low incomes, think of the *median personal income* as the middle point, meaning half the people make above and half the people make below that number; *real median income* simply means it's been adjusted for inflation.

Figure 2.2   Average, Median, and Real Median Personal Income, 1980–1921

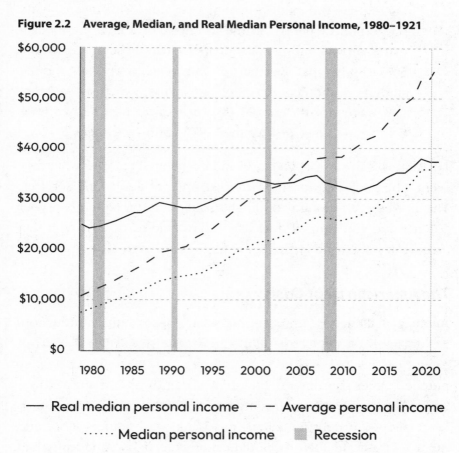

Source: U.S. Census Bureau, Federal Reserve Economic data. https://fred.stlouisfed.org/graph/fredgraph.png?g=TIQ7.

Shown this way, you can see two interesting things:

1. Looking at the real median income (the solid line), wages haven't stagnated, but they haven't gone up a ton since 1980, either. Compared to the median income in current dollars (the dotted line), when adjusted for inflation, you can see that real mean personal income has stayed relatively flat.

2. The gap between the average and median personal incomes is widening, with the average income being significantly higher than the median income over time. This means that a proportion of people in the top 50%, or above the median mark, are making significantly more than those in the bottom 50% to drive that average up. This matches up with another study from the Economic Policy Institute, which showed that real wages for the top 95–99% of earners have grown 80%, compared to just 28% for the bottom 90% of earners.[2]

All this is to say that increases in income aren't always what they seem when adjusted for the increased price of goods and services. This is why even though you might make more on paper than your parents did, you can still feel like you're able to do less with that income. It's not just a feeling – for some, it's a fact.

The American Debt Crisis

Another challenge worth covering, which needs little introduction, is the American debt crisis. For starters, the student debt crisis in America is no joke – over $1.59 trillion as of 2022.[3] That's a crazy number. Other consumer debt – think credit cards and auto loans – is even worse, with significantly higher interest rates designed to keep people in debt longer (to pay banks and lenders more and more interest). In total, excluding mortgage debt, Americans had almost $4.5 trillion worth of debt as of Q2 2022.[4] Taken together and combined with the 2008 recession that hit many millennials right out of college, and more recently, the pandemic, and it's no surprise that many millennials are struggling to catch up.

If you're looking to get out of debt more quickly, I'll cover your options in Chapter 5, including what to do if you can't keep up with your payments.

Political and Regulatory B.S.

Focusing on women and minorities in particular, money makers in either of these groups may feel like money is tight or that they're not "good with money" because they've had less access to it – legally and historically – not just in terms of income disparities but also in the ability to gain and learn from experience managing that income via access to bank accounts and investment vehicles. Women and minority groups have simply not had the same opportunities and protections to develop wealth that some of their nonminority male counterparts have had. For example, minority groups have been discriminated against in a myriad of ways throughout U.S. history, including by being denied access to credit – so much so that the Fair Credit Opportunity Act of 1974 disallowed this practice by banks on the basis of sex, race, color, religion, or marital status. Whether or not policies like this have always been enforced is another story. For example, in 2011, Bank of America agreed to pay a $335 million settlement after being accused of racial bias in home mortgage lending. To hit this from another angle, gender bias, women could not open a business bank account without a male relative willing to co-sign a business loan until 1988. So, in addition to stagnating wages, and the gender and minority pay gaps that still exist, certain groups have simply had less generational experience to learn what to do with their money, how to optimize it, and how to make it grow.

The Motherhood Penalty

In June 2022, the U.S. Supreme Court overruled *Roe v. Wade* – a decision that sent shock waves across the country, many appalled that women's reproductive rights could be so harshly reversed after nearly 50 years of protection. In light of this decision, unsurprisingly, many more women will end up having children, which will likely impact their economic mobility over time. Many mothers who cannot afford daycare will have no choice but to leave their jobs. Further, research has shown that women with children are less likely to be hired and promoted than women without children, directly impacting their income – it's called the Motherhood Penalty. Similar to the age gap, mothers are often paid 70 cents for every dollar paid to fathers, according to the American Association of University Women.[5] Lastly, the cost of raising a child from birth to age 18 was estimated in 2015 by USDA to be $233,610, but this number is wildly outdated. When updated for inflation, it's estimated to be $272,049.[6] Altogether, the ruling will make it more difficult for many women to build financial resilience than it has been in the past half-century. Low-income women and families will be impacted the most, making financial education more important than ever to help women and their families plan and react financially to life's unexpected moments.

Increased Home Values

While wages may not have kept pace with the rise in inflation or productivity over the years, many Americans still have improved their day-to-day lifestyles from 10, 20, or 30 years ago – whether that's in part due to an overreliance on credit or not is another debate. That said, despite our current lifestyles, it can be difficult for some money makers to feel like they're doing well with their money because their parents or grandparents bought a home in their 20s or 30s, and it's harder for you to pull off. This is where it's important to remember that CPI, as a measure of inflation, does not take into account the cost of purchasing a home. Instead, it takes the value of what it would cost to rent a similar home – which says very little about your ability to buy one. In other words, if wages adjusted for inflation considered purchasing a home, that graph we went over earlier would likely look even worse. In Figure 2.3, you can see that the average sale price of homes has more than tripled since 1990 alone. So, if you're like Claire and feeling down that you haven't been able to afford a home yet, this chart may help you understand why.

Figure 2.3   Average Home Sales Price, 1980–2022

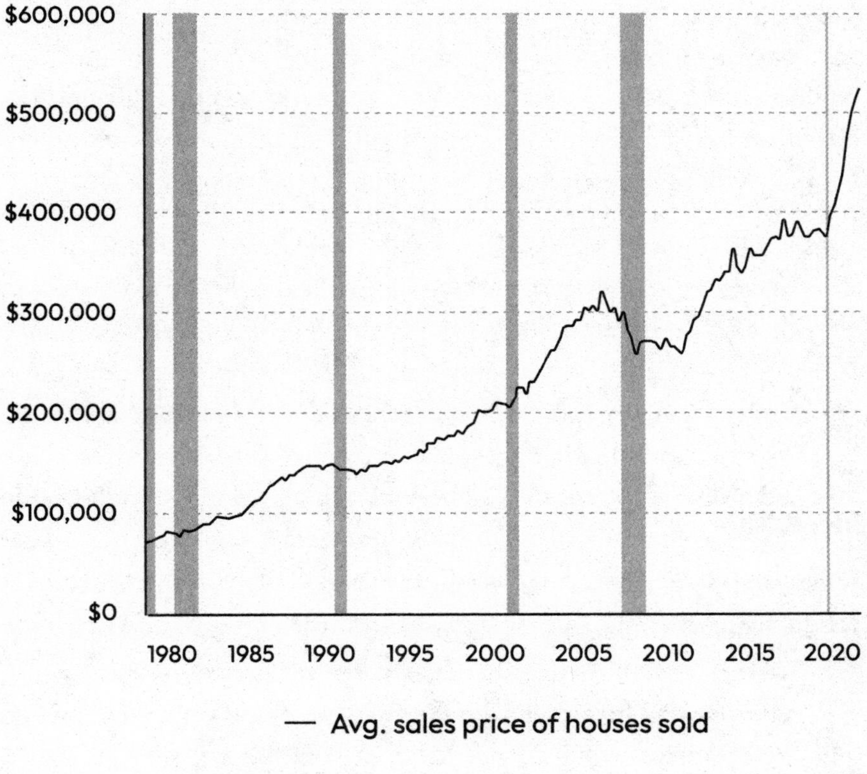

— Avg. sales price of houses sold

Source: U.S. Census, U.S. Department of Housing and Urban Development (HUD). Federal Economic Reserve data. https://fred.stlouisfed.org/graph/fredgraph.png?g=TIQ3.

Take all of these issues together, and it makes sense why Claire still feels like she's behind. Combined with a lack of financial education in America, and it makes sense why 34% of Americans suffer from financial anxiety[7] and other negative emotions I'll cover in Chapter 3. Luckily, by shifting her mindset and being more strategic about her money, Claire can shift not just her emotional state but also the state of her finances over time.

And you can, too.

Let's explore Claire's options.

A New Plan for Your Money

Claire knows she wants to make some changes to her money but isn't clear where to start. She wants to invest for the future and pay down her debt, but it's hard with so many competing priorities. Based on her situation, here's what I'd recommend. You'll learn how I came to these recommendations in the coming chapters.

- Claire doesn't have an emergency fund, but if she did, it could have helped her avoid taking on medical debt. Instead, she put it on a credit card where she has to pay *interest* or the money lenders charge borrowers when they don't pay their debt off in full. Moving forward, an emergency fund should be Claire's top priority to avoid taking on even more debt. She adjusts her spending to open up a high-yield savings account, contributing $83/month using an automatic transfer. It will take her a year to save her first $1,000, but at least she'll have something.

- Claire isn't taking advantage of the full *employer match* in her 401(k) – she feels like she has forever to do that, but meanwhile, she's leaving free money on the table. An employer match is when your employer offers to match your contributions to your 401(k) (or other workplace retirement plan) up to a certain amount. For example, let's say your employer offers to match 100% of your contributions up to 4% of your salary. This means that for every dollar you contribute up to 4% of your income, then your employer would match your contribution, adding another 4% and effectively doubling your investment – that's a 100% return on your investment (in this example). Claire should take advantage of it! So, before she goes beyond the minimum payment on her credit card, she increases her 401(k) contribution another 2% to meet her full employer match. Even if she never increased her contribution again (which she should, and I'll cover this in Chapter 7), that extra 2% plus another 2% from her match would make for $400/month total, growing to $487,988, inclusive of a $343,988 profit over the next 30 years.[8]

- Claire has $3,400 worth of medical debt that will cost her more in interest than anything she can safely make in a savings or investment account (except for that employer match, which is a 100% return). If she sticks to her current minimum payment of $102/month, it will take her over four years to pay off plus an extra $1,902 in interest.[9] She decides she wants to accelerate that as much as she can, which requires a few changes.

Claire *could* stop her gym membership but instead decides to reduce her spending on entertainment and personal care. She also lowers what she sets aside for vacation, deciding to do a staycation this year. In exchange, she'll keep her gym membership and can still go out to restaurants like normal. That said, because Claire wants to keep the majority of her spending the same, she temporarily picks up a side hustle for an extra $150/month after taxes. In total, these changes give her an extra $250 per month to put toward her credit card, which she sets up on autopay. She'll save over $1,500 in interest and pay the card off in 11 months just by going beyond the minimum payment.

Table 2.2 shows a before and after of Claire's budget with these changes:

Table 2.2   Claire's Money Moves

Before changes	After changes
$60,000/year salary	$60,000/year salary plus $150/month
2% to 401(k) (pre-tax) = $100 Employer match = $100	4% to 401(k) = $200 Employer match = $200
Take-home pay: $3,429	Take-home pay: $3,511
Fixed expenses: $1,848 • Rent: $1,550 • Utilities: $75 • Phone bill: $50 • Monthly MetroCard: $127 • Subscriptions: $46	Fixed expenses: $1,848 No change
Goals: $688 • Minimum student loans: $386 • Minimum credit card payment: $102 • Vacation fund: $200	Goals: $871 (increase) • Minimum student loans: $386 • Emergency fund: $83 • Minimum credit card payment: $102 • Extra credit card payment: $250 • Vacation fund: $50
Variable spending cap = $893 $893 ÷ 4.3 = $208 weekly • Groceries: $250 • Dining/drinks: $200 • Other transport: $50 • Entertainment: $125 • Fitness: $84 • Shopping: $84 • Personal care: $100	Variable spending cap = $792 (decrease) $792 ÷ 4.3 = $184 weekly cap • Groceries: $250 • Dining/drinks: $200 • Other transport: $50 • Entertainment: $75 • Fitness: $84 • Shopping: $83 • Personal care: $50
Total budget: $3,429	Total budget: $3,511

Claire still wants to live on her own at some point, but she has other priorities for the moment. Once her credit card is paid off, she resumes her vacation fund and quits the side hustle. She also plans on asking for a raise next year and hopes those additional funds might help her get a place of her own one day. She may also be able to lower her student loan payments, which I'll cover in Chapter 5. Tackle Your Debt.

While they may seem like small changes at first, Claire saves over $1,500 in interest on her credit card and will gain an extra $171,944 in her 401(k) over the next 30 years just from the extra 2% she put toward her retirement thanks to her employer match. She also has an emergency fund to support her if another financial surprise comes her way – and in the process, she's building million dollar habits by automating her savings and investment contributions. While life may not have turned out exactly how she thought it would, she knows she'll be able to attain her goals in the long run.

Summary

Despite the many real reasons why Americans– millennials, women, and minorities in particular – may struggle with money, the story doesn't end there. Just like Claire, you can make small changes that have a big impact on your financial picture over time. While life will always throw a few curveballs our way, with the right mindset and financial education, you'll be much more prepared to handle those situations to not only overcome any challenges, but also build wealth.

In the next chapter, I'll talk about what might be the hardest part of a financial journey for some money makers: how to shift your money mindset. Regardless of where you are in your financial journey, shifting your mindset to see the possibilities in front of you will be one of the most important steps you take – setting yourself up for all of the financial shifts that follow.

Notes

1. David Cooper, Sebastian Martinez Hickey, and Ben Zipperer, "The Value of the Federal Minimum Wage Is at Its Lowest Point in 66 Years,"

Economic Policy Institute, July 14, 2022, https://www.epi.org/blog/the-value-of-the-federal-minimum-wage-is-at-its-lowest-point-in-66-years/.

2. Lawrence Mishel and Jori Kandra, "Wage Inequality Continued to Increase in 2020," Economic Policy Institute, December 13, 2021, https://www.epi.org/blog/wage-inequality-continued-to-increase-in-2020-top-1-0-of-earners-see-wages-up-179-since-1979-while-share-of-wages-for-bottom-90-hits-new-low/.

3. Household Debt and Credit Report (Q2 2022), Center for Microeconomic Data, Federal Reserve Bank of New York, https://www.newyorkfed.org/microeconomics/hhdc.

4. Ibid. Table source: Federal Reserve Board of New York Consumer Credit Panel/Equifax.

5. "The Motherhood Penalty," American Association of University Women, https://www.aauw.org/issues/equity/motherhood/#Resources (accessed September 3, 2022).

6. Tim Park, "How Much Does It Cost to Raise a Child in the U.S.?" Investopedia, updated January 9, 2022, https://www.investopedia.com/articles/personal-finance/090415/cost-raising-child-america.asp.

7. Kendall Little, "Americans Are Just As Anxious About Money as They Were One Year Ago. Here's How to Manage the Stress," Next Advisor, *TIME*, August 5, 2021, https://time.com/nextadvisor/in-the-news/survey-americans-anxious-about-money-post-covid/.

8. Assumes a 7% annualized rate of return.

9. Assuming a minimum payment 22% interest rate, $102/month fixed payment, and minimum payment of 3% of the credit card balance.

Chapter 3

Money Mindset and Your Emotions

Meet Julia, a 25-year-old emergency room nurse born in the Bronx, New York, who moved to Raleigh, North Carolina, after being accepted into the nursing program at the University of North Carolina. A first-generation college graduate with a salary of $72,000, she already feels like she makes good money – definitely a lot more than anyone in her family has made before. Her parents split up when she was nine, and her mother still lives in New York with her brother and sister. Her mother works for a cleaning service, her brother is in high school, and her sister is in college studying civil engineering. Even though Julia worked hard for her nursing degree (and the commensurate salary), she sometimes feels guilty about having more than her family and frequently sends money back to support them (anywhere from $600 to $800 per month). She lives alone in a one-bedroom apartment, which she loves to fill with plants, even though she's not great at keeping them alive. They always cheer her up when she's had a rough week at work. Nursing isn't an easy job.

Julia has $48,000 in student loans and makes her monthly payments, although she expects the rest will be forgiven after 10 years through the U.S. Public Service Loan Forgiveness (PSLF) program. She has seven years to go and looks forward to the day when she's debt-free. She'd love to have a big house one day, but between helping her family and her student loans, she hasn't been able to save for *a down payment. "Maybe one day," she often thinks to herself. So far, she's managed to put $4,000 in an emergency fund, but doesn't have much else in the way of savings. She meets her employer's match, contributing 4% of her annual salary to her 401(k) but figures she has the rest of her life to work on retirement. She's just focused on her loans and her family right now.*

Let's take a look at Julia's current expenses in Table 3.1.

Table 3.1 Julia's Current Expenses

Julia, 25	Monthly Expenses
Raleigh, NC, $72,000 salary $4,000 emergency savings	4% to 401(k) (pre-tax) = 240 Employer match = $240
Take-home pay	$4,172
Fixed expenses: • Rent: $1,200 • Utilities: $80 • Phone bill: $50 • Car payment: $225 • Subscriptions: $56	$1,611
Goals: • Student loans: $449 • Emergency fund: $200	$649
$4,172 − $1,611 − $649 = $1,912 remaining for variable expenses	
Variable expenses: $1,912 • Groceries: $350 • Dining/drinks: $250 • Other transport: $75 • Entertainment: $80 • Shopping: $100 • Fitness: $100 • Gas: $200 • Family/not budgeted: $757	$1,912 = variable spending cap $1,912 ÷ 4.3 = $445 weekly
Total Budget:	$4,172

Julia is happy to help her family but supporting them can also be emotionally and financially draining. She wishes she had more funds to put toward her own lifestyle and goals. She'd like to save for a home and take a much-needed vacation but feels guilty whenever she spends money on herself – though she She does have a growing plant obsession. She thinks she probably spends too much money on them, usually around $100 a month between plants and supplies, but they make her happy when she's stressed out.

Julia has a lot of emotions regarding her money, and that's a common experience for most money makers. In this chapter, you'll do some mental jiujitsu to identify your own emotions and any mindset that may be hindering your ability to build wealth. I'll cover two types of mental roadblocks:

1. *Money mindsets* that influence how we think about money and accumulate wealth.

2. *Emotional spending habits* that influence how we manage our money in the short term or use money to avoid certain emotions.

Both are game changers when it comes to finding your financial freedom.

By identifying your mindset and emotional spending habits you'll be better prepared to improve your relationship with money and implement the six million dollar habits over time.

Your money mindset worksheet

To get started, use the Money Mindset Worksheet at the end of this chapter. Completing it as you move through the upcoming sections will help you to:

- Identify any mindset that might limit your ability to build wealth.

- Document any emotions (positive or negative) that influence how you use money in the short term.

- Determine a strategy to help you overcome any negative emotions or money mindset.

- Set a calendar reminder to revisit your spending habits 30, 60, and 90 days from now. Where did you succeed? Where did you struggle? What is holding you back, and how can you address it?

Emotions and Your Money

In 2019 I ran a workshop in Washington, DC, on emotions and money, and asked participants to share feelings they often associated with money. If you've ever experienced financial anxiety, some of the following terms may resonate with you.

Negative feelings about money	Positive feelings about money
• Shame	• Excited
• Guilt	• Motivated
• Sadness	• Free
• Helplessness	• In control
• Fear	• Making progress
• Confusion	• Abundant

- Judgment
- Complacency
- Undeserving
- Anxious

- Confident
- Worthy
- Proud
- Deserving

Many participants had both positive and negative associations with money, several of which weren't even tied to their current financial situations. For example, a lot of people in that workshop tied their negative emotions to childhood – observations about how their parents fought over money, constantly being fearful they might run out of money (even if they had sufficient income) or, interestingly, the reverse – being comfortable with debt because that was once the only option. They got used to growing up or living with it.

People have a lot of emotions when it comes to their money, in part because money ties to so many aspects of your life: your relationships, family, friends, social lives, education, income, daily needs, and things that simply make you feel good (or don't). The tricky part is identifying where those emotions stem from so that you can improve your relationship with money moving forward. To do so, I recommend three steps below, starting with Step 1: Identify your money mindset.

Step 1: Identify Your Money Mindset

Your money mindset is like a personality trait that each of us naturally brings to managing our money. Unlike the aspects of emotional spending that usually happen in a particular moment (covered in the next section), your money mindset is more a way of thinking – consciously or subconsciously – that can impact your financial future over time.

35

Take Julia from the opening story of this chapter. There are many emotions that contribute to why Julia spends the way she does – for example, she buys plants when she's stressed out – but that's very different from her money mindset as a whole. Her mindset is what drives her to take, or not take, certain actions. For example, in the short term, she's focused on immediate priorities like supporting her family. In the long term, she feels like she has the rest of her life to save for a home and invest for retirement, even though she would be better off starting as early as she can (Million Dollar Habit No. 6). Julia has what I'd call a *Someday mindset*. If she thought more long-term and was a bit more strategic, she could likely meet several goals much sooner, but she doesn't see the bigger picture.

Table 3.2 shows some of the common types of money mind-sets people have, in my experience. Find which one resonates with you most.

Table 3.2   Money Mindset Types

Mindset Type	Thoughts	How It Impacts Your Finances
You Only Live Once (YOLO) mindset	A budget is restricting. I live in the moment. I practice being present.	You resist allocating expenses and tend to make impulse purchases, as opposed to someone who might save up for an expense or comparison shops.
The "Someday" mindset	I have plenty of time to save or invest later. I'll catch up next year. I can only prioritize so much at one time.	By focusing strictly on what's in front of you, or looking short-term, you may fail to think about what you can do that can help yourself over time. You might be missing the bigger picture.
Abundance mindset	I see life as a glass half full. I believe that if I take specific actions, I'll achieve results. I feel like I can always make more money.	While this mindset is generally a positive one to have, you may skip certain milestones or safeguards that are in your best interest, such as establishing an emergency fund, because you're so confident that you can always make more. You might also take on significant risk.

36

Mindset Type	Thoughts	How It Impacts Your Finances
Scarcity mindset	I'm afraid of losing money. You can never have enough savings. Having more money makes me feel better or safe.	While having sufficient emergency savings and saving for specific goals are good, you might be missing out on the opportunity to make your money work harder by investing. You may hoard savings and have difficulty spending your money, even when planned for.
Overwhelmed	There's way too much information. Investing is overwhelming. I don't know where to start.	You avoid learning more about how money works, even though you're interested or want to tackle a problem, because it feels complicated. You're often intimidated by the unknown.
Status Quo	I'll never have a lot of money. I grew up with debt; it's no big deal. I'll be paying off my debt until the day I die. It is what it is.	You may not recognize the large impact that even small changes to your habits can make on your money. You may be complacent or scared of change, even if it's good.

By acknowledging your money mindset, you'll be in a much better position to make mental shifts that support your financial freedom and help you build wealth. For example, by acknowledging her Someday mindset, Julia can actively take steps to progress toward multiple goals at once, taking advantage of the time she has to save and invest sooner, putting more of her money to work.

> Reminder: Don't forget about your worksheet at the end of this chapter. Which mindset best matches your personality? How long can you remember feeling that way, and why do you want to change it? Write your answer in your worksheet.

Once you've identified the money mindset you relate to most, it's time to identify its root cause so you can shift any limiting beliefs. For example:

- Do your feelings toward money stem from how your family or the people around you spoke about money when you were growing up?

- Is it considered impolite or rude to talk about money in a particular way (or at all) in your family or culture?

- Does reaching a financial goal feel overwhelming? Or impossible? Perhaps it's prevented you from seeking help or learning about money to take smaller, more manageable steps?

- Do you feel guilty about spending money, even though you've worked hard to reach a certain income level?

- Do you feel anxious about spending money, even though you have sufficient income to do so?

- Do you feel like you need to "pay your dues"? Has it stopped you from progressing toward your own goals or asking for a raise that could accelerate you reaching them?

- Do you accept the status quo because it's all you've known to date? For example, you're comfortable with, or slow to tackle, debt because your family always "dealt with it" or "made ends meet."

Once you've identified where your mindset stems from, you should be in a better place to act. Table 3.3 includes a few examples that may be helpful depending on your mindset.

Table 3.3   Examples of Mindset Shifts

Mindset Type	Thoughts	Shift Your Mindset
YOLO mindset	A budget is restricting. I live in the moment. I practice being present.	→ A budget is a tool I can use to build wealth over time.
The Someday mindset	I have plenty of time to save or invest later. I'll catch up next year. I can only prioritize so much at one time.	→ I can set boundaries and goals that help me tackle multiple goals (within reason) at once. I don't have to limit myself to one or two.
Abundance mindset	I see life as a glass half full. I believe that if I take specific actions, I'll achieve results. I feel like I can always make more money.	→ By taking advantage of certain strategies, I can optimize my finances while also protecting what I already have.
Scarcity mindset	I'm afraid of losing money. You can never have enough savings. Having more money makes me feel better or safe.	→ Saving is a good habit but only to an extent. By learning to real-locate a portion of that to my debts or investing, I'll be able to build wealth more quickly over time.
Overwhelmed mindset	There's way too much information. Investing is overwhelming. I don't know where to start.	→ I'm going to learn more about money today. I already invest through my 401(k) at work; I can take it one step further. I'll start by investing in myself through learning about money in this book.
Status Quo mindset	I'll never have a lot of money. I grew up with debt; it's no big deal. I'll be paying off my debt until the day I die. It is what it is.	→ Even an extra $10 beyond my minimum payment will help over time. I may not be where I want to be right now, but I will be in a better position if I come up with a realistic plan today.

So which mindset do you have, and how might you shift certain behaviors to improve your relationship with money?

Regardless of your current mindset, it's important to note that even the smallest changes to your mindset or behavior can help. Unlike previous generations, the financial tools, and technologies available today allow us to track our finances more easily, save more quickly, and invest with a fraction of what was required to do so predictably in the past. Remember Million Dollar Habit No. 4, Start with day 1? Forget past money mistakes and start today. The path to wealth and financial freedom is wider than ever before, and even the smallest of mental shifts can help.

Keep in mind:

- **Your bank account is not a reflection of your worth:** How much debt you have or assets you have today is not a reflection of who you are or what you're capable of tomorrow.

- **You are not your peers:** Regardless of how your family, friends, or peers manage or accumulate money, aspire to follow your own path. Be the one that "makes it." Be the first. Be the one that educates others.

- **We all start somewhere:** A 2019 survey by Fidelity Investments found that 82% of all millionaires are self-made.[1] People change and excel in brand-new career paths well into their 40s and 50s. It's never too late to start learning about money, to build wealth, or pass down knowledge, but you need to be in the right mindset to accept that information first.

Hopefully you're starting to see the possibilities.

With Step 1 accomplished, it's time for Step 2: Tackle Your Emotional Spending, where I'll cover how to identify and react better to emotions that may influence your money in the short term.

Step 2: Tackle Your Emotional Spending

As mentioned earlier, people experience many different emotions regarding their money, both positive and negative. It's also a bit of a chicken and an egg problem – your emotions can influence how you manage your money, and how much money you have can influence your emotions (see Figure 3.1).

Figure 3.1   Emotional Spending Cycle

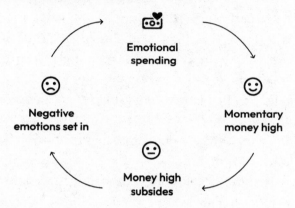

Other examples of emotional spending (or saving) include refusing to invest or put money in a bank because physically seeing your cash feels safer, spending too much money to fit in with friends, and buying something that doesn't actually make you happy.

Here are some common examples I've come across with clients:

- Booked a vacation you couldn't afford to avoid the fear of missing out.

- Said "screw it" and spent more than usual because you were stressed out or felt like since you were already in debt, "What's a little more?"

- Spent more than usual because you were excited to have visitors in town.

- Went into debt during the holidays because you felt guilty or obligated.

While these examples focus on negative emotions, positive emotions can impact your spending too. How many times have you bought something just because you were excited or felt like you deserved it? Good emotions can make us do things with our money too, not just the bad ones. This is not to say you can't treat yourself – quite the opposite; I think you should spend on what makes you feel good – but it's important to be intentional with your money. Ultimately, you want to hone in on the purchases or experiences that really make you feel happy and fulfilled, as opposed to a short-term solution.

On the flip side, it's likely not surprising that having more money can impact your level of happiness. In a 2021 study from the American Psychological Association of 1.6 million people across 150+ countries, having a higher income predicted more positive feelings, like confidence and pride, while having a lower income predicted negative feelings, like anxiety.[2]

Are you surprised? I didn't think so. Whoever said "money can't buy you happiness" may have been right – technically – but it can certainly buy a lot of things that make life enjoyable or, at the very least, more manageable.

What *is* surprising is that some studies show the income level to happiness ratio decreases after a certain point. The difference between $40,000 and $75,000 can have a tremendous impact on your emotional well-being. This makes sense, as a certain level of income is going to help you pay necessary expenses. But beyond $95,000, the corresponding increase in happiness starts to level off, according to a 2018 study from Purdue University.[3] In other words, money only makes you happy up to a point.

Whatever your emotions are when it comes to money, I assure you that they're completely normal. Even though most people don't talk about it, money impacts all aspects of our lives, so of course we're going to have emotions and feelings about it.

Remember Julia? Let's identify all the emotions influencing her money habits in the short term. Take another look at the paragraphs that introduced Julia at the beginning of this chapter. What words stick out to you?

Here's what jumps out at me:

- She's making "a lot" of money (she's comparing herself to others).
- She feels guilty whenever she's not supporting her family (supporting her family is fine, but she would benefit from setting some boundaries).
- She overspends a bit on plants because they make her happy when she's had a bad day (there's nothing wrong with buying something you like, but she would benefit from giving herself some boundaries here, too).

Maybe the emotions you feel are different, but it's important to identify what those are and how they impact your spending or saving. We all have emotions about money because we're human; the trick is working with those emotions and not in reaction to them. Sometimes, all it takes is a little structure. Other times, depending on how your emotions impact your money, you may want to eliminate a behavior entirely.

For example, if you tend to impulse buy when you're out because everything seems like a good deal or you're excited about something, you might: (a) consider waiting 48 hours to see if you're

43

still excited about the item, (b) remove yourself from email lists so you don't see sales you don't need, or (c) consider using an app to shop for only what you need at home, and get those items delivered or do curb pickup without having to shop around a particular store.

Target, anyone?

Julia wants to support her family but should also be able to spend on herself without feeling guilty. She, too, could benefit from some boundaries. Let's take a closer look.

- **What is the emotion:** guilt and/or obligation.

- **How this emotion impacts her money:** Julia's savings aren't where she would like them to be because she sends whatever extra money she has to her family. This prevents her from progressing on her goals.

- **The change:** Instead of sending whatever she has left at the end of the month, Julia sets a monthly goal. She thinks sending $5,000 to her family over the course of the year is a good amount. Divided by 12, that's $416/month. She factors this into her monthly budget, which leaves her with an extra $341 per month to put toward other expenses or goals. This way, she can still feel good about helping her family but also set some boundaries for herself. She realizes she'll be able to put a down payment on a home sooner than she thought.

- **The result:** Julia gives $5,000 to her family every year, while still making room for $100/month worth of shopping (probably plants) for herself while saving $250/month for a home.

Table 3.4 provides a few other examples that might be relatable to you.

Table 3.4 Setting Boundaries for Emotional Spending

Emotion	Impact	Action/Change	Result
Obligation or guilt *Example: financially supporting a family member, expectations for gifts around the holidays*	You feel negative about spending on your own goals, or maybe you spend too much on the expense you feel obligated about, leaving little for yourself.	Dedicate and transfer a specific amount of funds from your checking account to cover the obligation, while making sure there's enough room for yourself in your budget.	You're able to support the expense within a reasonable limit, so you can feel good while still covering your own needs.
Peer pressure *Example: overspending with friends*	When shopping or eating out with friends, you feel a need to keep up with their level of spending, or perhaps get embarrassed about the idea that you don't want, or can't afford, to spend as much.	Consider lower-cost activities, ask to split the bill before ordering begins, or get your friends involved, perhaps by agreeing to a monthly, low-cost activity that allows you all to save up for something a bit more fun or elaborate down the road.	Setting boundaries and expectations with your friends and family can help you from overspending in the moment.
Fear or anxiety *Example: shopping to avoid doing something you're anxious about or distracts you from a negative feeling*	Shopping can serve as a distraction from facing fears or anxiety in everyday life, but the feeling is often temporary and does not address the issue.	Consider other outlets or boundaries you can use to address this emotion. Is there an activity you can do instead to distract yourself like exercise or journaling? You may also consider a therapist to address the real concern.	Addressing the root cause and/ or finding a more productive or less expensive distraction can help pass the time when feeling anxious.

(Continued)

Table 3.4   (Continued)

Emotion	Impact	Action/Change	Result
Treating yourself *Example: spending more than your budget can handle because you felt you deserved it in the moment*	Spending money on yourself is fine so long as it's within your budget or variable spending cap (more on this in Chapter 4). The trick is not to go overboard, which can delay your progress on goals.	Treating yourself can be a good thing so long as you're in control of the situation. Instead of spending in the moment, implement a 48-hour rule or consider transferring funds to a bank account that you can use in the future, this way it's less impulsive but you still get to make the purchase.	Adding a bit more structure to how you treat yourself can still get you that dopamine rush you want without breaking the bank in the long run.

Using the worksheet at the end of this chapter, think through the top three emotions you have related to money and how they might impact your ability to build wealth. The goal is to identify feelings that impact your finances and be more intentional with your money moving forward.

Now that you've learned about some of the mindsets and emotions that could be holding you back, it's time to put that knowledge to work in Step 3: Take Action.

Step 3: Take Action

This section is all about confronting your money mindset and any potential emotional spending, including expenses that may not align with your values or make you feel negatively.

Don't know where to start? I suggest printing out your last credit card statement or using a personal finance app to track your expenses. Once you have two to three months' worth of expenses to reference, mark or highlight which expenses or experiences made you feel good in one color, and those that made you feel negative or weren't worth the money in another color. After a while, you'll start to recognize how certain categories of expenses align with your emotions or vice versa. Note them below.

List two or three expenses that made you feel good or contribute toward your goals:

1. _____

2. _____

3. _____

List two or three expenses that made you feel negative or weren't worth the money relative to other goals:

1. _____

2. _____

3. _____

Next, using your worksheet and the examples in Table 3.4, determine any boundaries you'll want to build into your budget or behaviors you might change, so you can feel good about where your money is going and how it's contributing to your goals.

Summary

Nice job, money maker! Doing the emotional work when it comes to your money can be harder than the financial side sometimes, so way to go for thinking through this section. As a quick recap, you learned:

- How to identify your money mindset and any beliefs that may be limiting your full financial potential.

- Which, if any, emotions may be negatively impacting your finances, whether that's by influencing how you manage or think about money.

- How to set boundaries and take action to improve your relationship with money in the long run.

Now that you've done the mental work, it's time to move on to your budget and something I call, the Money Moves System. This next chapter will take some effort, but I promise you, when it's all said and done, you'll be able to manage your money automatically and drastically reduce the financial anxiety that comes with everyday financial decisions.

I can't wait to see your money moves!

Notes

1. "The Intersection of Well-Being and Advice: Millionaire Outlook 2019," Fidelity, https://clearingcustody.fidelity.com/app/literature/item/9890298 .html.
2. "Income Robustly Predicts Self-Regard Emotions," American Psychological Association, 2021, https://www.apa.org/pubs/journals/releases/emo-emo 0000933.pdf.
3. A T. Jebb, L. Tay, E. Diener, and S. Oishi. "Happiness, Income Satiation and Turning Points Around the World," *Nature Human Behaviour* 2 (2018): 33–38, https://doi.org/10.1038/s41562-017-0277-0.

Worksheet: Shift Your Money Mindset

Reminder: You can download this and all other worksheets included in this book at www.wealthonadime.com/resources.

Step 1. Identify Your Money Mindset	
Which money mindset do you identify most with, and why? How long can you remember feeling that way, and why do you want to change it?	
How may that contribute in a good way to your financial future? What about in a negative way?	
Dive deeper. Where do you think your money mindset stems from? What about it would you like to change?	
Step 2. Tackle Your Emotions	
List the top three emotions you think of when it comes to your money. Can't think of any? Revisit the list at the start of this chapter.	
For each emotion you listed, why do you think you feel that emotion?	
Step 3. Take Action	
Based on the emotions you identified in Step 2, how might you work around them instead of reacting in the moment?	
List two or three expenses that made you feel good or contribute toward a goal.	
List two or three expenses that made you feel negatively or did not contribute toward a goal or were not worth the expense.	
What are some of the actions you could take regarding your finances that would help you address your negative money habits?	
What are some boundaries you may put into place to help you reach your goals – with yourself and with others?	
Set a calendar reminder to revisit this worksheet in 30 days. What emotions are you still struggling with? Do you need to rework any strategies?	

Did any of your emotions or the work here surprise you? I'd love to hear about it! Send me an email at hello@beworthfinance.com.

Chapter 4

Flip the Script on Budgets

Meet Eric, a 26-year-old living in Portland, Oregon, originally from Seattle, Washington. Eric makes $57,000 a year as an elementary school teacher and lives with his girlfriend in a rented, one-bedroom apartment. They talk about getting married and starting a family in the next few years, but for now, they enjoy watching Netflix and hiking on the weekends. Eric manages his money pretty well on a month-to-month basis, but planning a financial future feels like a whole different ball game. He wants to build wealth but doesn't know how to play his cards right. He feels good day-to-day but doesn't have any particular plan.

Eric grew up in a single-parent home where debt was normal; he accredits this to why he doesn't have any (except his car payment). After watching his mom struggle with credit card debt, he was determined to avoid the same path. He went to school on a partial scholarship and worked two jobs to cover his housing. Since graduating, he's never used a credit card that he didn't pay off on time and in full. But before he met his girlfriend, money was easy; he didn't think twice about going out with friends and probably spending a bit too much on drinks. But his expenses are different now. His goals are different. He's saving up for an engagement ring and gets nervous about the expenses that come along with having a child one day – daycare, college costs, and family vacations. He's not sure how all of them are supposed to fit into a system that makes sense. He wants money to be simple again but hates the idea of sticking to a budget.

Let's take a look at Eric's current expenses (see Table 4.1).

Table 4.1   Eric's Current Expenses

Eric, 26	Monthly Expenses
Portland, OR, $57,000 salary $3,600 emergency savings	4% to 403(b) (pre-tax) = $190 Employer match = $190
Take-home pay	$3,277
Fixed expenses: • Rent: $800 (his girlfriend pays the other half) • Utilities: $150 • Car payment: $280 • Subscriptions: $26	$1,256
Goals: • Engagement ring: $400 • Emergency savings fund: $300	$700
$3,277 – $1,256 – $700 = $1,321 remaining for variable expenses	
Variable expenses: $1,321 • Groceries: $250 • Dining/drinks: $300 • Other transport: $0 • Entertainment: $150 • Fitness: $90 • Shopping: $175 • Gas: $125 • Personal care: $25 • Not accounted for: ~ $206	$1,321 = variable spending cap $1,321 ÷ 4.3 = $307 weekly
Total Budget:	$3,277

Like Eric, many of us grow up thinking a budget is restrictive, complicated, or stressful. We assume that it involves allocating and tracking every nickel and dime, reminding ourselves of the things we can't have for the things we want later – and depending upon the type of budget you've tried, that might have been the case in the past.

Well, it's a new day, money maker!

In this chapter, you'll learn to change that. We'll follow Eric as he builds a new system for managing his money. You'll also learn:

- How to organize your expenses.
- How to set realistic money goals.
- How to build a budget that leaves you with only one weekly spending cap to track.
- How to automate all of your cash flows using what I call the Money Moves System.

By the end of this chapter you should have a fully automated system – a fool-proof plan – to reach your goals. Lastly, if hearing the word "budget" makes you cringe, then please don't call it that! Call it a *spending plan* or a *prosperity plan*. Call it your *path to wealth*. Call it whatever you want, but for the purpose of this chapter, I'll call it a budget because I like to keep things simple here.

What a Budget Should Be

At its core, a budget should be goal driven, simple, and seamlessly fit into your everyday life like any other habit you do on the reg.

Goal-Driven, Not Restrictive

The *real* purpose of a budget isn't to be restrictive – it's to help you reach your goals and live the life you really want.

Think of your budget as the MVP of your financial toolkit. While it doesn't have to be extremely detailed, your budget is a **necessary** tool to make sure you are consistently contributing to your goals – and what those goals are will be unique to you and your lifestyle.

When you think about it that way, the focus on your spending almost becomes secondary. It's not about how much you make; it's how much you can contribute toward your goals. Yes, they are related – your goals and your spending – but your goals should inform your spending, not the other way around. This is often referred to as the *pay yourself first method*.

By prioritizing your goals, your budget becomes a tool that *you* control to live your best life, whatever that life looks like to you.

- Does it involve your current or future family?
- Does it involve lavish vacations or events?
- Does it involve switching careers or starting a new business?

Let your goals guide you through this chapter.

Without a doubt, there is no way I could have paid off my debt or grown my investment portfolio without a budget – and if any finance professional tries to tell you differently, I wouldn't believe them. They may use a percentage instead of a dollar amount, they may use a budget that's extremely high level, but they still use something. When someone asks me how much I save or invest every year, I'm not guessing. I know it, in absolute terms, and can project where it's going to get me over time. That's the level of control and certainty a budget can provide you if you use it correctly. I want you to have that same level of confidence with your money.

The major takeaway I want you to have is that your budget shouldn't be restrictive or something that controls you. As you move through this chapter, *you* will determine your own budget and *you* will control it moving forward, not whatever spreadsheet or app you might use (though those can definitely help!). Stick to it, and your budget will be your compass as you continue to build wealth over time, regardless of where you're starting now. Don't forget your million dollar habits – start small, dream big, and start with day 1.

Simple, Not Complicated

The second thing a budget should be is simple. That's why when you finish this chapter, you'll have just one weekly or monthly number to track, depending on your preference. By bucketing your expenses into four main categories (income, fixed expenses, money goals, and variable expenses), you end up with one number to watch after all your fixed expenses and goals are already accounted for. We'll call this your variable *spending cap.*

Your spending cap is a magic number for your money – a key part of the system I used to pay down my debt and still use to manage my money today. Your spending cap will be a ceiling for all your variable expenses, and how you allocate it across those expenses will be up to you, so long as you don't go over it on a weekly or monthly basis.

Figure 4.1 is an example of what a budget and spending cap would look like for Eric based on his expenses.

Figure 4.1   Budget Example

🔘	Take-home pay	$3,277
🏠	Less fixed expenses	− $1,256
🐷	Less money goals	− $700
🏷️	= Variable spending cap	$1,321 monthly cap % 4.3 = $307 per week

In this example, based on Eric's take-home pay, fixed expenses, and goals, his spending cap would be $1,321 per month or $307 per week, depending on his preference – that's his magic number. You'll have one too. Then, by automating your expenses – I'll teach you how in Step 4 – it will be super easy to track your variable spending cap because everything else (you're your fixed expenses and money goals) will automatically be taken care of.

Together, I call it the Money Moves System, and it's been pure magic for myself and clients over the years.

By keeping things simple and automating your expenses, you cut out a lot of noise and anxiety that makes sticking to a budget so stressful and annoying. *Anyone* can set up a budget – sticking to it is the hard part. Using the Money Moves System, you won't worry about the day-to-day details because all your variable expenses will come from the same bucket. You'll just need to stick to your spending cap and you'll be good to go.

Now, will it take some effort to get your finances set up this way initially? Yes, it will. That said, better to do the work now and have a simple system moving forward than create more work for yourself and room for error in the long run.

So, do budgets have to be complicated? Not at all. Sometimes, less is more – it can be as simple as one number.

Habitual, Not Stressful

Let me be the first to acknowledge that sticking to a budget can be stressful when you're making a low income or paying off debt – even the easiest of things can be made difficult by tough circumstances. That said, the main point of this section is that your budget shouldn't and doesn't have to add to any existing stress. In fact, it can reduce it, but to say it would eliminate stress completely for those in already stressful situations wouldn't be fair to those trying to make ends meet. I do truly believe that situations can become more manageable and hope this chapter (and the book overall) helps those of you in tough situations to gain back a little more control in your lives.

The last thing your budget should be is something that's going to stress you out on the reg. This is why keeping your budget simple is so important; it's easier to automate, it's one less thing for you to think about, and it's much easier for you to stick to. By simplifying and automating your finances, managing your money can become habitual, like brushing your teeth or playing your favorite game. Most habits don't stress you out; they're just something you've learned to do over time; it's also what makes the bad ones so difficult to break! Much like a positive habit, your budget can play a huge role when it comes to your money, if it's set up to function with minimal effort – by automating it.

There is one catch though . . . your budget must be realistic based on your actual expenses. This part is going to take some work, but once you've done it, it's a seamless system. Don't worry, I'll walk you through each step in this chapter, complete with templates and worksheets to make it as easy as possible.

Now that you know what a budget should and shouldn't be, it's time to build your own.

Here's what you'll work through in the following sections:

- Step 1: Get Organized
- Step 2: Set Your Money Goals
- Step 3: Build Your Budget
- Step 4: Automate Your Money

As you move through each of the steps, we'll refer back to Eric, who was worried about how all the pieces and priorities of his money fit together. By the end, he'll realize it doesn't have to be as complicated as it might seem. And you will, too.

So what do you say? Let's get to work.

Step 1: Get Organized

One of the biggest favors you can do for yourself while building wealth is to be realistic about the goals you want to achieve and how your current spending is helping you get there (or not). It can be humbling to realize that some of your habits or expenses in the moment might be hindering the dreams you have for your future self, but it's a necessary evil– and you won't know exactly how much you're spending or saving toward your goals unless you get organized.

Repeat after me: To build wealth, you must have an accurate picture of how and when you're contributing to your goals. No one builds wealth by accident, but luckily, you can take small but mighty steps to get there.

Let's start with your spending.

If you ask a friend or family member how they allocate their spending, you might hear some of these common phrases:

- "I don't know where my money goes." This person admittedly doesn't know how much of their money is going where.

- "I probably spend [insert random guess] on food per month, give or take a bit." This person thinks they know how much they spend but are likely way off.

- "I save 20% of my income – it's the 50/30/20 rule." While rules of thumb like the 50/30/20 rule, where you budget 50% of your income toward needs, 30% toward wants, and 20% toward savings – can be helpful, 20% is a useless metric if it's not tied to an end goal. I have no idea whether this person is on track to reach their goals or not. It tells me nothing about their future financial life.

Statistically speaking, people are pretty bad at the specifics of how much they spend . . . but they may have a sense of where they are at a high level. For example, if someone is consistently spending over what they make, they generally know that. If you're in debt, you might even *feel* that. But for most people, the barrier to building wealth has nothing to do with what they spend on small purchases – it's that they don't know how much they're contributing to and progressing on their goals. When will they reach it? Do they even know what number they're planning to reach?

Most people don't – but you will soon!

What you spend on groceries versus gas money versus shopping doesn't matter so long as you know what you're contributing toward your debt, saving, and/or investing goals. When you think about it that way, building wealth becomes more of a money management issue and less of a far-fetched dream.

It's not how much money you make or where you spend it, but how you allocate it toward your goals. It's having confidence that a plan will *actually* work that gives you financial freedom from stress or anxiety, and the execution of that plan will build your wealth over time. For most people, financial freedom isn't a dollar figure – it's a feeling.

To get there, you'll start by getting organized. This involves splitting your finances into four buckets:

1. Net take-home pay (monthly)
2. Fixed expenses
3. Goals
4. Variable expenses

Each of these buckets should be based on your total monthly income and spending. Remember, while getting organized might be a little tedious at first, it's all with the goal of having one simple number to track at the end. So hang in there, money maker, and let's get to work.

1. Net take-home pay (monthly)

This is the amount of money you actually bring home every month, after any deductions that may come out of your paycheck like any pre-tax retirement contributions, income taxes, Social Security contributions, and health insurance premiums.

If you get paid monthly or twice a month, calculating this number is easy.

If you get paid every other week (bi-weekly), multiply your paycheck by 26 and divide by 12.

If you get paid weekly, multiply by 52 and divide by 12.

Bi-weekly paycheck: $2,400 × 26 = $62,400 ÷ 12 = $5,200 per month

Weekly paycheck: $1,200 × 52 = $62,400 ÷ 12 = $5,200 per month

If you have inconsistent income

The system I outline in this book is best suited for those who have consistent income, like a salaried position. If your income is inconsistent, things get a bit complicated, but not impossible! Instead of using a random month's take-home pay, you'll plug in a monthly *take-home pay* that you'll pay yourself – sometimes through your income, and sometimes through a mix of income and savings. It's called a *Hill and Valley Fund*, and I'll give you an example of how it works in the worksheet at the end of this chapter.

2. Fixed expenses

Fixed expenses include anything that stays the same every single month, like your rent or mortgage payment, car payment, and subscription services. While non-mortgage debt payments may also stay the same every month, like student loan payments, I suggest putting any non-mortgage debt under the next category – goals – in an effort to accelerate that debt payoff and build wealth faster.

Common fixed expenses include rent, mortgage, utility bills (okay if they fluctuate *slightly*), gym memberships, subscriptions, and monthly-based public transportation cards.

Find your fixed expenses

Not sure what fixed expenses you have in a given month? You have a few options:

1. Use a personal finance app to get your full financial picture. I recommend Rocket Money to not only build your budget but also to track your finances and wealth using their net worth feature. Full disclosure, I also work for Rocket Money at the time of this writing, but they are not affiliated with this book – I just recommend awesome products.

2. Look at your past three months' worth of bank and credit card statements. Highlight any fixed expenses in red and any variable expenses or goals in green.

3. Check your online bank account(s). The majority of major banks categorize your expenses for you as well – though they tend to not be as accurate as finance apps in my experience. Adding up expenses across accounts can also be tedious, but it is an option!

4. Categorize and/or monitor your expenses using an Excel spreadsheet or keep a money diary. A physical money diary will require a lot more manual math but will still get the job done for those not comfortable with online banking.

3. Goals

The next bucket of expenses in your budget includes your *money goals* and *sinking funds*. Throughout this book, I'll often reference them together as your goals but will break them down for this section.

Your *money goals* are financial milestones you want to achieve, like paying down debt or growing your investment portfolio. They're one and done. As part of Step 1, Get Organized, it's okay to keep these goals at a high level for now (no dollar amounts needed). In Step 2, Set Your Money Goals, you'll get specific about what your goals are, how you'd like to prioritize them, and the specific dollar amounts to contribute toward them on a monthly basis.

Sinking funds will also be part of this bucket, even though they may not feel like what we'd normally consider a goal. A *sinking fund* is a savings account that you set up specifically for revolving but irregular expenses. These are things you plan to spend on throughout the year, but not every month, and often include things like vacations, annual insurance payments, quarterly tax payments, holiday shopping, and gifts. Sinking funds are somewhat predictable, and even though you don't spend money on them every month, you should still budget for them. This is where you'll plan for such expenses so there's not a hit to your bank account later.

What are your non-negotiables?

When I work with clients one-on-one, I often ask them what their *non-negotiables* are so we can include one or two of them in their budget. Your non-negotiables are the expenses that are extremely important to you, so much so that you're likely to spend on them no matter what (separate from necessities, like food and shelter). For example, my two non-negotiables are taking two vacations every year and spending money on gifts, including never showing up to someone's house empty-handed – all those desserts and bottles of wine add up! What your non-negotiables are will be unique to you; my clients' non-negotiables have been all over the place, from making donations to their church to a random spice they like cooking with, to the latest iPhone. No one will know what your non-negotiables are but you, but once you identify them, you should plan accordingly, either as a sinking fund (if non-monthly) or appropriate spending category.

4. Variable expenses

The last bucket of expenses includes any expenses that vary month to month. Common variable expenses include variable transportation costs like gas and rideshare services (e.g., Lyft, Uber), groceries, eating out, personal care expenses, entertainment, and shopping.

Ideally, anything in this category will be covered by whatever dollar amount is left after you subtract your fixed expenses and money goals from your take-home pay. If that's not the case, I'll discuss what to do in Step 3, Build Your Budget but don't worry about it now. The important part in this section is that you understand how variable expenses differ from your fixed expenses and goals.

Now that you understand how these four categories work together, use the Get Organized Worksheet at the end of this chapter to categorize your expenses and note their respective accounts. For goals, estimates are fine at this stage – you'll work to refine them in Step 2: Set Your Money Goals. In Step 3, we'll put it all together, and in Step 4, we'll automate the entire system so it's one less thing you have to think about.

Feeling pumped about your money? I love when that happens! Let's keep going . . .

Step 2: Set Your Money Goals

Ready to set some money goals? This is my favorite part! In this section you'll specify the money goals you want to achieve as you build wealth, down to the date and dollar amount. We'll start at a high level and get more granular as we move through each of the sections.

Setting realistic money goals is a crucial part of finding your financial freedom because having confidence that you'll reach your goals is half the battle of reducing any anxiety associated with your money.

Progressing on those goals is the other half – you'll do that too, slowly but surely, with the methods in this book.

To get started, I suggest categorizing your goals by priority (high versus low) and type (financial versus other). Figure 4.2 presents a goals matrix of how someone might build out their goals across the four quadrants.

Figure 4.2   Goals Matrix

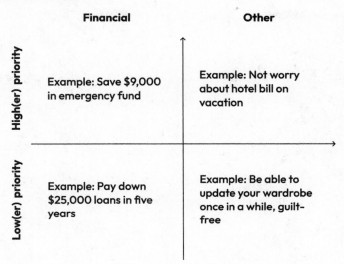

- *High-priority goals* may include things like setting up emergency savings, eliminating credit card debt, or saving for a home.

- *Low-priority goals* might include other savings goals like saving for a vacation, a luxury purchase, or something else that's nice to have (but perhaps not necessary).

- *Financial goals* are those more traditionally attributed to your finances, like saving for retirement or making a down payment on a home.

- *Other goals* are those that may feel more emotional or sentimental but very much relate to how you manage your money. For example, being able to go on vacation and not worry about the cost or holiday shopping without having to worry about paying off a credit card. Some of these will be addressed by sinking funds, others by changes to your monthly spending.

Using the Goals Matrix in your worksheet, list out any goals or sinking funds you'd like to include. If you know specific dollar amounts or dates, you're targeting – for example, to put $9,000 in an emergency fund in the next three years – then include that detail in the matrix.

If you don't know where to start or how to prioritize your goals, that's okay, too! Many people have several goals but prioritizing them against other priorities can be difficult.

Any of this sound familiar?

- How much should I save for an emergency?
- Should I pay down debt before I invest for retirement?
- I'm not sure where to start.

You're 100% not alone.

To help you get started, I've included a section on common financial goals, as well as a Goals Flowchart (see Figure 4.3) to help determine and prioritize your goals.

Lastly, in prioritizing your goals, consider how reaching them (or not) might make you feel. For example, imagine the freedom you'd feel if you paid off your debt, or how happy you'd be to afford a big trip with your family. Are there goals or the ability to pay for certain expenses that make you feel happy, accomplished, or fulfilled? Maybe there are expenses that don't make you feel that great, like a subscription service you don't use often or buying clothes you don't need. Keep these in mind as you build your budget moving forward.

Common Financial Goals

As I mentioned earlier, it is completely normal to need some help in figuring out your financial goals. While the exact dollar amounts and target dates will be unique for everyone, below are some common financial goals I recommend you have in your budget if applicable.

1. **Emergency savings:** Your emergency savings are important, not only so you can continue making progress on your goals, but also to prevent you from going into debt when an unexpected expense occurs. If it's something that can be more or less anticipated, like holiday shopping or a home repair every few years, include that as a sinking fund, not a goal.

   As a benchmark, I recommend starting with an initial goal of $1,000 worth of emergency savings before eventually working your way up to at least three months' worth of living expenses. Because of its importance, I recommend saving at least $1,000 before making any extra payments on your debt (still pay the minimum in the meantime) or investing beyond whatever your employer match is, if you have one as part of your employer-sponsored retirement plan, like a 401(k). Beyond that initial $1,000, I realize that three months' worth of living expenses is an enormous goal for most people, so don't feel like you need to conquer it right away, nor that you can't work toward other goals simultaneously – you totally can! But in the meantime, $1,000 will provide a buffer should the unexpected come along.

2. **Debt payoff:** Debt not only hinders your ability to build wealth, but it also impacts your credit score and debt to income (DTI) ratio. We cover both of these metrics in detail in Chapter 6. Your Full Financial Picture. For now, just know that both your credit score and DTI ratio are important because they impact what credit offers you may be eligible for moving forward, which can cost you more (or less) money in interest over time. That said, perhaps most importantly, debt can take a huge toll on your financial and mental well-being.

If your interest rates are above 7%, it can be really hard to build wealth, because that means your debt is growing faster than most relatively predictable investments in the stock market can. Further, debt payments mean you have less to save or invest for future wealth. For this reason, debt elimination makes a great goal, especially if you have any high-interest debt (any debt with an interest rate of 7–8% or above).

Because there are so many specifics to paying off your debt, it's okay to list this as a vague goal for now in your matrix. I'll revisit the specifics in Chapter 5. Tackle Your Debt.

Note: I don't include mortgage debt payoff as a goal so long as your interest rate is below 7%. Generally speaking, I consider mortgages a standard living expense, but if it's higher than 7%, then it starts to compete with the growth you could see in the stock market – at which point I might consider paying it down more quickly if you couldn't refinance for a lower rate.

Lastly, take a few seconds to imagine what paying off your debt would enable you to do. If you weren't spending money on your debt right now, what might you spend it on or invest in? If it meant you could build wealth – let's say reaching $1 million – years or decades earlier (which is possible), would you do it?

Before you forget, write down what you'd do here or in the Debt Warrior Question area below. It's also included in your worksheet at the end of this chapter.

Debt Warrior Question

Q: What would you do with your money if you were had less debt? How might you spend, save, or invest that money instead?

A: _____

_____

_____

_____

_____

3. **Invest early and often:** For many, saving for retirement is the ultimate long-term goal; but it's never too early to start. When it comes to building wealth, I can't say this enough: invest as early and as often as you can. If your workplace offers a retirement plan with an employer match, take advantage of that ASAP – that's free money your employer will give you so long as you contribute, up to a certain amount. Now, what most people don't tell you is that meeting your employer match or even maxing out your 401(k) (a $20,500 contribution in 2022) may still not be enough to retire on depending on when you start and how much you plan to spend in retirement. But investing early will get you significantly, exponentially closer to that goal.

All this said, investing is a goal I recommend any money maker include in their budget. If you want to build wealth, this is how you do it.

Not sure how much you need to save for retirement? Find my favorite retirement calculator from NerdWallet at www .wealthonadime.com/resources.

Note: The calculator will use, in part, your current income to determine what you need in retirement. It uses it as a basis to project what your *pre-retirement income* will be in the future, and estimates what you'll need from there. If you don't think you'll need quite that much in retirement (or maybe you'll want more to live large – I like your style), you can adjust this figure under the "Optional" section of the webpage.

Got a time machine?

I often get asked what my top money regret is or something I would have done differently if I had known more about money when I was younger. It's an easy answer for me. If I could go back in time, the top thing I would have done differently is invest earlier. While I always met my employer match on my 401(k), I didn't know for a long time that I should have gone beyond it – and I definitely didn't know I could invest on my own. I first started working when I was 16 years old. If I had understood just how much investing earlier would have helped me, I would have opened a Roth IRA the second I turned 18. I could have even asked my parents to open one up for me, called a *custodial account*, before I was 18 – maybe I would have contributed $100 here and there – but I didn't know those things existed. And I certainly didn't appreciate the power of starting early.

Today, I invest aggressively in hopes of being work-optional by the time I'm 45. It requires investing over 40% of my paycheck every month. Had I started when I was 16, it would have cost me a fraction of that. The point is, don't underestimate the power of starting to invest as early as you can.

4. **One-off savings goals:** The last category of common savings goals is *one-off savings goals*; things like saving for a new car, a wedding, or a down payment on a home. These are things you need to save for, but don't purchase frequently. Take Eric, for example. He's saving up for an engagement ring – that's a great example of a one-off savings goal, and different from a vacation he may want to take once or twice a year, every year, which would go in a sinking fund.

Lastly, in coming up with your goals, it can be helpful to look at your last few months of transaction history and highlight the expenses that made you feel amazing or relaxed, and those that you could have gone without. Consider prioritizing the former in your budget and reducing or eliminating the latter to help reach your goals faster.

I hope these recommendations are helpful as you start to map out your goals.

While figuring out your financial goals is one thing – prioritizing them is another. To help you do that, use the flowchart in Figure 4.3. It's also included in your worksheet.

Figure 4.3   Goals Flowchart

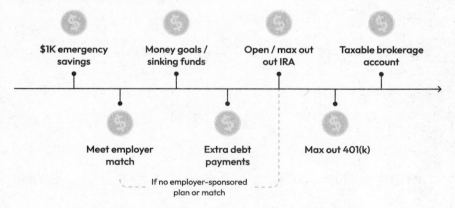

Note: Figure 4.3 assumes you're already making any minimum debt payments. **Don't forget:** Make sure to add any new goals to your Goals Matrix.

Determine Your "Other Goals"

Now that you have your financial goals mapped out, it's time to tackle the last bucket – your *other goals*. These are things you may associate more with emotions or wishful thinking, but upon closer examination, are very closely tied to your money.

Some examples of other goals might be:

- Wishing you had a car to spend less time commuting to work.
- Going on a vacation to reconnect with family.
- Being able to go out with friends at a moment's notice.
- Not feeling anxious when you purchase a gift.

Use Table 4.2 to list out three or four goals you might want to include in this section of your matrix.

Table 4.2   Your Other Goals

Something you'd like to be able to do (or avoid).	Estimate the annual expense associated with the item.	Estimate the monthly equivalent.	Does this relate to a fixed expense, variable expense, or goal?	Summarize goal: "Save/ Invest/Pay down [insert $] to [insert what you'd like to do or avoid].

Nice job! Now add them to your matrix from highest to lowest priority.

Now depending on the type of expense, you might address it through a one-off savings goal, a sinking fund, or your variable expenses. You'll make this determination in Step 3. Build Your Budget in just a bit!

The Money Moves Checklist

Congrats! By now, you should have already given some serious thought to your money goals, which is a huge part of finding financial freedom and building wealth over time, no matter your starting point.

But just to make sure you haven't missed anything, I've included a checklist in your worksheet at the end of the chapter to make sure you factor in a few high priority goals.

Feeling like you got everything? Amazing!!

Now it's time to put everything together – but first, take a minute to celebrate how far you've come! It takes effort to think about all the places you'd like your money to take you, so congratulations on mapping all of that out, at whatever level of detail you've been able to achieve so far.

Next, in Step 3, we'll put all your expenses together to figure out your variable spending cap. This will also help determine how realistic your goals are, so you can adjust as needed. Then, in Step 4, you'll automate everything so you barely have to think about it. I promise, all this detailed work will be worth it in the end!

Let's get to it.

Step 3: Build Your Budget

Note: To make this easy for you, I've included a Budget Worksheet at the end of this chapter, also available for download at www.wealthonadime.com/resources.

As a quick reminder, here's a recap of the four buckets you'll include in your budget.

- Net take-home pay (if you have inconsistent income, I've included a section in your Budget Worksheet to estimate this amount).
- Fixed expenses.
- Money goals (and sinking funds): I recommend starting with your top three highest-priority goals and seeing if your budget can work from there.
- Variable expenses (this will also be your spending cap).

Don't forget to include your one or two non-negotiables!

Next, you'll build your budget in two separate steps. First, you'll draft your budget and make sure it's realistic. Once you have that down, you'll calculate your weekly spending cap.

To assist in preparing your budget, use the Budget Template included in your Budget Worksheet at the end of this chapter.

Draft Your Budget

Use the following steps to draft your first budget. If you split finances with a partner, you may want to sit down and complete this exercise together as you reflect upon your expenses and priorities.

1. **Add up your expenses in each category** to arrive at the totals for each bucket. Feel free to use the template at the end of this chapter as a guide. For your fixed and variable expenses, you've already prepared monthly estimates in your Get Organized Worksheet, so this should be pretty easy. For your money goals and sinking funds, you may have to do some math to arrive at your monthly estimate by dividing any given

annual expense by 12. This will give you your monthly contribution.

> Note: I'll cover debt repayment in detail in Chapter 5. For now, include at least the minimum payments for all your debt under goals, plus whatever extra you may want to include. If you're not sure, I'll help you determine how much extra you'll want to include in Chapter 5.

2. Check those totals against the following equation:

Take-home pay – fixed expenses – money goals – variable expenses = 0

a. If you're at 0, perfect! This means everything fits, just make sure there's nothing you want or need to adjust based on your priorities.

b. If you're above 0, this means you have some extra funds to spare! I recommend accelerating your goals, but you may prefer to increase your spending – it's up to you!

c. If you're below 0, you're over budget and will have to make some changes.

Ideally, when you run the above formula, you'll either have some money left over or be at 0 – but in reality, this rarely happens on your first try. The downside of dreaming big is that you may not be able to fit all of your top-priority goals in your budget on the first shot. That's completely normal. If you're like most people, you'll have to adjust to get to that 0 balance. To prioritize your goals, I recommend seeing if you can reduce your expenses in the following order: variable expenses first (these are usually the most flexible) followed by your fixed expenses (these usually make the largest difference overall).

Million dollar habit no. 5: keep it real

It's important to be realistic when adding up your expenses and compiling your budget. Reducing your groceries to something that isn't feasible just to make your budget "work" won't do you any favors in the long run, so be as honest with yourself as possible.

Similarly, you ideally want all your goals to be specific, measurable, achievable, realistic, and time-bound (SMART). You may not have all the details right now, but they should be SMART by the time you're finished building your budget. If you need help, I've included an example of a SMART goal and table you can use to map your goals out in the worksheet at the end of this chapter.

If you've adjusted your budget and still can't get it to 0, you still have a few options:

1. You extend the timeline on your goals to reduce your monthly contributions.

2. You can lower the overall amount you hope to put toward each of your goals.

3. You can generate more income (I include a section on this below).

Now, depending on your income, developing your budget may force you to consider some tough questions like:

- How aggressive do you want to be in reaching your goals? Would you prefer to be a bit more flexible with your spending now, if it means reaching certain goals later? Or cut back on spending in certain areas to reach your goals more quickly?

- If, based on your budget, you're not tackling your goals as quickly as you'd like, are you willing to generate additional income? I include a few recommendations for negotiating your salary and side hustle ideas in Chapter 5.

- What expenses do you consider must-haves, and at what cost?

Notice my questions focus on your goals and must-haves – a.k.a. the things that are important to you. Personal finance is *personal*, so don't shy away from prioritizing what you care about, even if it might sound ridiculous to someone else. Now, that doesn't mean throwing all best practices out the window, but it does mean you have a lot of flexibility in choosing how to spend or save.

If you still can't fit in your goals or expenses, I recommend taking a second look at your major expenses (rent/mortgage, transportation, and food). These costs are usually the most expensive line items in a person's budget, so it may be worth considering moving into a less expensive home, or taking more public transportation, if it means reaching your goals more quickly. If you really love the fancy neighborhood you live in, that's cool too, so long as you're willing to deprioritize some of your other goals. Once you get your budget to 0 after accounting for all four buckets, then you can calculate your weekly spending cap.

Note: If you can't cover your expenses and/or are struggling with debt, I'll talk about your options in Chapter 5. Tackle Your Debt, which includes a section on credit counseling and debt management plans. Hang in there, money maker.

Calculate Your Weekly Spending Cap

Don't worry, this is the easy part!

By now, you should already have the monthly total for your variable expense category. To calculate your weekly spending cap, simply divide this number by 4.3. It's 4.3 and not 4 because some months have slightly more than 4 weeks, so that math wouldn't work out quite right. Dividing by 4.3 gives you an accurate target to stick to with your variable spending on a weekly basis.

You can also use the monthly spending cap if you prefer not to track your expenses weekly.

Regardless of whether you go with a weekly or monthly amount, you have complete flexibility to adjust amongst specific categories like groceries, eating out, shopping, and so on. So long as you stay within your cap, the rest of your budget should work pretty seamlessly – especially after you learn to automate it in the last and final step of this chapter.

For example, remember Eric? Table 4.3 shows how his expenses are plugged into the four-bucket system.

Table 4.3   Eric's Budget

Eric, 26	Monthly Expenses
Portland, OR, $57,000 salary $3,600 emergency savings	4% to 403(b)(pre-tax) = $275 Employer match = $275
Take-home pay	$3,277
Fixed expenses: • Rent: $800 (his girlfriend pays the other half) • Utilities: $150 • Car payment: $280 • Subscriptions: $26	$1,256
Goals: • Engagement ring: $400 • Emergency savings: $300	$700

Eric, 26	Monthly Expenses
$3,277 − $1,256 − $700 = $1,321 remaining for variable expenses	
Variable expenses: $1,321 <ul><li>Groceries: $250</li><li>Dining/drinks: $300</li><li>Other transport: $0</li><li>Entertainment: $150</li><li>Fitness: $90</li><li>Shopping: $175</li><li>Gas: $125</li><li>Personal care: $25</li><li>Not accounted for: ~ $206</li></ul>	$1,321 = variable spending cap $1,321 ÷ 4.3 = $307 weekly
Total Budget:	$3,277

Eric's weekly spending cap is $307 per week, but he also has $206 not accounted for in variable expenses. Ideally, he wants to put that toward something specific, so he starts a new sinking fund to put toward a vacation in the future. He's always wanted to go to hike Banff National Park in Canada. At that rate, he'll have $2,472 by next year he can use toward flights and equipment.

Third time's the charm

If you've never used a budget or tracked your expenses before, it may not be realistic based on your spending despite your best intentions, which means it may take a month or two to get it to a point where this system will actually work. That doesn't mean the system doesn't work. Rather, it likely means your estimates were off, which makes sense because most people have no clue how much they actually spend on various expenses. While this system is intended to be hands-off once it's working, you may need to

(Continued)

(Continued)

track some of your spending in the beginning so that you can adjust as needed. Trust me, it is really important to get this right before running on autopilot. Once your numbers are reasonable and accurate, that's when you'll start progressing toward your goals and feeling less anxious about your financial future.

Reminder: Don't move forward until your take-home pay, less fixed expenses, goals, and variable expenses is at or pretty damn close to 0. If you couldn't get it to 0, that means you're set up to spend more than you make in a month, putting you at risk for additional debt. Consider how you might reduce or change your expenses or generate more income to get to 0.

Step 4: Automate Your Money

All right money maker, how ya feeling? You've accomplished a lot in the last few steps to set up your budget, but if budgets alone were going to solve all of your financial problems, you likely would have done that already. The truth is a budget isn't enough. What you really need is a system that makes your budget easy to implement and stick to – and that's exactly what the Money Moves System is designed to do (see Figure 4.4).

The Money Moves System is simply a series of automatic transfers you'll set up to and from accounts over the course of the month, depending on how often you're paid. Figure 4.4 should be helpful in illustrating where your money goes throughout the month, although whether you use cash or credit to spend is up to you. Luckily, since you already know the totals for your four major buckets, this is going to be super easy to set it up. Simply follow the steps below.

Figure 4.4   Money Moves System

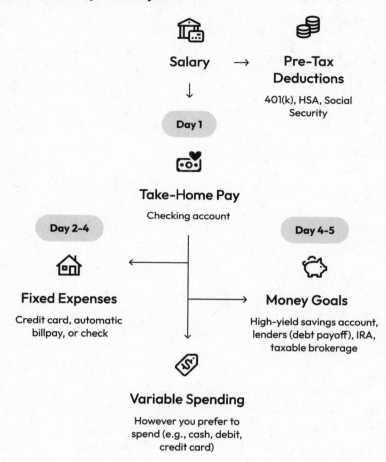

Direct Your Take-Home Pay

For your take-home pay, I recommend setting this up as a direct transfer to your checking account, though the system can still work if you're paid by check or in cash – simply deposit that into a checking account as soon you're paid. If you have the flexibility, ideally this will be before or around the 1st of the month.

If your payroll schedule doesn't fall on the 31st or the 1st of the month, you can start day 1 of the cycle as soon after you get paid.

Set Up Any New Savings Accounts

I recommend that you have at least two savings accounts, if not more: one for your emergency savings and one for everything else. Ideally, I recommend keeping several accounts and/or sub-savings accounts for two reasons:

1. It's much easier to track progress on each of your goals if they're separated. Want to know how much you have saved for that vacation? Just look at your dedicated vacation fund.

2. It becomes difficult to withdraw from one account for the wrong purpose. For example, you won't take money from your emergency account to pay for a birthday gift or pull from your car fund to pay for a dental emergency.

Several banks now offer sub-savings accounts including Ally (my personal favorite), Capital One 360, and Synchrony. I recommend using a high-yield savings account to get a higher return on your savings as opposed to the ridiculous .01% some of the big banks offer – I'm looking at you, Citibank. Using a high-yield savings account, depending on the market, you can get anywhere from 50 to 250x more interest, which can make a big difference in your money over time.

Change the Due Dates on Your Bills

To make sure you pay your bills on time and can easily track your variable spending cap, you may need to move the due dates on some of your bills. This can usually be done by contacting your lenders or subscription service providers and asking them to do so. I recommend scheduling these bills be paid on days 2–4 of your monthly spending cycle, as soon as possible after you get paid.

If using credit cards, so long as you're staying within your variable spending cap, you'll be able to cover any monthly charges consistently and in full. If you have trouble paying your credit cards, I'll cover this in Chapter 5, Tackle Your Debt, and offer a Quick Guide to Improving Your Credit in Appendix A.

Set Up Your Automatic Transfers

Now that you have your savings accounts in place, it's time to set up your automatic transfers. Your Get Organized Worksheet from Step 1 should be helpful here, listing all your different accounts, and the account and routing numbers where your money currently "lives."

Using this system, your fixed expenses will be paid or withdrawn from your checking account first, followed by transfers toward your money goals (and sinking funds), leaving you with your variable spending cap that you'll monitor in one of the following ways:

- If you use credit cards for your variable spend, you'll monitor your credit card balance (or use a personal finance app). If you prefer to make credit card payments throughout the month, as opposed to monthly, you may also monitor what's left in your linked checking account.

- If you use a debit card or cash for your variable spend, you'll monitor the balance in your checking account (or use a personal finance app).

- If you prefer to use cash, you can withdraw your weekly or monthly spending cap and track in that way.

Depending on your payroll cycle and whether you prefer using cash or credit cards, you may need to adjust when you transfer money toward your money goals, but this should not impact your weekly spending cap. For example, if you're paid twice a month, you may split the transfer to your money goals in two, contributing half after each paycheck. Remember, so long as any new credit charges for your variable expenses stay within your spending cap, you'll be able to pay them in full on a monthly basis.

So there you go, that's the whole system!

Now that you've learned how to set up your budget and automate your finances, all that's left is for you to put it into action. It may take a month or two to get things running seamlessly, but once they do, you'll be amazed at how easy it can be to manage your finances moving forward. You'll also be able to see progress on your goals more easily because they'll be in dedicated accounts. Once implemented, you'll likely notice a major reduction in your financial anxiety as you spend less and less energy managing your money, thanks to automation.

Using this same system, Eric no longer feels overwhelmed. He automated his finances and even moved his emergency fund into a high-yield savings account so he can generate more interest over time. It took him about two months to work out all the kinks – he originally underestimated how much he spends on gas, and adjusted his shopping budget accordingly – but now, managing his money is easy. He's automatically saving for his engagement ring, will have a fully funded emergency fund by the end of the year, and is already planning trip to Banff. So long as it's within his weekly spending cap, he can still buy a round of drinks for friends every once in a while, too. Table 4.4 shows the before and after in Eric's budget.

Table 4.4   Eric's Money Moves

Before changes	After changes
$57,000/year salary	$57,00/year (no change)
4% to 403(b) (pre-tax) = $190 Employer match = $190	4% to 403(b) (pre-tax) = $190 (no change) Employer match = $190
Take-home pay: $3,277	Take-home pay: $3,277 (no change)
Fixed expenses: $1,256 • Rent: $800 • Utilities: $150 • Car payment: $280 • Subscriptions: $26	• Fixed expenses: $1,256 (no change)
Goals: $700 • Engagement ring: $400 • Emergency savings: $300	Goals: $906 (increase) • Engagement ring: $400 • Emergency savings: $300 • Vacation fund: $206
Variable spending cap = $1,321 $1,321 ÷ 4.3 = $307 weekly • Groceries: $250 • Dining/drinks: $300 • Other transport: $0 • Entertainment: $150 • Fitness: $90 • Shopping: 175 • Gas: $125 • Personal care: $25 • Not accounted for: ~$206	• $Variable spending cap = $1,115 (decrease) $1,115 ÷ 4.3 = $259 weekly cap • Groceries: $250 • Dining/drinks: $300 • Other transport: $0 • Entertainment: $150 • Fitness: $90 • Shopping: 175 • Gas: $125 • Personal care: $25
Total budget: $3,277	Total budget: $3,277

Money can be complicated, but it doesn't have to be. It's a huge weight off Eric's shoulders, knowing all the different pieces and priorities of his financial life are working together.

Summary

In this chapter you learned how to organize your expenses, set realistic money goals, and not only build a budget but work it into an automatic system that affords you two major benefits: (1) a variable spending cap and (2) a major reduction in financial anxiety.

Now that you've got the system down, the remaining chapters in the book will focus more on investing and the strategies you can use to build wealth, even if you're starting small. The one exception to this is Chapter 5. Tackle Your Debt, if that's applicable to your financial journey.

If you don't have any debt, skip ahead to Chapter 6. Your Full Financial Picture.

Worksheet: Build Your Budget

Step 1: Get Organized

Use the following table to organize your expenses in preparation of building your budget in Step 3: Build Your Budget.

Reminder: You can download this and all other worksheets included in this book at www.wealthonadime.com/resources.

Goals Matrix

Use this matrix to prioritize your money goals. Include dollar amounts and dates where you can.

Make Your Goals SMART

Use this table to make sure any goals included in your budget are SMART (specific, measurable, achievable, realistic, time-bound).

SMART Category	Example	Goal 1	Goal 2	Goal 2
Specific	I want to save $12,000 for an emergency.			
Measurable	I want to save $12,000 over the next two years.			
Achievable	I will achieve this goal by saving $500 every month for the next two years.			
Realistic	This goal is achievable so long as I cut back on my gym membership and dining out.			
Time-bound	I want to achieve this goal in the next two years.			

Category	Monthly Estimate	How does money move in or out of this account? (e.g., checking, savings, card, cash)	Current Date of Deposit or Payment	Financial Institution	Account Number	Routing Number If Applicable
Monthly Take-Home Pay						
Job 1						
Job 2						
Side hustle						
Total monthly take-home pay						
Fixed Expenses						
Rent/ mortgage						
HOA						
Cable/Internet						
Utilities						
Insurance						
Cell phone						

Category	Monthly Estimate	How does money move in or out of this account? (e.g., checking, savings, card, cash)	Current Date of Deposit or Payment	Financial Institution	Account Number	Routing Number If Applicable
Subscriptions (e.g., Netflix)						
Money goals (list separately as needed)						
Savings account(s)						
Credit card(s)						
Loan(s)						
Variable expenses						
All variable expenses						
List any other accounts						

Debt Warrior Question

Q: What would you do with your money if you had less debt? How might you spend, save, or invest that money instead?
Write your answer here:

A: _____

_____

_____

_____

Other Goals Table

Something you'd like to be able to do (or avoid).	Estimate the annual expense associated with item.	Estimate monthly equivalent.	Does this relate to a fixed expense, variable expense, or goal?	Summarize goal: "Save/ Invest/Pay down [insert $] to [insert what you'd like to do or avoid].

Money Goals Checklist

- Do you have an emergency fund of at least $1,000?
- Do you have any high-interest debt you want to make extra payments on?
- Are you meeting any employer match you might have?
- If you don't have an employer-sponsored retirement plan, have you opened up an IRA? I'll go over all the retirement details in Chapter 7. Invest Early and Often.

- Do you have an emergency fund of at least three to six months of living expenses?

- Not sure if you're currently saving enough for retirement? Use my favorite retirement calculator from NerdWallet at www .wealthonadime.com/resources.

> Note: The calculator will use, in part, your current income to determine what you need in retirement. If you don't think you'll need as much in retirement (or maybe you'll want more to really live large), you can adjust this under the "Optional" area of the webpage.

- Are there any expenses that surprise you over the course of any given month or year? If so, include them as a sinking fund.

- Are there any activities or events you wish you could do more of over the course of a year? Might they be included as a sinking fund?

- Do you anticipate making any major expenses in the future? For example, for a down payment on a home or a wedding.

- If you have children, what expenses do you anticipate paying for them in the future? For example, a camp or college tuition?

Step 3: Build Your Budget

Use the budget template below to map out your expenses and calculate your totals for each major budget category.

Category	Yearly Estimate	Monthly Estimate
Monthly Take-Home Pay		
Job 1		
Job 2		
Side hustle		
Total monthly take-home pay		

Category	Yearly Estimate	Monthly Estimate
Fixed Expenses		
Rent/mortgage		
HOA		
Cable/Internet		
Utilities		
Insurance		
Cell phone		
Subscriptions (e.g., Netflix)		
Total fixed expenses		
Money Goals		
Standard: Swap out with your own goals		
Goal 1. Emergency savings		
Goal 2. Debt		
Goal 3. IRA		
Sinking funds:		
Goal 4. Vacation		
Goal 5. Other		
Total money goals		
Monthly variable spending cap (take home – fixed – goals)		
Weekly spending cap (monthly cap divided by 4.3)		
Variable Expenses		
Groceries		
Dining out		
Shopping		
Entertainment		
Gas		
Transportation		
Personal care		
Other		
Total variable expenses		
Remaining funds (aim for this to be "0")		

Budgeting with Inconsistent Income

Budgeting with inconsistent income can be hard, but it's not impossible. To find this number, estimate what you think you're going to make over the course of the year and divide by 12, keeping in mind any taxes that might be due if you're an independent contractor. Use this as your monthly take-home pay.

Now, because your income is inconsistent, some months you'll make more than this amount; other months less. Let's say your average is $5,000 per month. Anything you make above $5,000 per month, will go in a separate sinking fund we'll call a *hill and valley fund*. The idea is that over time, by building up that hill and valley fund, so for months where your pay is lower than your average "monthly salary," you can use money from your hill and valley fund to cover the difference. In months where you make more than the average, you'll transfer the extra to that account.

Visually, a hill and valley fund would look something like this:

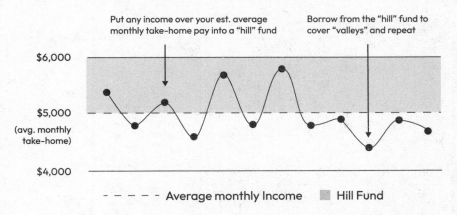

In practice, using a hill and valley fund would look something like the table on the following page.

Budgeting with Inconsistent Income

Budget	Jan	Feb	Mar	Apr	May	Jun	Jul	Aug	Sep	Oct	Nov	Dec
Take home	5,400	4,800	5,200	4,600	5,700	4,800	5,800	4,800	4,900	4,400	4,900	4,700
Fixed	2,000	2,000	2,000	2,000	2,000	2,000	2,000	2,000	2,000	2,000	2,000	2,000
Goals	1,700	1,700	1,700	1,700	1,700	1,700	1,700	1,700	1,700	1,700	1,700	1,700
Variable	1,300	1,300	1,300	1,300	1,300	1,300	1,300	1,300	1,300	1,300	1,300	1,300
Under (over) budget	400	(200)	200	(400)	700	(200)	800	(200)	(100)	(600)	(100)	(300)
Deposit to Hill and Valley Fund	400	0	200	0	0	0	800	0	0	0	0	0
Withdraw from Hill and Valley Fund	0	200	0	400	0	200	0	200	100	500	100	300
Total Hill and Valley Fund	400	200	400	0	700	500	1,300	1,100	1,000	400	300	0

Chapter 5

Tackle Your Debt

Unlike the other chapters in this book, based on fictional characters, I will use a real-life example for this one – my own. The dates, figures, and feelings I mention are real and have been fact-checked against bank statements, tax forms, and other financial records to the best of my ability. It was important that I share my story with you because while *now* I know that I was never alone in my financial journey, I felt very much alone back then – and I don't want anyone with debt to ever feel that way.

So, let's take a look at what my expenses were in December 2012, right when my student loans kicked in, using the four-bucket system (see Table 5.1).

Table 5.1   My expenses from December 2012

Myself, 24	Monthly Expenses
Washington, DC, $40,000 $3,500 emergency savings	4% to 401(k) (pre-tax) = $133 Employer match = $133
Take-home pay	$2,492
Fixed expenses: • Rent: $712 • Utilities: $125 • Phone bill: $0 (family plan) • Subscriptions: $25 • Metro pass: $0 (work benefit)	$862
Goals: • Student loans: $504 • Emergency fund: $120	$624

(Continued)

Table 5.1   (Continued)

Myself, 24	Monthly Expenses
$2,492 – $862 – $624 = $1,006 remaining for variable expenses	
Variable expenses: $1,006	Variable spending cap = $1,006
• Groceries: $150	$1,006 ÷ 4.3 = $234 weekly cap
• Dining/drinks: $200	
• Other transport/travel: $250	
• Entertainment: $25	
• Fitness: $0	
• Shopping: $130	
• Personal care: $50	
• ATM/uncategorized: $201	
Total Budget:	$2,492

While everything looks neat and organized in this table, in reality, this is before I got organized with my money. As a result, I often transferred money back and forth between accounts and used cash more frequently, which made my spending more difficult to track. Fortunately, in the few months between graduating and my loans kicking in, I was able to build a starter emergency fund. That said, I still had no idea where my money was going, making my $503.93 debt payment that much more intimidating.

Debt can be isolating, embarrassing, and anxiety-provoking. It certainly was for me at the time. I hope this chapter, combined with Chapters 7–9 on investing, will give you the tools you need to take some giant leaps forward and turn your debt from a taboo topic into a story of triumph.

■ ■ ■

You might recall my story from the start of this book when I was struggling to pay off my debt. When I first moved from New York to Washington, DC, I was making $15/hour at a consulting firm as an intern with a master's degree. While that internship eventually became a permanent position, my starting salary as a full-time employee was $40,000 per year. That's a lot less than what I thought I'd be making out of graduate school.

For everyone who says I had a master's degree and should have negotiated my salary, I did. The starting offer was $37,000, only three months after I declined a job I would have hated for $52,000. Life doesn't always go as planned.

While I realize a $40,000 salary would likely be a bit higher now, assuming employers have kept up with the rise in inflation, I'm also not afraid to admit that having more debt than I made in a year sucked. I imagine that having more debt than you make in a year is hard, no matter how much you make.

And just so you know where I stand, I don't think all debt is bad. I believe credit is an extremely useful tool when used properly and diligently. For example, student loans can drastically improve your career opportunities and the amount of income you can make over time. Credit cards combined with the right technology tools can help you keep better track of your money than using cash. You can also use credit card rewards points to pay for things like travel, exchange them for cash, or even pay off your student loans (true story, I did this with Citibank). You can use a mortgage to buy a home or to start investing in real estate in a way that would otherwise be impossible if you had to buy a property outright. And if you've ever spoken to someone who needs credit and can't get access to a line of credit, then I don't need to explain to you why credit is important.

Not sure if you should use credit for something? Ask yourself the quick set of questions in Figure 5.1.

Figure 5.1   Should You Use Credit?

Should I purchase this on credit?

☐ Is it in your budget?

☐ Can you pay it off in full?

☐ If an emergency, have you exhausted your emergency fund?

☐ If you can't pay it off in full, can you at at least meet the anticipated minimum payment?

Is it a good offer?

☐ Do you know the interest rate?

☐ Is the interest rate variable or fixed?

☐ What will the total payoff cost be when you include interest over time?

☐ Does it include an introductory offer?

☐ If so, what happens when the introductory offer ends?

☐ Are there fees to take out the new line of credit?

☐ Have you considered the repayment period?

Without a doubt, there are advantages to using credit, but they're not worth the pitfalls if you don't use credit responsibly, especially credit cards, which I recommend paying off in full every month. If you can't do that, and the expense is not an emergency, I recommend setting up a specific savings goal or sinking fund for whatever you're planning to purchase. Otherwise, you're essentially losing money on interest that you could be using to invest instead.

Lastly, it's worth noting that the emotional toll of using credit is usually worse for *unsecured debts* like credit cards, student loans, or medical debts. The major difference between *unsecured debt* and *secured debt* is whether or not they are backed by collateral – like your home or a car that can be taken from you in the event of nonpayment (see Figure 5.2). Unrelated to their technical definition, people often view unsecured debts as "bad debt," compared to secured debts, which most people are able to reframe in their mind as a regular living expense, like a mortgage or car payment.

Figure 5.2   Secured versus Unsecured Debt

Secured Debt	Unsecured Debt
Mortgage	Student loan
Auto loan	Credit cards
Secured card	Medical debt
Home equity loan	Payday loan

That's definitely how I felt about my student loans, especially when I didn't feel like my salary out of school matched what I had paid for my degree.

Looking back, I think the anxiety about my debt was less about my inability to pay it and more about the size of it. The *enormity* of it. It filled me with nothing but doubt. The thought that I would owe anyone $500+ a month for the next 10 years of my life was exhausting. It wasn't about the minimum payment – I knew I could take on extra side jobs if I needed to. The emotional toll came down to the size of my debt relative to my income: I had taken on almost $45,000 worth of debt – the original $40,000 plus interest that had accrued while I was in school.

So, in a magical world where even if I could put 100% of my paycheck toward my student loans, I still wouldn't be able to pay it off in a year. That idea drove me crazy – it gnawed at me, anxiously, like a nightmare where you know something bad is going to happen, but you can't quite wake yourself up yet.

"This is ridiculous." became a very frequent thought for me.

Under the standard 10-year repayment plan, my monthly payment was $503.93 or almost 20% of my take-home salary – closer to 25% after I paid rent. That was an expensive pill for me to swallow.

And it's tough for millions of other Americans, too.

Debt in America, particularly credit card debt and student loans, is a big, anxiety-producing problem. Including mortgage debt, Americans had over $16 trillion worth of debt in 2022.[1] To put that in perspective, you could spend $1 million a day, every single day, for over 43,000 years (YEARS!!) and *still* not reach that amount.

That is not a typo. The number is just *that* wild.

Here are some other newsworthy stats:

- Total American student debt: $1.59 trillion[2]
- Number of Americans with student debt: 45 million[3]
- Average American federal student loan debt: $37,358[4]
- Total American credit card debt: $89 billion[5] in Q2 0222[6]
- Average American credit card debt: $5,769[7]

Further, according to the Federal Reserve's 2021 Economic Well-Being of U.S. Households Report that surveyed 874 respondents, approximately 84% of adults had a credit card in 2021, and 12% were behind on their student loans.[8] So if you're struggling with debt, either because you hate that you have it, you wish you could pay it off faster, or you're struggling to meet your payments – you're not alone. Luckily, there are strategies you can use to get ahead. I'll cover them in three sections:

1. Develop your debt payoff plan.
2. Find extra money to pay down your debt.
3. Accelerate your debt payoff.

I also include an entire section on student loan repayment, as there are some nuances and plans specific to my student debt warriors out there!

As we go through each step, keep in mind Million Dollar Habits No. 1 and 4: Start small, dream big and Start with day 1. Like me, you may not have understood the impact of the debt you were taking on or had no choice but to rely on credit at the time. Don't fault yourself for that – all you can do is your best from this point forward.

So let's get to it.

Develop Your Debt Payoff Plan

In this section, you'll complete four steps to understand your debt payoff options and develop your debt payoff plan.

- **Step 1: Get the basics down:** You'll learn some boring but important terms (don't worry, there are only five!) to help you understand your debt payoff options.

- **Step 2: Know your numbers:** You'll get crystal clear on how much debt you have, where those balances are coming from, and your minimum payments.

- **Step 3: Consider your options:** You'll learn about a few options (debt consolidation, refinancing, and/or balance transfer) that might make repayment easier by either lowering your interest rate, your monthly payment, or both.

- **Step 4: Determine your payment:** Using your budget, you'll decide how much of a payment you can afford to make. Depending on what this is (below, at, or above your minimum payment), we'll determine the best way for you to move forward from there.

Step 1: Get the Basics Down

Here are those five (boring but) important concepts we have to get out of the way:

- **Principal balance:** The amount you owe to pay off your remaining debt, not including any interest or other fees.

- **Statement balance:** The amount you owe based on your last billing cycle, not including any pending charges. This is different from the *current balance*, which includes any new charges and reflects what you owe at any given time.

- **Interest:** What you owe the lender, in addition to the principal balance, for lending you money. You'll often hear the term *annual percentage rate* (APR), which reflects the interest rate and any fees you'll pay over the course of a year if you don't pay your debt off in full. APR relates to your debt, and the higher this rate is, the more expensive it is to borrow. This is not to be confused with *annual percentage yield* (APY), which refers to money you earn when saving or investing. In those cases, the higher the APY, the better.

- **Minimum payment:** The minimum amount you must pay to not be noted as "past due" with your lender or incur additional fees (but you'll still incur interest). Most often associated with credit cards, a minimum payment covers interest and a small portion of your principal balance. How it's calculated varies depending on your credit card or debt.

- **How debt works:** When paying down debt, any payment you make must first pay down any interest accrued before it can pay down the principal balance. This is why it can easily take years to pay off a credit card if only paying the minimum because most of a minimum payment goes toward interest (and credit cards use *compound interest*, which builds up very quickly). Other types of debt with fixed loan amounts, like mortgages and student loans, use something called an *amortization schedule*. This is a fancy way of saying you repay a debt over time using fixed payments, though the majority of those payments in the first few years *also* go toward interest. You can see an example of how this works using a fixed payment over time in Figure 5.3.

Figure 5.3   How Amortization Works

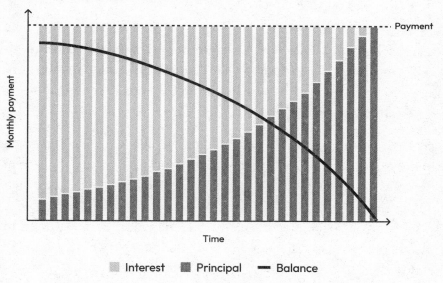

Using this example, you can see how it might take years to pay down a loan or build equity in a home. Unlike when you save or invest, interest is this scenario is your worst enemy. As a result, tackling your debt quickly requires going beyond the minimum payment, using one of two strategies I'll cover later in this chapter.

Now that you understand each of these concepts, the next step is to know your numbers.

Step 2: Know Your Numbers

To tackle your debt, you have to know the details about how much you have, including any balances, interest rates, and minimum payments. You can find this information in a few different ways:

1. Use a finance app that links all of your accounts to find your current balances. You may have to do a little digging to find precise interest rates.

2. You can collect your most recent statements from your various banks and/or lenders.

3. You can download a free copy of your credit report to view all reported balances. **I recommend this in addition to option 1 or 2** because it will catch any accounts you may have missed. You can get your free credit report at www .freecreditreport.com.

If you want to improve your credit, I include a quick credit guide in the Appendix. For now, your current action step is to simply hunt down any current balances, minimum payments, and associated interest rates.

Once you've identified all of your credit balances, you'll want to fill out Table 5.2, also included in your Debt Payoff Worksheet at the end of this chapter.

Table 5.2   Debt Info Summary

Lender	Total Balance	Interest Rate	Minimum Payment
Example: Debt 1: Citibank Card	$1,234	19%	$36
Insert any additional debt			
Insert any additional debt			
Total:		N/A	

Once complete, you should have an accurate view of how much you owe in total, your various interest rates, and the minimum payments due. Next, let's see if there are any actions you can take to make a big change to your debt upfront.

Step 3: Consider Your Options

Three actions you may be able to take to drastically change your debt payoff plan include debt consolidation, debt refinancing, or, for credit cards only, a 0% balance transfer. All of these are separate from any additional payment you may want to make on your debt to speed up the repayment process.

1. **Debt consolidation:** This involves taking out a new loan or credit card to pay off multiple existing debts, leaving you with one monthly payment that's a lot easier to track instead of having to deal with multiple minimum payments. Sometimes, but not always, debt consolidation can also provide for better terms (e.g., lower your interest rate). While you could do this on your own, there are also a few companies that can handle the process for you, from getting you approved to dealing with lenders. You can find my recommendations at www. wealthonadime.com/resources.

   Pros: Simplifies your monthly payment and might improve the terms of your offer (for example, a lower interest rate).

   Cons: Time required to pay off individual lenders if not using a debt consolidation service provider; doesn't necessarily reduce your interest rate or repayment term.

   For student debt warriors: If you have multiple federal student loans, you can consolidate them and keep your federal protections (e.g., income-driven repayment plans, public student loan forgiveness, etc.) by applying for a federal Direct

Consolidation Loan at https://studentaid.gov/manage-loans/ consolidation. While you *could* use a private lender to consolidate federal loans, I don't recommend it because you would lose those protections. If you have private student loans, that risk doesn't apply and you can use any lender you like.

2. **Debt refinancing:** This is similar to consolidation in that it involves taking out a new loan or debt to pay off existing debt, but while consolidation must involve more than one debt, refinancing can involve one or more. The lower interest rate is what you really want to decrease through refinancing, as this is what will save you the most money over time. If a lender offers to lower your monthly payment without lowering the interest rate, make sure to read the fine print. A lower monthly payment does not necessarily mean the interest is lower. For example, a lender could keep your interest rate the same, or even increase it, while extending the repayment period to decrease your monthly payment. Make sure to look at the total payoff cost of the loan.

If your priority is to build wealth, you want your interest rate to be as low as possible. If your priority is lowering your monthly payments to make managing your finances easier, then you might consider a longer repayment period in exchange for a lower monthly payment. The latter will cost you more money over time.

Pros: Simplifies your payment, can lower the amount of interest you pay over time (read: keep more of your money to build wealth) and might lower your monthly payment overall.

Cons: A lower interest rate is not guaranteed and may prolong your repayment period depending on the terms.

For student debt warriors: Refinancing your student loans will require using a private lender. This is not to be confused with changing your federal repayment plan, which I'll cover later in this chapter. Refinancing your federal loans is risky because it would take away all of your federal protections, including the ability to use income-driven repayment plans, apply for public service loan forgiveness (PSLF), or take advantage of other federal benefits such as the federal loan repayment pause during the pandemic. Further, any interest the government may have been covering through an income-driven repayment plan can be *capitalized* or added to your existing balance. If you're not sure what type of student loans you have, check with your loan servicing provider, or visit www.studentaid.gov.

3. **0% APR balance transfer (for credit cards only):** Involves taking out a new credit card, usually with a 0% interest rate, and transferring any existing debts to that new card. Because of the 0% interest rate, this allows you to pay off your transferred debt much more quickly. The catch here is that the lower interest rate is usually only offered for 15 to 21 months before it goes back up – sometimes to a higher interest rate than you had before the transfer.

For example, if you had one credit card with a $3,500 balance, 22% APR, with a $140 monthly payment, and another card with $2,300 worth of debt, 16% APR, with a $92 payment, you'd have a total of $5,800 worth of debt. If you were to pay that off with the combined minimum payment of $232, it would take you almost three years due to the high interest – debt is the worst!

But if you transferred that to a 0% APR card with a 16-month introductory offer and continued to make that same minimum payment of $232, you'd save over $1,500 in interest payments, and pay off your debt in a little over two years. That's a huge difference!

107

Lastly, if you're thinking of hopping from balance transfer to balance transfer, know that most people don't get approved for that. In fact, getting approved the first time around will usually require a credit score of 660 or above. To see whether a 0% transfer makes sense for you, I recommend using a calculator from Credit Karma that I link to at www.wealthonadime.com/resources.

Pros: You can save hundreds, potentially thousands of dollars in interest by putting 100% of the payment toward your principal balance.

Cons: The 0% introductory rate doesn't last forever, and the rate it increases to after the introductory may be higher than your current card(s).

Still deciding whether consolidation, refinancing, or a balance transfer is right for you? Use Table 5.3 if you need help, also included in your Debt Payoff Worksheet.

Table 5.3   Debt Options Decision Table

Question	Debt consolidation (Y/N)	Debt refinancing (Y/N)	$0 balance transfer (Y/N)
Will it simplify your payment?			
Will it reduce your minimum or monthly payment?			
Will it lower your interest rate?			
Will it decrease your repayment term?			
Will you give up any protections?*			

*This is particularly important to consider if you're thinking about refinancing your student loans.

Whew! That was a lot to cover. In addition to these options, it's always worth contacting your lenders to see if they are willing to reduce your APR or pause interest payments. They may be willing to work with you if you're struggling. Next, I'll cover why you'll want to go above the minimum payment to accelerate your debt payoff if you can.

Take a money minute

If you are considering or have already pursued any of these options, make sure you update your Debt Payoff Summary with the new interest rates and monthly payment before proceeding to Step 4.

Step 4: Determine Your Payment

By referring back to your Debt Info Summary table, you can calculate the total minimum payment across all of your debts. Consider this the bare minimum. If you aren't able to keep up with your minimum payment(s), you might consider contacting the National Foundation for Credit Counseling (NFCC) to help you with a *debt management plan*, not to be confused with a *debt settlement plan* (or company), which are often known for scams. If this applies to you, I include a section on debt management plans at the end of this chapter.

If you are keeping up with your total minimum payment, know that you'll have to go above the minimum to pay down your debt more quickly. There are two reasons for this:

1. Paying only the minimum payment can take years due to how compound interest and minimum payments are calculated.

2. It is likely to cost you hundreds, if not thousands, of dollars more in interest if you don't go beyond the minimum. This is

money that you could be used to live your best life and build wealth.

To some people, the idea of spending more years of their life in debt is enough to keep them motivated. I was more motivated by Reason No. 2, interest paid over time. Originally, I was just going to make my $503.93 per month minimum payment. I thought I would take the slow and steady route.

Then I changed my mind.

When I found out that my minimum payment would cost me an additional $16,000 in interest over time, it was game over. I had other plans for that money! I decided I didn't care if I had to work extra jobs or make some sacrifices to go beyond my minimum payment. I started small at first with whatever I could, but over time, I got a bit obsessive about it, doing whatever I could to pay almost 3× my minimum payment in the final year of paying down my student loans.

I'm not saying you have to go as hard as I did – quite the opposite. ANYTHING you can put on top of your minimum payments will help. Even an extra $25 monthly payment can take off years depending on your type of debt.

Let's take Claire and Julia from Chapters 2 and 3, and pretend they both have $37,000 worth of student loans, with a minimum payment of $386 per month. For the sake of this example, let's say Claire kept her side hustle it after she paid down her credit card to pay down her debt more quickly with an extra payment of $150/month.

By making an extra $150 payment Claire would save over three years and $3,203 worth of interest payments (see Figure 5.4). That's three years of her financial life back! Even if she only put an extra $50 per month, she'd still save an entire year and over $1,000.

Figure 5.4   Debt Acceleration Example

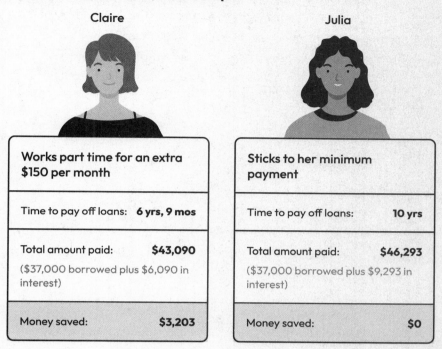

Claire	Julia
Works part time for an extra $150 per month	**Sticks to her minimum payment**
Time to pay off loans: **6 yrs, 9 mos**	Time to pay off loans: **10 yrs**
Total amount paid: **$43,090**	Total amount paid: **$46,293**
($37,000 borrowed plus $6,090 in interest)	($37,000 borrowed plus $9,293 in interest)
Money saved: **$3,203**	Money saved: **$0**

Now, what *you* might save by accelerating your debt payment depends on a few factors:

- Your debt balance
- Your interest rate
- How much of an additional payment you can make

The more you pay down, the larger the impact will be on your finances. To find out what might be possible for you, I recommend using the Student Loan Hero calculator available at www.wealtho-nadime.com/resources.

Let's take that example one step further. Let's assume that once Claire pays off her loans completely, she reallocates that payment of

$536 ($386 + $150 = $536) for the remainder of what would have been her debt payoff period (three years and three months). Instead of spending that money, she invests it in her 401(k). In total, she contributes $20,904 in three years and three months. For the purpose of this example, let's say she doesn't touch it after that. We'll assume a 7% rate of return.

Did You Know?

While the stock market continually goes up and down, every day (and so will your investments), historically, the S&P 500 (which tracks some of the largest 500 companies in the stock market) has never generated less than a 7% annual return over any 30-year period in U.S. history. So, while the market enters a recession every once in a while, and it can be a scary time, it also recovers, usually in just a year or two. Numerous studies show you can't time the market, but over long periods, it is reasonable to expect a return of 7% or greater, after inflation.

After 10 years, without adding another dime, Claire's investment would double to $44,453 (see Figure 5.5). That's over $24,000 generated in total gains (growth) because Claire reallocated what would have been her debt payment toward her investments.

That's the game changer, debt warriors! Figure 5.4 shows the real benefit of accelerated debt payoff: It puts you in a position to invest more quickly. It's not just about paying off your existing debt, though it may be all-consuming now. The decision to make an extra payment can impact the rest of your financial life.

Using my own experience as an example, by being so aggressive with my debt payoff plan, I was able to pay off my debt in 3.5 years

Figure 5.5   The Opportunity Cost of Being Debt Free

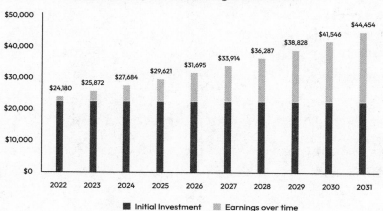

instead of 10, saving myself $10,000 worth of interest. Then I reallo-
cated my former debt payments to invest for my first home, keeping
my fixed and variable expenses the same, and set up an automatic
transfer into a taxable investment account through a robo-advising
company called Wealthfront. So not only did I save $10,000 in inter-
est by paying off my debt earlier, but I also saved up for my down
payment using that same discipline.

All this to say, in determining your debt payment, I recommend
you aim for as high as you can without feeling uncomfortable. This

Note: While my debt repayment strategy was sound, I wouldn't
necessarily recommend the same approach to save up for a
home or any other major savings goal. If you're not comfortable
with the idea of potentially losing some of your money in the
short term (the next one to five years), then I recommend saving in a high-yield savings account instead of a brokerage
account for any major goal. You'll learn all about this in
Chapters 7–9.

113

will require doing one of two things: cutting expenses or increasing your income. And while those options may not be for everyone, if you're looking to really build wealth over time, that means getting rid of any high-interest debt ASAP so you can reallocate that cash toward investments. I'll cover a few ways to do this later in the book.

Find Extra Money to Pay Down Your Debt

Don't know where you'll find the money to accelerate your debt payoff? You have two options:

1. Reduce your expenses.

2. Increase your income.

The latter will make the largest impact on your financial life, enabling you to accelerate more and more of your money goals. But because it can be a bit overwhelming to some money makers, and not everyone has time for a side hustle, I'll start with Option 1: Reduce your expenses.

Ways to Reduce Your Expenses

Some people might think of reducing your expenses as playing small because there's only so much you can cut out of your budget. A person or a family can only restrict so much – while your options to generate income through your salary, part-time job, or side hustle are much more open. That said, if you can't find a way to increase your income at the moment, then I recommend reviewing your expenses in the following order for areas you may be able to reduce.

- **Housing:** Your rent or mortgage is likely your largest expense. If renting, even though you may love the location, or the fancy

114

apartment, consider whether you are living within your means. It might be worth making the extra 20-minute commute if it could save you $200 per month or $2,400 per year to pay down your debt.

- **Dining out:** Listen, we all love a good brunch, but it can be a little too easy to spend your money eating out or ordering in. When asked to estimate how much they spend on dining and groceries, most clients I've worked with are off by *at least* $100 per month. To get this down, consider cooking more or even ordering a recipe or meal delivery service like Blue Apron. While services like these might sound expensive at first, they're likely less expensive than dining out.

- **Transportation:** If you live in an area with public transportation, this can be a much more affordable option than buying a car, making a car payment or using rideshare services.

- **Utilities:** Utility bills like electric, gas, water, Internet, or cable can also be pretty expensive these days – especially with the recent rise in inflation. Using an app like Rocket Money can help you keep track and even negotiate to reduce your bills for things like cable and other subscription services. Find it at www.wealthonadime.com/resources.

- **Subscription services:** There are so many subscription services these days I literally can't name them all, especially when it comes to streaming services. Other subscriptions you might not think of as frequently include clothing subscriptions (e.g., Stitchfix) and lifestyle subscriptions (e.g., FabFitFun). While they may not seem like much in the moment, they add up over time. Consider canceling or pausing some of your subscriptions, especially if you have multiple in one area (like several streaming services). Finance apps like Rocket Money can help.

Now that I covered a few places you may be able to cut back, let's dive into some ways you might increase your income, which will have much more of an impact on your financial life.

Ways to Increase Your Income

- **Negotiate a higher salary:** In addition to all the side jobs I worked, negotiating my salary year after year also had a huge impact in paying down my debt. In fact, not a year went by where I didn't give it a shot, increasing from a $40,000 salary in September 2012 to $72,000 in 2016. That said, while this can be easier said than done, it is *always* worth asking in your current job or in taking on a new position. The worst-case scenario is that your employer will say no, which gives you plenty of opportunity and leverage to set the stage for a performance bonus or raise down the line. A few tips here:

  - **Come prepared:** You want as much data as possible for this conversation. What specific metrics can you use to present the quality of your work? What specific new roles or responsibilities have you taken on? When was the last time you received a raise or a bonus? What are people with similar titles in your industry paid? You can use a website like Glassdoor.com, Payscale.com, or ask the *over-under question* to colleagues or those with similar titles on LinkedIn – where you ask if they get paid above or below a certain salary – to gather the data you need to back this up.

  - **Role-play your conversation:** Practicing your pitch and how you'll react to the actual conversation with your supervisor will pay off in spades the day of your request. To do this, list of all the possible reasons you think your supervisor might decline your request and come up with a rebuttal for each scenario. Then, grab your best friend, a family member, or trusted colleague and run through each of the scenarios in real-time. Practice your pitch and what you'll say if things don't go your way. Not getting flustered and delivering your talking points can help you land the pitch when you need to most.

o **Don't stop at your salary:** Instead of focusing solely on your salary, zoom out to your entire compensation package. This includes performance bonuses, cost of living increases, retirement plan matches, paid time off, parental leave policies, daycare coverage, pet insurance, and so on. Anything that can help you put a dollar back in your pocket. If your employer can't or refuses to give you the salary or raise you're hoping for, you can ask them to revisit the other aspects of your compensation package.

o **Plan for next time:** If your employer isn't willing to give you any type of increase this time around, take advantage of the opportunity to set yourself up for next time. Work with your supervisor to establish realistic benchmarks that you can hit 6 to 12 months out, with their word that so long as you hit them, they'll be able to give you some type of increase then. Type up the plan and have your supervisor sign off on their intent so there's no debate down the road.

Salary negotiation is something I often work on with my coaching clients because it can truly change the entire trajectory of your financial life. Are there plenty of reasons your employer might say no? Absolutely, whether they are legitimate or sound more like an excuse. It took me a long time to realize that employers are willing to pay A LOT for top talent, and it's up to all of us to make the best case possible. Does that mean they will always say yes if you're crushing it at work? Unfortunately, no – all you can do is make it as difficult as possible for them to say no, and easy to say yes. Establish key performance targets, prepare your case, and deliver your best argument. Remember that no one will be a better advocate for you, than you.

- **Get a side hustle:** While the idea of a second job or side hustle may not seem like a lot of fun, keep your eye on the prize! Anything extra, however small, will help to pay down your debt more quickly and build wealth over time.

  There are almost endless options for side hustles these days that don't require starting your own company, despite the popularity of doing so during the *Great Resignation*. For example, can you rent your home through Airbnb, or maybe just a storage space through a company like Neighbor. No joke, I once read a story on Bloomberg about a guy renting the side of his chain-link fence for $4 a month per person to people looking to lock up their bikes.[9] Don't tell me there's not a way you can make a few extra bucks – get creative! Can you make something? Sell it on Etsy. Are you handy? Sign up and perform odd jobs on TaskRabbit. Love dogs? Apps like Rover will pay you for your time. You can drive a car for Uber, deliver with DoorDash, or teach something online using a platform like Teachable – the options are endless. I've included a list of all the side hustle sites I could think of at the end of this chapter.

- **Sell items you no longer need:** With the rise of online marketplaces like Poshmark, Mercari, even the O.G. marketplace like eBay, there is no shortage of companies willing to resell your gently used items, including but not limited to clothes, handbags, furniture, and home decor. Consider cleaning out your closet to decide what you can sell to generate extra income for your debt payment.

- **Credit card reward programs:** Repeat after me: This is not a reason to spend more on your credit cards! But for any spending you *already* do, you may be able to redeem reward points for cash that can go toward paying down your debt. I actually used Citibank's Thank Your Reward Program to make extra payments on my student loans – it was never a lot, but every little bit helped, one of several ways I was able to pay off all my debt so quickly.

These are just a few ideas to increase your income, but feel free to think outside the box! While building wealth isn't about being frugal, being debt-free will give you a huge step up, so anything you can do to pay down your debt quicker will help.

The things I (almost) did for money

I often speak about the times when money made me anxious daily, before I paid off my debt or increased my income, and definitely before I made a career talking about all things money. It wasn't pretty, but I do affectionately look back on that time as having formed me into the financial coach I am today – even if it involved some extra work.

Committing to my debt payoff plan required working odd jobs in addition to my full-time job. I kept an eye out for used items on the curb and at yard sales that I could sell on Craigslist. I was the girl who gave out samples in a liquor store. I was a mystery shopper at fast food restaurants and random companies like Western Union. I got paid $10–$15 to do surveys online. I'm sure there were others.

(Continued)

119

(*Continued*)

> I did whatever I could to get out of debt during that time – though I did draw the line when I saw a job ad to be a hostess for what I'm pretty sure was a sex club in Washington, DC. The job advertised on Craigslist (surprise) didn't *say* that it was a sex club, but it advertised what seemed like a ridiculous amount of money at the time to serve as a hostess for some "exclusive gathering" in the middle of the night . . . How bad could getting paid $400 to greet a few strangers at the door be? Ultimately, I wasn't willing to find out ... but I definitely considered it.
>
> That's how badly I wanted to be free from the prison of my student loans.
>
> I cried when I made my last payment on my student debt. I was proud because I knew I had worked hard to make it happen. I was exhausted because it took a lot of work. But knowing I was going to be able to decide what I did with that money every month going forward felt incredible. Don't knock a side hustle, or several, if it helps you reach your goals.

Accelerate Your Debt Payoff

In this section, you'll learn how to accelerate your debt payoff using either the *avalanche method* or the *snowball method* to make extra payments on your debt. With the avalanche method – my favorite – you'll apply any extra payment to your highest-interest debt, regardless of the remaining balance. For the snowball method, you'll apply the extra payment to your lowest-balance debt, regardless of the interest rate. You'll choose one or the other, each with its own set of pros and cons that I'll outline shortly.

By coming up with a plan to repay your debt more quickly, you'll:

1. **Save time and money:** By going beyond the minimum payment on your debt, you'll tackle more of your principal balance to cut down on your debt quicker. This can take years off your debt repayment plan and save you hundreds, if not thousands, of dollars over time.

2. **Save mental energy:** By knowing in advance where you'll apply any additional payment, it's one less thing you'll have to think about every month.

3. **Know exactly when you'll be debt-free:** Having a debt payoff strategy takes out all the guesswork because you'll know exactly when you'll be debt-free so long as you stick to the plan. This can remove a lot of financial stress and anxiety from your life, just knowing you'll reach your goal if you stick to the process.

So let's get to it!

The Avalanche Method

While either the avalanche or snowball method will work to accelerate your debt payoff, I always recommend the avalanche method first because it will save you the most money in interest over time – money that you can use to build wealth!

Using the avalanche method, first, you'll list all your debts in order from highest to lowest interest rate, regardless of their balances. Let's use Table 5.4 as an example, where the total minimum payment across all debts listed is $341. Then, in addition to meeting the minimum payments across all of your debt, you'll apply any extra payment to the highest-interest debt – let's say that's an extra $50. In this example, you'd apply that extra payment to the Chase card with an interest rate of 22%, even though it's not the highest balance debt (see Table 5.4).

Table 5.4   Avalanche Method Example, Step 1

Lender	Balance	Interest Rate	Minimum Payment	Extra Payment	Total Payment
Chase card	$3,000	22%	$85	$50	$135
Visa card	$1,000	19%	$28	-	$28
Student loan	$22,000	4.5%	$228	-	$228
Total monthly payment			$341	$50	$391

So while the minimum debt payment across all the debts in this example is $341 (adding up the numbers in the Minimum Payment column), the total payment would be $391 including the extra $50 payment.

Money Tip: Every extra payment counts, but make sure it's being applied to your principal balance instead of being stashed away as a future payment. If you're not sure how an extra payment is being applied, get on the phone with your financial provider to make sure. An extra payment being applied to interest or a future payment will do little to nothing to help you or save you money. You also want to make sure it's applied at the same time or immediately after your minimum payment.

Once you've paid off your initial highest-interest debt – in this example, the Chase card – you'll move to the next-highest interest rate debt (e.g., the Visa card). This time, your extra payment will be what you were previously applying to the Chase card ($85 payment + $50 extra payment = $135 total, see Table 5.5) until you pay off that debt and continue with the process till all your debt is paid off.

Table 5.5   Avalanche Method Example, Part 2

Lender	Balance	Interest Rate	Minimum Payment	Extra Payment	Total Payment
~~Chase card~~	~~$0~~	~~PAID~~	~~PAID~~	~~PAID~~	~~PAID~~
Visa card	$1,000	19%	$28	$135	$163
Student loan	$22,000	4.5%	$228		$228
Total monthly payment			$135		$391

By focusing on the highest-interest debt and working your way down the list, you'll save the most money in interest over time – which means more money in your pocket to invest.

The Snowball Method

Similar to the avalanche method, the snowball method also involves making payments beyond the minimum amount required across all your debts, but instead of applying it to the highest interest debt, you'll apply it to the smallest-balance debt (regardless of the interest rate). The major benefit of the snowball method is that you're more likely to wipe out an entire *individual* debt quicker because you're starting with the lowest balance. If you are motivated by a quick win, this might be a more effective method for you.

Using the same debts from the avalanche example, this time you'll order your debts from the lowest-balance to the highest-balance debt, regardless of the interest rate. That puts the Visa card, in this example, at the top of the list (see Table 5.6).

Table 5.6   Snowball Method Example

Lender	Balance	Interest Rate	Min. Payment	Extra Payment	Total Payment
Visa card	$1,000	19%	$28	$50	$78
Chase card	$3,000	22%	$85	-	$85
Student loan	$22,000	4.5%	$228	-	$228
Total monthly payment			$341	-	$391

You'll notice the total monthly payment across all debts is the same amount – $391 – but the extra $50 is applied differently: to the lowest-balance debt, instead of the highest-interest debt.

When you've paid off the lowest-balance debt (e.g., the Visa card), you'll move on to the next-smallest debt in the group – in this example, the Chase card.

Although I always recommend the avalanche method first because it saves you the most money over time, several studies show that the snowball method can be easier to stick to. Pick whichever strategy you think fits your personality best. If you decide you prefer the snowball method because you get to knock out one of your debts completely, then do that! Either will put you ahead of the money game.

For the Student Debt Warriors

Given the craziness that is student debt in America, and as a former student debt warrior myself, I felt that student loans deserved their own section. At the time of this writing, the Biden Administration has extended the pause on federal student loan repayments through December 31, 2022 – the fifth extension of the pause since the start of the pandemic. During this time, the interest rate on all federal loans is 0%, which is actually an incentive to keep paying your loans (unless you're seeking PSLF), as it means 100% of any payment you make during this time will go toward your remaining balance. As you've already learned, this is unusual because generally any payment has to pay off any interest incurred before reducing your remaining balance. For this reason, if you have the means, I highly encourage you to continue making payments if you can during the pause.

When the repayment period resumes, either the avalanche or the snowball method will work to accelerate your debt payoff regardless of the type of debt you have. That said, student loans are so complex that I wanted to cover a few unique situations, including PSLF and the different payment plans below.

This section also illustrates how absurd student loan repayment is in America (and I'm not even talking about private student loans). Private lenders aside, there are currently seven different repayment plans for federal student loans. With so many options, it's no wonder we get overwhelmed! Here, I'll attempt to demystify the differences between them. There will always be nuances depending on your income, family size, and so on, but I hope this at least helps you decide where to start.

> Note: The following sections assume you already know whether you're on a basic repayment plan (standard, graduated, or extended), an income-driven repayment plan, or planning to seek PSLF on your federal loans. If you're not sure, you can find your plan by logging into www.studentaid.gov.

If You're on a Basic Repayment Plan

There are three main types of basic repayment plans for federal student loans:

- Standard: fixed payment, 10 years.
- Graduated: payments start low but increase every 2 years, 10 to 30 years.
- Extended repayment: payment is fixed or graduated, 10 to 30 years.*

In my opinion, if you can handle the monthly payments, I recommend sticking to the standard 10-year repayment plan because you'll

---

You must have at least $30,000 in "direct" federal student loans to qualify for this plan.

125

generally pay the least amount over time – unless you're eligible for PSLF, in which case an income-driven repayment plan makes sense (more on this below).

While all three plan types pay down the same balance, because the graduated and extended repayment plans start with lower payments, you'll likely pay more in interest over the life of the repayment term. This is why I generally recommend the standard, fixed plan if you can swing it.

While income-driven repayment plans (if you're eligible) can lower your monthly payments, there are a few reasons why I don't recommend them out of the gate:

- While income-driven repayment plans can lower your monthly payment, they also extend the repayment term. This usually costs you more in interest over time.

- Just because an income-driven repayment plan might lower your costs initially, it doesn't mean your payment won't increase significantly over time.

- While your monthly payment may start or be lower under an income-driven plan, you barely touch any of your principal balance, if at all. This is why some people actually see their balance increase over time, despite making payments, called *negative amortization*.

- Even if your remaining balance is forgiven under an income-driven plan after 20 or 25 years of payment, you're still on the hook for paying taxes on the amount that is forgiven.

For these reasons, I recommend sticking to and accelerating the 10-year repayment plan if you can. While there's a small argument that using an income-driven plan and investing the difference can help you build wealth, in my opinion the cons outweigh the benefits.

Plus, I'd vote for a predictable payment over one that has the potential to increase significantly over time – anyone else a Type A planner or just me?

Ultimately, you should do whatever feels most feasible and comfortable for you – if the standard plan is a stretch or you prefer a lower monthly payment, by all means, take advantage of that option.

A potential reform to federal loan repayment

On August 24, 2022, the Biden Administration proposed a rule as part of their Student Loan Relief plan that, if implemented, would drastically reform the current student loan repayment system. For example, there is a proposal to cover any portion of a borrower's interest that their monthly payment does not cover under an income-drive repayment plan. This would prevent negative amortization so long as a borrower continued to make their payments on time, enabling them to actually pay down their debt. There are other proposed changes, too, that would reduce the monthly payment on income-driven repayment plans from 10% of discretionary spending to 5% of discretionary spending. We'll have to stay tuned to see what happens.

If You're on an Income-Driven Repayment Plan

If you're under one of the several income-driven repayment plans, you should expect your monthly payment to increase over time, relative to your income, and spend more over the life of your repayment period (between 20 and 25 years depending on the plan) than you would with the standard, 10-year plan.

There are four main types of income-driven repayment plans:

- Repay-As-You-Earn (REPAYE): 20 or 25 years, monthly payment can exceed the payment under a 10-year plan.

- Pay-As-You-Earn (PAYE): 20 years, monthly payment can't exceed the 10-year plan.

- Income-based Repayment (IBR): 20 or 25 years, monthly payment can't exceed the 10-year plan.

- Income-contingent Repayment (ICR): 25 years, monthly payment can exceed the 10-year plan.

Out of these four, I'd recommend PAYE and IBR if you're eligible, with both plans never exceeding the monthly payment you would have paid under the standard, 10-year plan. PAYE has a slight advantage due to the fact it may subsidize some interest and potentially have a shorter repayment period than IBR, but it can be harder to qualify for.

Because an income-driven plan gives you a lower payment, that means you're touching less of the principal balance. It can be incredibly frustrating, but this is why despite years of payments, some people's debt balances actually go up because interest is growing on top of interest when their payment isn't large enough to cover all the interest based on their income.

Note: Table 5.7 is current at the time of publication. For the most recent information, please visit https://studentaid.gov/manage-loans/repayment/plans.

Table 5.7   Public/Federal Student Loan Repayment Plans

Type of Plan	Monthly Payment	Years in Repayment	Monthly Payments Go Higher Than the Standard 10-Year Plan?	Good for PSLF?	Reminders
Standard repayment	Whatever is required to pay off the loan	Up to 10	N/A	N	Will likely cost you the least over time.
Graduated Repayment	Lower at first, increasing every 2 years	Up to 10*	Y	N	Likely costs more than the standard plan over time.
Extended Repayment (fixed or graduated)	Lower than Standard, but whatever is required to pay off the loan	Up to 25	Y	N	Likely costs more than the standard plan over time.
Revised Pay As You Earn (REPAYE)	10% of discretionary income, likely to increase over time	Forgiven after 20 or 25 for undergrad or graduate loans	Y	Y	Likely costs more than the standard plan over time, with the exception of PSLF. You may have to pay taxes on any amounts that are forgiven.
Pay As You Earn (PAYE)		Forgiven after 20 years	N	Y	
Income-based Repayment (IBR)	10–15% of discretionary income	Forgiven after 20 or 25 years	N	Y	
Income-Contingent Repayment (ICR)	Lesser of: 20% of discretionary income or what you would pay on a fixed, 12-year repayment plan	Forgiven after 25 years	Y	Y	

Between 10 and 30 years for Consolidation Loans.

Beware of student loan capitalization

Capitalization is when any unpaid interest on your student loans is added to the principal balance of your loan. So long as you make your payments on time on a basic repayment plan, you don't have anything to worry about. Under income-driven repayment plans, however, there is likely a chunk of interest that's being paid by the government or that will be forgiven down the line upon completion of your payment plan. That said, you want to make sure any unpaid interest is not capitalized, adding to the amount you already know. This can occur if you ever refinance through a private lender or voluntarily leave a REPAYE, PAYE, or IBR plan. It can also happen if you fail to update your income on some of the income-driven repayment plans, or no longer qualify based on income under the PAYE or IBR plans. Hopefully, this problem will be considered in future efforts to reform the student loan repayment system, but in the meantime, make sure to stay on top of your payments and any required paperwork to avoid this potential setback.

If You're Seeking Public Service Loan Forgiveness (PSLF)

First off, for those of you in public service who may qualify for PSLF, thank you for everything that you do. Especially given that many of the professions that qualify for this category require advanced degrees, in my opinion, forgiving a portion of your debt is the least we can do to say thank you after your years of service and responsible repayment of your loans.

For those of you unfamiliar with PSFL, it's when an individual in public service can get the remainder of their student loans forgiven after 10 years' worth of qualifying payments – specifically, 120 separate monthly payments. This includes any that may have been made during the federal pause on student repayment during the COVID-19 pandemic. This is AMAZING for those of you who qualify for this benefit, and one of the few times I would recommend an income-driven repayment plan – because you're not planning to pay it for all of those 20 to 25 years.

You may qualify for PSLF if you work for a nonprofit organization or government employer. According to Studentaid.gov, nonprofit organizations include any tax-exempt 501(c)(3) or non-exempt 503(c)(3) organization that provides services such as emergency management, military service, public safety, law enforcement, public interest law, early childhood education, public health organizations, public education, and more. A government employer includes any U.S. federal, state, local, or tribal agency, the Peace Corps or AmeriCorps, or any military branch. A government contractor is not considered a government employer.

IMPORTANT: Because PSLF requires 120 separate AND monthly payments, do NOT make additional payments if seeking this benefit. Because your remaining debt can be forgiven after 10 years, there's little reason to pay it down more quickly. If you have the extra money, I recommend putting it toward your other debt or increasing your retirement contributions instead.

Not sure if you might qualify for PSLF? Check out the PSFL Help Tool as well as the guide, which is actually worth reading. I promise.

Read this first: https://studentaid.gov/articles/become-a-pslf-help-tool-ninja/.

Then, visit the help tool: https://studentaid.gov/pslf/.

Summary

Whew – congrats on making it through this chapter!

Debt can be exhausting, and probably the only thing worse than knowing you have to pay it down is spending more of your valuable time learning about how it works. I get it.

But you did it!

And I'm legit proud of you for leveling up what you know about money.

Here's a quick recap because it has been a longggg chapter:

- The first step to paying off your debt is to **figure out the details of how much debt you have and on what terms.** This includes balances, interest rates, and understanding the concept of compound interest.

- When paying down debt, the higher the interest rate, the more you pay. This is why **making extra payments is important to cut down more of the principal balance.** The only way to do this is to go beyond your minimum payment.

- **Debt consolidation and refinancing may help if you can get a lower interest rate** but beware of refinancing federal student loans as you would lose some key protections.

- **Avalanche and snowball methods are two strategies you can use to accelerate your debt payoff plan.** The avalanche method will save you the most money over time, but use whichever feels right to you!

- If you have federal student loans, you may be eligible for other payment plan options that may lower your monthly payment but increase the amount you pay over the entire payment period. **Carefully consider the pros and cons of student debt repayment plans** before changing your plan.

Lastly, if I can leave you with a final vote of confidence for this chapter, it would be this: Debt may be exhausting, but you *are* stronger.

While he has no background in personal finance, I love this quote from Chris Pratt (yes, the actor from the Lego movies – with an estimated net worth of $80 million, btw) that I think could be applied to any difficult period of your life, including debt repayment:

Fifteen years ago, I felt the same passion I feel today, but I had very little opportunity. I had to hustle hard. . . . And I never had a plan B. I never stopped believing. Ever. Don't give up. Apply constant pressure for as long as it takes. It will break before you do. Go get it.

– Chris Pratt

So go get it, money maker! Every extra payment you make toward your debt will put you that much closer to the life of wealth you want. I remember what it's like not to be able to see past that first step, but I promise if you stick to a plan, there is light at the end of the tunnel. Use your budget to determine what's realistic and adjust as necessary to find what works for you.

> Remember: It's not just about paying down your debt, it's about freeing up that cash to build wealth down the road. I have every confidence you can do it, and I hope this chapter has given you the confidence you need to move forward.

Resources

When I was paying down my debt, nothing motivated me more than putting some actual numbers on paper – or let's be honest, in a spreadsheet.

If you're looking for ways to determine whether and how much of an additional payment makes sense for you, I recommend the following resources to help you get there. You can find them all at www.wealthonadime.com/resources.

My Favorite Calculator for Complex Debt Situations: Bankrate Debt Repayment Calculator

This calculator can include multiple and different types of debts (e.g., credit cards, auto loans, student loans, etc.), as well as promotional and introductory offers to present you with a solid debt payoff strategy.

My Favorite Resource for Student Loans: Student Loan Hero

Student Loan Hero is a top-notch resource for all things student loans. While the studentaid.gov website is where you should go for the latest updates on federal loans and PSFL, Student Loan Hero can help you figure out your next steps with a variety of different calculators, including those specific to your current and/or income-driven repayment plans. I link to them all at www.wealthonadime.com/resources.

My Favorite Money App: Rocket Money

Just like getting organized is such a big part of setting up your budget, monitoring and sticking to that budget is how you reach your financial goals. By using a tool like Rocket Money, you can easily estimate what you have to put toward your debt payments and track your spending over time. Rocket Money also helps you save money by canceling your subscriptions and negotiating your bills, so you have more cash to accelerate your debt payoff. Plus, they use a lot of emojis – who said personal finance has to be boring?

My Top Resource for Those Having Trouble Meeting Their Minimum Payments: The National Foundation for Credit Counseling (NFCC)

The NFCC is an incredible resource to help those with debt in collections or otherwise struggling to meet their debt payments. Through the NFCC you can connect with a nonprofit credit counseling agency that can work with your lenders to get you a lower interest rate, pause payments, etc. to help you pay down your debt. They'll do this through what's known as a debt management plan, not to be confused with a debt settlement plan.

A debt management plan is an agreement you enter with a non-profit credit counseling agency to help pay down your debt. To get started, you would first contact the NFCC, which will direct you to a reputable credit counseling agency to go over your options. If you do decide to enter a debt management plan, the agency will do its best to work with your lenders to get you certain breaks like pausing payments, coming up with a lower monthly payment, lower interest rate, or other option to make paying your debt(s) easier. Instead of having multiple payments to lenders or collections, you'd only have one and the credit agency would distribute it to your lenders. While it is not guaranteed that your lenders will agree to the plan, this is a great option to pay down your debt responsibly and quickly if you find yourself in deep waters.

A few things to keep in mind when considering a debt management plan:

- Debt management plans are useful for unsecured debts, like credit cards and student loans, but are not useful for secured debts, like mortgages or auto loans.

- You will still be responsible to pay down the entirety of your debt; the goal is to make it easier for you to do, not to have your debts forgiven.

- Your creditors will not be alerted that you have entered a debt management plan until you formally agree to enter one, following your initial counseling session.

Notes

1. "Household Debt and Credit Report," Center for Microeconomic Data, Federal Reserve Bank of New York, https://www.newyorkfed.org/microeconomics/hhdc.
2. Ibid.
3. "A Look at the Shocking Student Loan Statistics for 2022," Student Loan Hero, updated July 29, 2022, https://studentloanhero.com/student-loan-debt-statistics/.
4. Lyss Welding, "Average Student Loan Debt Statistics in the U.S.," Best Colleges, updated July 13, 2022, https://www.bestcolleges.com/research/average-student-loan-debt.
5. "Household Debt and Credit Report."
6. Ibid.
7. Doug Milnes, "What Is the Average Credit Card Debt in America in 2022?," MoneyGeek, updated August 19, 2022, https://www.moneygeek.com/credit-cards/analysis/average-credit-card-debt/.
8. "Economic Well-Being of U.S. Households in 2021," Federal Reserve, May 2022, https://www.federalreserve.gov/publications/files/2021-report-economic-well-being-us-households-202205.pdf.
9. Sarah Holder, "The Airbnb for America's Extra Crap Is Here," Bloomberg, July 3, 2019, https://www.bloomberg.com/news/articles/2019-07-03/rent-out-your-closet-with-an-airbnb-for-storage.

Worksheet: Debt Payoff

Reminder: You can download this, and all other worksheets included in this book at www.wealthonadime.com/resources.

From Step 2: Know Your Numbers

Debt Info Summary

Lender	Total Balance	Interest Rate	Minimum Payment	Debt Payoff Date
Total:	$_____.___	N/A	$_____.___	

From Step 3: Consider Your Options

Use the following table to determine the best options available to you by marking Yes (Y) or No (N) in the below columns. If you marked N in any of the columns, you may want to consider another option or keep your current financing arrangement.

(Continued)

(Continued)

Debt Options Decision Table

Question	Debt Consolidation	Debt Refinancing	$0 Balance Transfer
Will it simplify your payment?			
Will it reduce your minimum or monthly payment?			
Will it lower your interest rate?			
Will it decrease your repayment term?			
Will you give up any protections?*			

* This is particularly important to consider if you're thinking about refinancing your student loans. Refinancing federal student loans requires using a private lender and would rid you of the ability to use income-driven repayment plans or apply for PSLF at any point in the future. You will lose any and all federal protections, including the federal pause on student loan payments you may have benefited from during the COVID-19 pandemic.

Side Hustle Ideas

For a full list of side hustle ideas, including courses I recommend if you're still looking to create something to sell or start your own business, visit www.wealthonadime.com/resources.

- **Have a car?** Drive for Uber or Lyft on your own schedule

- **Have a car or bicycle?** Deliver for DoorDash, GrubHub, UberEats

- **Love animals?** Walk dogs with Rover or pet sit by signing up for TrustedHousesitters.com

- **Creative or crafty?** You can sell things you create, even printables (think, downloadable signs other people print for their home, parties, etc.) on Etsy

- **Random things to sell?** Don't forget about the O.G. marketplace, eBay

- **Handy or capable of doing odd jobs?** Check out TaskRabbit, a marketplace where you'll be able to advertise and/or respond to requests for services, from holding someone's spot in line to organizing closets

- **Own your home, parking spot, or unused storage space (a closet, empty room, etc.)?** Consider Airbnb, Vrbo, HomeAway, Spacer (for parking spots) or Neighbor (for storage space).

- **Full of opinions?** Participate in research studies or focus groups with Limelight Insights, Mediabarn Research, or User Testing.

- **Have some used clothes or other items?** Resell what you already own (or find) on Mercari, Poshmark, Facebook Marketplace, Craigslist, OfferUp, and Decluttr

Chapter 6

Get Your Full Financial Picture

Now that you've learned how to build and automate your budget, you'll likely become more and more eager to invest whatever you can to build wealth. Investing money can become similar to a game in that way for many money makers with the means to do so. After all, wealth is probably one of the major reasons you got this book to begin with; money can be a strong motivator.

In the next few chapters, you'll learn exactly how you can start investing, even beyond your 401(k), as we cover the different types of accounts you might utilize, the investments you might consider, and how to open an account of your own. Before you get there, however, it's important to ask yourself a few key questions to assess what I refer to as your *full financial picture*. To be clear, this doesn't mean your financial picture has to be perfect before you start investing, but rather, you want to know if any other areas of your finances need improvement so you can invest safely and confidently.

For example, let's take Julia from Chapter 3, who wanted to save up for a home. Let's assume she saves up enough for the down payment but has a poor credit score or empties out her emergency fund to afford the home. Both of those are areas that could either prevent her from getting approved for a mortgage or put her in a risky financial situation once she goes through with it. Apart from the dollar figures themselves, emotional aspects also come into play. For example, if Julia is constantly stressed about money, she may want to work on that before taking on the responsibility of a home or whatever the large expense might be. This is why it's important to look at your full financial picture when thinking about your goals, including how you plan to use your investments.

To assess your full financial picture, I recommend asking yourself three questions:

1. **How do your numbers look?** Separate from your bank accounts, there are four key metrics you can calculate to get a better picture of your overall financial health, especially if you track them over time. They include your net worth, credit score, liquidity ratio, and debt-to-income (DTI) ratio. I'll cover how to calculate them in just a bit.

2. **How do you feel about your money?** While metrics are important, it's also important to think about your relationship with money. So, how do you feel? Do you worry about meeting your monthly expenses? Are you confident you'll reach your goals over time? If any of these answers make you anxious, you should consider revisiting the goals section of this book to gain clarity. You might also consider investing more conservatively, which I'll cover in Chapter 7.

3. **How do you use your money?** Are you able to cover all your bills? Do you consistently contribute to savings or goals? Do you usually spend more than you make?

Thinking about these three areas should give you a better sense of how you're doing in the bigger picture. You'll want to strike a balance across all three as you continue to build wealth (see Figure 6.1).

Figure 6.1   Your Full Financial Picture

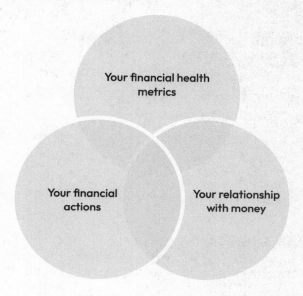

The most technical part of this process is calculating the financial health metrics associated with Question 1; so let's cover what each of them mean.

Net Worth

Your net worth is a great measure of your financial health because instead of accounting for just your assets or debt, it looks at the bigger picture. Your net worth is calculated by taking the value of all of your *assets* (anything you own of value) minus all your *liabilities* (any debts you owe).

Net worth = assets − liabilities

When talking about your financial health, whether your net worth is positive or negative isn't as important as whether that number is going up over longer periods of time. So, even though Julia has a negative net worth due to her student loans, the important part is that as she continues to pay down her debt and builds assets, her net worth will go up in the long run. If you're in a similar situation, by paying down debt and saving or investing, your net worth will likely get closer to 0 and become positive over time.

Now, if you're a bit closer to retirement (e.g., 10 to 15 years till you retire), your net worth becomes more important because it's indicative of the number that's going to support you in retirement. If this resonates with you, in the next chapter, I'll cover some options for investing if you're playing catch-up.

Your Credit Score

Your credit score is a number used by lenders to quickly determine how likely (or risky) it is that you are (or aren't) going to pay back the money you borrow. It's important because it impacts not only whether you get approved for a loan or new line of credit (e.g., a credit card, mortgage, personal loan, etc.) but also the terms of that offer, which can end up costing you more or less money over time. If your credit score is low, you may receive less favorable terms, or not get approved for a credit offer at all. Examples of less favorable terms would be a higher interest rate or balloon payments on a mortgage – anything that would cost you more money over time. The opposite is true as well – the better your credit score, the better the offer.

Most big banks and finance apps provide your credit score and likely indicate whether it's considered poor, fair, good, very good, or excellent. That said, there are different types of credit score models that lenders consider. For example, you may have heard of a FICO score before, but that's just one type of credit scoring model. FICO and Vantage are the most popular. Table 6.1 shows how they compare.

Table 6.1   FICO versus Vantage Credit Model

Credit Score Rating	FICO Model	Vantage Score Model
Exceptional/Excellent	800–850	781–850
Very Good/Good	740–799	661–780
Good/Fair	670–739	601–660
Fair/Poor	580–669	500–600
Poor/Very Poor	300–579	300–499

Regardless of the scoring model, it's worth noting that both of them look at the same five or six factors to determine your score, with payment history being the highest weight factor in both.

- Payment history: Whether or not you make your payments on time. This factor alone makes up 35–40% of your credit score depending on the scoring model.

- Balances: What balances are you currently carrying across your debt?

- Credit utilization: How much of your available credit limits you're using; you want to keep this ratio low as often as possible.

- Account age/length of history: How long have you been using credit? The longer you've had a history of credit, or a particular line of credit, the better (so long as it's good!).

- Account mix: Lenders like to see that you have experience with different types of debt, like a credit card, student loan, or a mortgage. Does that mean you should go out and apply for a few credit cards just for the hell of it? I wouldn't recommend it, unless you're confident you can do so responsibly.

- Recent behavior: This includes recently opened lines of credit and *hard credit checks*, where a lender views your full credit history. This usually lowers your score a few points, temporarily, especially if you get multiple checks in a short amount of

145

time. This is in comparison to a *soft credit check*, also known as a *soft credit pull*, when you review your own credit report or a company checks your credit as part of a background check – like a potential landlord or employer.

You can see how this is presented visually in Figure 6.2.

Figure 6.2   FICO Credit Factors

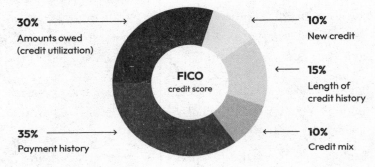

30%
Amounts owed
(credit utilization)

10%
New credit

FICO
credit score

15%
Length of
credit history

35%
Payment history

10%
Credit mix

Credit Score Not Looking Too Good?

It happens to the best of us. Instead of focusing on the past, focus on what you can do to get that number up! I provide a few ideas in Appendix A, including which factors you can impact immediately, as opposed to the things that could take years to change.

Your Liquidity Ratio

Your liquidity ratio is a measure of how prepared you'd be to cover your monthly expenses if you experienced a sudden loss of income. It is calculated by taking all of your liquid assets, or anything you own of value that you could convert to cash in a short period of time and dividing by your monthly expenses.

Liquidity ratio = Value of total liquid assets ÷ Monthly expenses

At a minimum, you want this number to be at least 1.0 or higher, which would indicate you could cover at least one month's worth of expenses. Ideally, over time, you'll want to increase this ratio to at least 3.0.

Common liquid assets included in this ratio include any cash in a checking or savings account, investments in brokerage accounts that you can withdraw without penalty (more on this later), or anything you could sell quickly if you had to, like jewelry, a handbag, or sneaker collection. While you might have money inside your 401(k) or IRA, I wouldn't include that in this calculation because it should be reserved for retirement, and in most cases, you'd face a 10% penalty for withdrawing before age 59 1/2.

Your Debt-to-Income (DTI) Ratio

The last number you'll want to know in assessing your full financial picture is your DTI ratio. This number is used when applying for a mortgage, as well as some other types of credit, such as personal loans. Most often, a *back-end* calculation is used by taking all of your monthly debt payments, including your rent or mortgage, loans, and credit cards, and dividing it by your gross monthly income (what you make before any taxes or deductions are taken out of your pay).

Back-end DTI ratio = monthly debts ÷ gross monthly income

Mortgage lenders, however, usually prefer a front-end DTI, which only accounts for housing costs like the future mortgage and property taxes you'd be responsible for if you got approved.

Front-end DTI ratio = monthly housing expenses ÷ gross monthly income

If you have an annual salary, your gross monthly income is your salary divided by 12. If you're paid hourly, multiply your hourly rate by how many hours you work in a month.

Debts commonly included in a DTI ratio include your monthly mortgage or rent, student loans, car payments, personal loans, credit card payments, and any other monthly debts. A front-end ratio only accounts for housing costs, while a back-end ratio adds in all other debts.

Let's say you have an annual salary of $50,000 for a gross monthly income of $4,166 and total current monthly debt payments of $1,500 ($1,000 rent plus $500 student loan payment). If you're applying for a personal loan that would add an additional monthly payment of $300, your back-end DTI ratio would be $1,800 ÷ $4,166 = 43%.

Ideally, you want your *back-end DTI* to be below 36% across all of your debts; 43% is considered pretty high. Any higher, and you may still get approved for a mortgage or credit application but with less favorable terms. You are likely to be rejected for a mortgage if that number is above 43%. It's not uncommon that people will save up for a down payment on a home, only to realize that despite having what they need, their DTI is too high to get approved due to student loans, for example.

For mortgages specifically, you ideally want your *front-end DTI* to be below 28%.

If you are approved for a mortgage with a back-end DTI above 43%, it's likely that the lender is offering a *non-qualified mortgage*. This is when a lender uses non-traditional methods to verify a borrower's income or credit history, enabling you to get a mortgage, but may also include riskier terms such as a *balloon payment* which requires a larger-than-usual payment after a certain amount of time. Student loan refinancing may also be difficult above a DTI of 50%.

Ultimately, a high DTI ratio should be a signal to you that taking on the debt is risky, and you might stretch yourself too thin trying to pay it. In other words, it's in your best interest – not just the lender's – to keep this number low.

How Often Should I Check These Numbers?

Don't want to calculate all of these numbers by hand? No problem. You can find calculators for each of these and a link to find your credit score at wwww.wealthonadime.com/resources. You'll also want to monitor them over time based on the following guidelines (see Figure 6.3).

Figure 6.3   Schedule a Check-In

Net Worth	Liquidity Ratio	DTI Ratio	Credit Score	Credit Report
Quarterly or annually	Quarterly until ≥ 1.0	Quarterly before credit application	Monthly	Semi-annually

Now that you have your numbers down, it's time to address the second and third sets of questions in assessing your full financial picture.

2. How do you feel about your money?

1. Are you confident or anxious? Yes / No

2. Do you worry about meeting your monthly expenses? Yes / No

3. Are you confident you'll reach your goals over time? Yes / No

4. Do you feel like your money is adequately protected? Yes / No

Your answers to these questions should give you a glimpse of how positive or negative your relationship with money is. Keep in mind that you can still worry about money even if the rest of your financial picture is in good shape. If that's the case, consider where the emotions you associate with money may stem from and what boundaries you may be able to put in place to get yourself in a more comfortable position.

Yup, financial therapy is a thing

Financial therapy is a growing field of professionals dedicated to helping people overcome stress and anxiety associated with their money – that's how much of an impact your finances can have on mental and emotional stability. Pretty wild, right? Financial therapists may be former financial professionals or mental health professionals that have been certified through an organization like the Financial Therapy Association, which was formally established in 2009. That said, this shouldn't stop you from raising financial anxiety issues with another financial professional or qualified therapist, as they might also be able to help you address some of the aspects leading you to experience stress or anxiety over money.

3. How do you use your money?

1. Are you able to cover your monthly expenses? Yes / No

2. Do you generally spend less than you make in a given month? Yes / No

3. Do you save or invest on a regular basis? Yes / No

4. If you have debt, do you feel like it's manageable? Yes / No

If you answered no to any of these questions, it's likely you're spending beyond your means and/or struggle with debt. If you haven't already addressed these in your budget and Money Moves System, you may want to revisit both to make sure your income can adequately cover your monthly expenses. If you're consistently unable to make your debt payments, reconsider a debt management plan – your lenders will not be alerted until you formally agree to enter a plan with a credit counseling agency.

Summary

Congrats, money maker! You made it through some potentially tough questions in this chapter. Remember, if you identified any areas you might need to work on in the above prompts, that doesn't mean you can't pursue your goals in the meantime, only that you may have a few priorities to work on simultaneously.

Next, in Chapter 7, you'll learn about Tanya as well as how much you might need to invest over time. Then, in Chapter 8. Investing 101, I'll dive deep into the different types of accounts and investments you might consider, including but not limited to mutual funds, index funds, and exchange-traded funds (ETFs). As a financial educator, I'll cover the pros and cons of each type of account and investment, but ultimately the decision will be yours – so get ready to level up your money!

Worksheet: Get Your Financial Picture

1. How do your numbers look? Take some time to find or calculate your financial health metrics using the sections below.

Calculate Your Net Worth

Net worth = Total assets − Total liabilities

Reminder: You can easily track your net worth across all of your accounts using an app like Rocket Money or you can use the table below.

Quarter/Year					
Total Assets		Total Liabilities		Net Worth	
Type of Asset	Value	Type of Debt/Liability	Value		
Total	$_____.00	Total	$_____.00	$_____.00	

Current date (MM/DD/YY): _____

Total Assets _____ − Total Liabilities _____ = Current Net Worth _____

Regardless of whether your net worth is positive or negative, you'll want to make sure it goes up over time. Consider checking quarterly at most, as it's likely to fluctuate in the short term, especially if you currently have any investments in the stock market (including through your 401(k) or employer-sponsored retirement plan).

Compare your net worth to last quarter; did it go up or down?

If negative, list two or three things you can do to try and change its trajectory:

1. _____

2. _____

3. _____

Check Your Credit Score

You can use a finance app, your bank's web interface, or check your credit score at www.freecreditscore.com without hurting your credit.

Check your credit score and insert it here: _____.

Where does your credit score rank on the following scale?

Credit Score Rating	FICO Model	Vantage Score Model
Exceptional/Excellent	800–850	781–850
Very Good/Good	740–799	661–780
Good/Fair	670–739	601–660
Fair/Poor	580–669	500–600
Poor/Very Poor	300–579	300–499

If you're looking for quick ways to improve your credit score, check out the Improve Your Credit Score Guide in the Appendix.

Calculate Your Liquidity Ratio

Liquidity ratio = Current liquid assets % Monthly living expenses

Enter your liquidity ratio here: _____

(Continued)

(Continued)

Calculate Your DTI

Step 1. Add up your monthly debts. Step 2. Divide by your gross monthly income.

> Back-end DTI = total monthly debt % gross monthly income

Enter your DTI ratio here: _____%

2. How do you feel about your money?

1. Are you confident or anxious? Yes / No

2. Do you worry about meeting your monthly expenses? Yes / No

3. Are you confident you'll reach your goals over time? Yes / No

4. Do you feel like your money is adequately protected? Yes / No

3. How do you use your money?

1. Are you able to cover your monthly expenses? Yes / No

2. Do you generally spend less than you make in a given month? Yes / No

3. Do you save or invest on a regular basis? Yes / No

4. If you have debt, do you feel like it's manageable? Yes / No

Chapter 7

Invest Early and Often

*M*eet Tanya, a 34-year-old project manager living in Chicago, *Illinois. She works for a construction company and lives in a two-bedroom apartment with her fiancé and their German Shepherd, Luna. On weekends, she likes checking out new restaurants and loves live music. Her parents are originally from the Dominican Republic, but most of her family lives in Boston now. She visits them often.*

Tanya feels good about her spending habits but wishes she had more clarity on her goals. She saves regularly, contributes to her 401(k), and lives pretty comfortably – nothing crazy, but can afford to splurge every once in a while. She and her fiancé talk about buying a home in the next few years, but hasn't started saving yet. She recently paid off the last of her student loans– $70,000 in total – and wants to level up her money but doesn't know where to start.

The first in her family to make six figures – $100,000 even – Tanya sometimes feels guilty knowing she has other family members who struggle with money. She was the first in her family to graduate from college – an opportunity her family members never had. A few years later, she went back to graduate school, paying off her student loans in just six years using the avalanche method. The extra cash feels like she might as well have won the lottery.

Tanya wants to build wealth – real wealth – the kind she can pass down to a future family. She recently listened to a podcast where someone was talking about retiring early and wonders if that might be a possibility for her, too.

Tanya has several options when it comes to building wealth, but first, I want to cover how she got to where she is today – by paying down her debt quickly and investing as soon as she felt she could. She started when she was 28, fresh out of grad school, making $83,500 at the time.

Let's take a look at Tanya's expenses back then (Table 7.1):

Table 7.1 Tanya's Expenses

Tanya, 28	Monthly Expenses
Chicago, IL, $83,500 salary	4% to 401(k) (pre-tax) = $278
No emergency savings	Employer match = $278
Take-home pay	$4,694
Fixed expenses: • Rent: $1,500 • Utilities: $100 • Phone bill: $45 • Subscriptions: $78 • Metro pass: $75 • Pet insurance: $50	$1,848
Goals: • Student loans: $713 minimum plus $325 extra for a total monthly payment of $1,038 • Emergency fund: $300 • Vacation fund: $250	$1,588
$4,694 – $1,848 – $1,588= $1,258 remaining for variable expenses	
Variable expenses: $1,258 • Groceries: $300 • Dining/drinks: $300 • Other transport: $150 • Entertainment: $200 • Fitness: $69 • Shopping: $139 • Personal care: $100	$1,258 = variable spending cap $1,258 ÷ 4.3 = $293 weekly spending cap
Total Budget:	$4,694

As we go through Tanya's story, you may notice this chapter is a bit different from the others in the book for two reasons. First, while the stories of Claire, Julia, and Eric may have resonated with you earlier, Tanya's story might be more of a glimpse into your future – the six-figure salary, her investment accounts, and so on. Maybe you're learning all this for the first time – that's okay. One of the easiest ways to get ahead in your financial journey is to listen and learn from others who are further along. I still do this *all the time*. I hope you'll learn something from Tanya's story, too.

Second, this chapter is a love letter to anyone who considers themselves to be "the first" in their inner circle of family or friends. Maybe you're a first-generation college graduate, the first in your family to become debt-free, the first to start a business, or just hell-bent on becoming a millionaire. If you're trying to set a new financial bar, this chapter is for *you*.

So, in the spirit of being "the first" I'll use Tanya's story to double down on why you want to start investing as soon as you can, even though it might be intimidating. Through her story I'll cover:

- The magic of investing with compound growth.
- The power of investing as early and as often as you can.
- Why you should always take advantage of your employer match.
- What to do if you feel like it's too late for you to start (spoiler alert: it's not).
- How much you should invest monthly.

So, let's get to it!

Remember day 1

As we dive deep into investing, I want you to recall Million Dollar Habit No. 4, Start with day 1, because we're going to be talking about things like tax-advantaged accounts, with contribution limits and income limits – a lot of terms and concepts that may be new to you. Don't get intimidated or frustrated that you didn't know them sooner; get excited! When it comes to your money, knowledge is power, so soak up every ounce you can and put it to use as soon as you have the opportunity to do it.

The Magic of Investing: Compound Growth

Back in Chapter 5, Tackle Your Debt, we talked about compound interest, how it's applied to your principal balance plus any interest incurred to date, and how it can make paying off your debt really, *really* hard.

When you're investing in the stock market, the concept of compound growth has the opposite effect, enabling you to build wealth faster and faster as your investments grow, either through *appreciation* or by reinvesting *dividends*. Not sure what this means? Let's go over some quick lingo:

- **Appreciation versus dividends**
  - *Appreciation* is when the value of your share(s) in a company or fund increases. Appreciation is one of two ways your investment can grow, the other being *dividends*.
  - A *dividend* is a portion of the profit that a company pays out to an investor or shareholder. Generally speaking, companies will pay dividends on either a quarterly or annual basis. You can reinvest these dividends to experience compound

growth, or cash them out. Either way, dividends are generally taxed in the year they are received, which I'll cover in detail in Chapter 8.

- **Investment versus investment account**

  o An *investment* is anything you purchase with the expectation that it will likely generate more money for you over time, known as *a return* on your investment. For example, stocks, bonds, funds, and annuities are all different types of investments.

  o *Investment accounts*, like a 401(k), IRA, or taxable brokerage account, hold your investments – although you have to select your investments within that account, otherwise your money might just sit in a cash fund or settlement fund, doing nothing. You want to make sure that money is invested! Luckily, you can usually avoid this mistake by selecting an automatic investment for the investment(s) of your choice.

- **Share versus fund**

  o A *share* is a quantifiable piece of ownership in a particular company or investment fund. For example, a company may have 100,000 shares, and you may own one or more of those shares. You buy shares at a particular price, and while the value of that share may go up or down depending on the market, you would still only own one or however many shares you purchased – unless you bought more shares along the way.

  o Similar to buying shares of a company, you can also buy shares in a *fund* (see Figure 7.1). A fund pools investors' money to make a variety of investments, which may be in different stocks, bonds, or other assets, such as real estate. A single fund can cover hundreds or thousands of different companies and investments at a time. There are many different types of investment funds, but the most common are index funds, mutual funds, and exchange-traded funds (ETFs). I'll cover each of these in detail.

Figure 7.1   Share versus Investment Fund

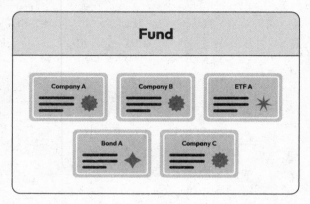

- **Stock versus bond**
  - *Stock* describes having ownership in a publicly owned company and is much less specific than owning a *share* in a company. You can say you "own stock" in a company or multiple companies, and that might be true, but that doesn't really tell you how many shares you own.

  - A *bond* is another type of investment you can purchase, usually from a government or municipality, that pays you in interest over a definitive period of time while the bond matures. Bonds are considered a much more conservative investment than stocks because they're more predictable but usually have significantly lower returns than the stock market.

- **Dividend stock versus growth stock**

  o *Dividend stocks* are stocks known for paying dividends out to their investors, usually on a quarterly basis, as opposed to growth stocks that are more likely to appreciate in value but don't pay dividends often (if ever). Dividend stocks are usually considered safer than growth stocks, preferred by investors who like the idea of reinvesting their dividends to compound over time. Alternatively, investors can also opt to cash out dividends as they are received.

  o *Growth stocks* are shares from companies that anticipate they'll experience high growth over time, beyond the average rate of the market, as they continue to reinvest and grow their company. That said, this growth is never guaranteed.

Got the basics down? Awesome. Back to compound interest. . . .

How compound growth works when investing in the stock market is first, you'll purchase a share to invest in a company or fund. Then those investments hopefully grow by (a) appreciation and/or (b) dividends that you'll either reinvest to buy additional shares or cash out – but you'll likely want to reinvest them for compound growth to work its magic. Then, as your investments grow, that growth will *compound* based not only on what you initially invested but also on growth incurred to date.

For example, let's say you buy a share for $100, and it appreciates annually at a rate of 7%. That first year you'd make $7, or 7% of $100, increasing the value of that share to $107. The next year, at a rate of 7%, you make $7.49 (not $7.00) – that same share is now worth $114.49, and $122.50 the third year. This is opposed to making the same $7 every year based on your original investment. Now, this might not seem like a big deal at the $100 or $1,000 level, but on the scale of hundreds of thousands, it's extremely powerful.

When your portfolio reaches its first $100,000, a 7% annual return would be a $7,000 gain. When your portfolio grows to a million, that would be a $70,000 gain in one year – from doing nothing other than investing your money.

This also means your money is worth more invested now, than it would be a few years from now, known as *the time value of money.* Figure 7.2 shows the impact over time, using an example of a one-time investment of $10,000 over 30 years.

Figure 7.2   Compound Growth Example

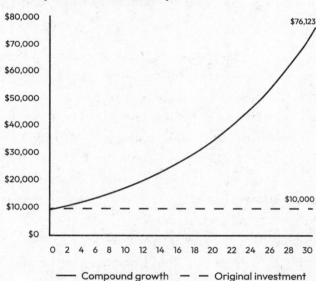

The impact of compound growth is significant – a $66,163 return on your investment over 30 years. Compound growth also means your investment starts to grow quicker over time. You can see this in Figure 7.2 as well, how the solid line starts to accelerate as time goes on. The earlier you start, the vastly higher returns you'll likely to see over time. The later you start, the more you have to invest to catch up.

Let's follow Tanya's story as an example.

Tanya's Wealth Journey

Tanya is 34 years old now, but she only started investing in her 401(k) when she was 28. Before that, she didn't know much about investing at all. Her first job out of college offered a 401(k), but she didn't feel like it was worth contributing to at the time. Plus, she was too busy saving up to go to graduate school. By the time she graduated and learned how important it was, she was 28 – so she started then.

When Tanya finished graduate school, she had about $70,000 worth of student loans to pay off at a fixed interest rate of 7%, comparable to the average annualized return of the stock market over long periods of time.[1] Because of this, it made sense for her to invest while she chipped away at her debt – especially to take advantage of her employer match. So, fresh out of grad school, Tanya invested 4% of her $83,500 salary in her 401(k) (about $278 per month) and paid extra when she could on her minimum student loan payment of $731 per month.

Student loan warriors, did you know?

Investing in your 401(k) or any pre-tax retirement account reduces your taxable income, and as a result, what's considered your discretionary income. This means investing can actually lower your monthly student loan payment for federal loans under any income-driven repayment plan, because your payment is determined based on the money you have left after taxes. Talk about a win-win scenario!

By investing only 4% of her starting salary from age 28, Tanya did two really amazing things.

First, instead of getting overwhelmed by her debt, she started small. Relative to her salary, $278 per month wasn't a crazy amount for Tanya to invest. Especially because she had never invested before, she went with what she was comfortable with, and that's always a great place to start. Whatever she had left over, she would make an extra payment on her student loans. The HR department at her job also helped her pick a *target-date retirement fund*, which automatically diversified and rebalanced her investments, lowering her risk. By starting small and automating her investments, this investment alone would grow to well over $1 million by the time she's 65.[2]

Don't worry, you'll learn all about the different types of accounts and investments you can make in Chapter 8.

The second smart thing Tanya did was take full advantage of her *employer match*. In this example, Tanya contributed 4% of her monthly paycheck of $278 per month, her first year out of grad school. Her employer offered a 100% match on every dollar she contributed, up to 4% of her total compensation. This means that for every dollar Tanya invested, her employer contributed another. This doubled the amount invested in her 401(k) every month.

Investing without an employer match

The investment scenarios in this chapter all assume employer matches on employer-sponsored retirement plans, like a 401(k) or 403(b) – but what if you're self-employed? Don't worry, you can still invest! Though you'll want to invest more than someone with an employer match. Hang tight, I'll cover all your options in Chapter 8. Investing 101. For now, stay focused on the goal – to start investing as early and as often as possible.

Your vesting schedule

Vesting is the process by which you get to keep any contributions your employer may make into your 401(k), determined by your "vesting schedule." These are separate from whatever contributions you make to your account. Some companies' vesting schedules might be 25% per year, others might fully vest immediately – each schedule will vary from employer to employer. In the 25% example, this means that if you left that employer after year one, you would get 25% of your employer contributions. Your contributions as an employee are always yours to keep, no matter what, so don't let a vesting schedule stop you from investing on your own.

After six years of investing, thanks to her employer match and compound growth, Tanya's 401(k) has grown to $51,215. She's definitely on the right track! Of this, she contributed $21,604, her employer contributed another $21,604, and her investments grew $8,007 in just six years. This example assumes a 3% annual salary increase and a 7% annual rate of return.

If Tanya continues to invest at the same rate, with the same assumptions, she'd have $1,733,411 or $1.7 million by age 65, making her the first millionaire in her entire family (see Figure 7.3). Of that amount, Tanya would have only contributed $237,992, for a profit of over $1.4 million including gains and her employer match. Without her employer match, her investments would have only totaled $866,720 – an approximate $733,280 difference.

Figure 7.3   Tanya's Portfolio Growth

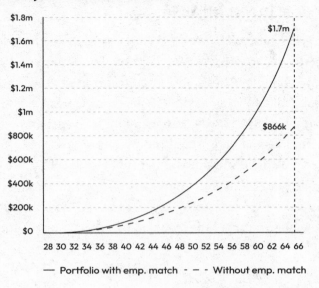

Now, using a more simplified example, let's say that Claire, Tanya, and Eric all invest the same amount dollar amount of $278 per month, with the same employer match (100% up to 4% of compensation) and kept with it till age 65 starting at ages 22 (Claire), 25 (Eric) and 28 (Tanya). Unlike the previous example, we don't assume any salary or contribution increases in this scenario, just a flat investment of $556 per month (employee and employer contribution combined). You can see in Figure 7.4 the advantage that starting early gives you.

Figure 7.4   The Benefit of Investing ASAP

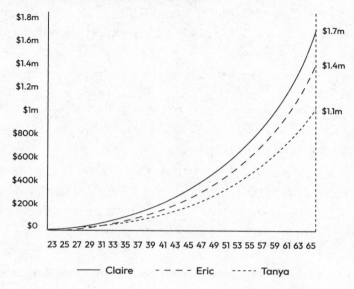

If Tanya had started investing just five years earlier, like Claire, her portfolio would have generated an additional $584,199 in growth, for a total portfolio value of $1,775,558. Even a one-year difference could have cost Tanya $80,593 – because at an annual return of 7%, the money starts to add up quickly as your portfolio grows. And this example doesn't even account for the additional growth they would have experienced if they increased the dollar amount of their investments over time. This is exactly why you want to invest as early as possible. I give this example not to shame anyone who may be late to the game, but to underscore how important it is to start investing whenever you can. I don't want you to miss out on this opportunity to make your money grow!

Note: Unlike the example in Figure 7.4, you should be aiming to increase your rate of investment every year, even if it's only by 2 or 3% of your salary.

To look at it one more way, Figure 7.5 shows how much more money Tanya and Eric would need to invest, inclusive of any employer contributions available to them, to reach the same amount as Claire at 65 because they started later. To catch up, Eric would need to contribute an extra $45,912 over the years because he started investing three years later. Tanya would have to contribute an additional $97,680.

Figure 7.5   Claire versus Tanya versus Eric: Contributions Required to Reach the Same Amount

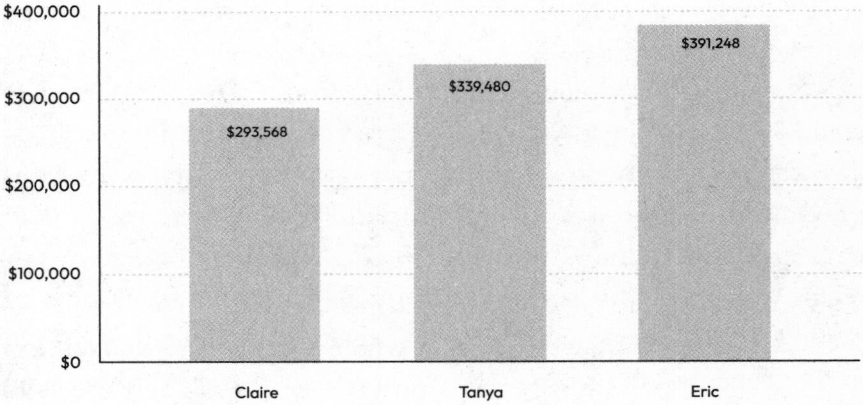

Curious how long it would take for your investments to grow? Test out my favorite retirement calculator at www.wealthonadime. com/resources.

Hopefully the examples above illustrate the importance of investing as early and as often as you can, even if you're just starting today.

Remember that more important than the amount you're contributing right now, is getting into the habit of investing regularly. You can easily do this through your 401(k) or by setting up an automatic contribution to an IRA (or both). Of course, there are other types of accounts you might consider as well, and I'll cover them all in the next chapter.

Like Tanya, for now, the important part is that you get started – and the easiest way to do that is likely through your 401(k) or IRA. Now that we have that covered, your next question is probably, *How much should I invest?*

So let's explore.

How Much Should I Invest?

Referring back to Tanya's story, you might think the $1.7 million she's able to save for retirement by the time she's 65 is pretty good, right? The truth is, it might be, but we can't be sure yet for a few reasons.

First, the major question we should be asking is: *What are Tanya's goals for investing?* Is she investing to retire at 65 or 55? Or maybe she wants to build some extra wealth to pass down to her family? Any of these would drastically change the amount of money she needs to invest over time. For the purpose of this chapter, let's assume she's just thinking about retirement at 65 right now – though early retirement does sound nice! We'll get to the possibility of early retirement a bit below, and dive deep into what makes it possible in Chapter 9. Beyond the Basics.

Beyond her goals for investing, whether or not $1.7 million is a good number for Tanya depends on (a) how much she expects to spend in retirement, known as a *withdrawal rate,* and (b) how long she expects to live in retirement. While the latter isn't the most fun thing to talk about in the world, it is important if you want your investments to be sufficient in retirement.

Plus, I don't know about you, but I want to be living my best life when I retire! Vacations, margaritas – I'm going to need my portfolio to support all these things, plus the basics like housing, food, and so on.

Long story short, there are a few variables that go into how much you should invest for retirement. Luckily, there are also a few guidelines to help you get a ballpark of how much you need to save over time. They include the 25× rule and the 4% rule.

The 25× Rule

The *25× rule* is the idea that if you can save 25× the amount you plan to withdraw (or spend) from your investment accounts your first year in retirement, then you can safely withdraw 4% every year thereafter and live happily ever after in retirement bliss.

For example, let's say you plan to spend $55,000 your first year in retirement. Keep in mind you'll want to adjust what you spend annually today for inflation to keep up with the increased cost of living 10, 20, or 30 years down the road. Let's also assume, in this example, that $15,000 of that $55,000 will be covered by Social Security benefits or other source of income (for example, a pension). This means you'd need to withdraw $40,000 that first year from your investment account to cover the difference. Following this example, you'd want to have 25× $40,000 in or across your investment accounts, for a total of $1 million, knowing you'll have to pay taxes on whatever you withdraw depending on the type of account.

$$25 \times \$40,000 \,/\, \text{year anticipated withdrawal} = \$1\,\text{million}$$

Going back to Tanya's example, based on her current rate of investment, we project she'll be able to save $1.7 million by the time she retires. Reversing the 25× rule, then $1.7 million would be enough for her to retire so long as she didn't need more than $68,000 her first year in retirement ($1.7 million ÷ 25 = $68,000). Again, this does not include any benefits she may get from Social Security.

Based on Tanya's current annual expenses, minus housing, debt payments and investment contributions, plus a $800 monthly buffer would be $34,272 worth of annual expenses today. Adjusted for inflation at the rate of 2% per year till age 65, and we estimate she'll need $66,316 her first year of retirement. According to the 25× rule, this would make her current contributions enough to meet her needs for approximately 30 years, separate from any Social Security benefits she'd receive.

A word on social security

One assumption of the 25× rule is that it does not include an additional income you may receive from Social Security benefits. This is probably a good thing, as Social Security benefits are expected to dry up by around 2035 and will only provide about 80% of its intended benefits to retirees at that time.[3] This is largely because population rates have declined over the years, so there are less people contributing to social security with longer life expectancies. That said, this doesn't mean it won't be replaced by something else, so we'll have to stay tuned . . . but it is another reason to start investing as soon as possible.

Want to estimate what your Social Security benefits might be? Use this calculator from the Social Security Administration: https://www.ssa.gov/myaccount/retire-calc.html.

One caveat about the 25× rule: It's based on the 4% rule, discussed below, which *does* account for inflation once you retire, but also assumes a retirement period of only 30 years – for example, from age 65 to 95. That said, if you hope to retire early or plan to live a long life in retirement, you'll either need to increase your investment goal or plan to lower your withdrawal rate.

My suggestion? If you want to play it safe, or plan to retire early, instead of the 25× rule, aim to save 30× or 33× your pre-retirement income, with a 3.3% or 3% withdrawal rate. So long as your portfolio grows to 30 or 33×, you'll be able to withdraw a smaller percentage and get the same dollar amount you need in pre-retirement income. See Table 7.2 for an example, assuming you want $60,000 in pre-retirement income your first year in retirement.

Table 7.2   Example of Multiplier vs. Withdrawal Rate

Multiplier	Investment Portfolio	Withdrawal Rate	Amount Withdrawn
25×	$1,500,000	4%	$60,000
28×	$1,680,000	3.5%	$60,000
30×	$1,800,000	3.3%	$60,000
33×	$1,980,000	3%	$60,000

The 4% Rule

As a rule of thumb, financial advisors will often recommend 4% as a safe withdrawal rate, where you withdraw 4% of your total investment portfolio your first year in retirement and adjust it by the change in inflation every year following. For example, if your investment portfolio was $950,000, then you could safely withdraw $38,000 your first year of retirement and adjust for inflation every year after. That said, there are a few caveats I'd like to point out:

- It assumes a 30-year retirement period – in other words, the 4% only lasts you long enough if your retirement doesn't exceed 30 years. If you retire early or live longer than 30 years, you might be out of luck unless you either (a) invest more, (b) have another source of passive income, (c) use a more conservative withdrawal rate, or (d) your portfolio grows faster than expected in retirement.

- It assumes you're paying any taxes or fees on the investments you withdraw with that same money – so you don't actually get to spend all of your withdrawal. This is particularly important if a large portion of your investments are in tax-deferred or taxable accounts, which I'll cover in detail in the next chapter.

- The rule is based on a research paper called the Trinity Study that assumed a 50% stock/50% bond portfolio, during a time when bonds had much higher returns. In other words, it assumed a certain level of growth that you probably couldn't get today with that same setup – but I'll cover how to rebalance your portfolio under *asset allocation* in detail in Chapter 9.

So, there are few caveats to the 4% rule, but it's still not a bad rule of thumb and can be helpful in planning a target for what you want to save or spend in retirement.

So . . . What's the Exact Number I Need?

Because retirement, like personal finance, is so nuanced, it's hard to make a specific recommendation without knowing you. That said, my favorite retirement calculator is from NerdWallet because it's easy to read but still lets you change a lot of the assumptions if you need to.

Want a few tips? Make sure to include any employer match in the monthly contribution. You may also note that this calculator uses your current income as one of its assumptions, adjusting that for inflation to arrive at your *pre-retirement income*. That said, the calculator doesn't know you! And your expenses now might be very different from what you'll spend in retirement. For example, you may not want to save or invest as much in retirement, or may have paid off a mortgage by then. Thankfully, NerdWallet lists all the assumptions built into the calculator, most of which you can change by clicking the "Optional" tab.

Find it on my website at www.wealthonadime.com/resources.

But What If It's Too Late? (Spoiler Alert: It's Probably Not)

If you're already in your 40s and 50s and you haven't started investing yet, or maybe you've just done the bare minimum, it can be easy to feel behind. When I started learning about investing, I was mostly just angry I hadn't learned about it earlier. It was incredibly frustrating – but the worst thing you can do is sit back and do nothing. While your investments likely won't grow as much as someone who started in their 20s or 30s, you'll still be significantly better off than if you never started at all. I don't know about you, but I'd rather have $100,000 or $200,000 to my name than nothing.

Wondering what you can do if you're a bit closer to retirement? Here are a few things you'll want to consider:

- **Play catch-up:** Most tax-advantaged retirement plans allow a *catch-up contribution* for individuals age 50 or over, allowing them to contribute beyond the standard contribution limit. This includes up to an extra $6,500 for 401(k)s, 403(b)s, 457(b)s, and Salary Reduction Simplified Employee Pension Plan (SARSEP) plans (if you had one before 1996), and an additional $1,000 for IRAs, so take advantage of that if you can!

- **Play it safe:** The closer you get to retirement age, the safer you'll want to be with your investments to prevent getting hit with a dip in the market or recession when you need it most. When investing for the long term, you can ride out any dips till the market recovers, but as you get older, you have less and less time for that to happen. In the next chapter, I'll cover what asset allocation is and how it can help as you get closer to retirement, but long story short, you'll want to invest in more conservative investments, like bonds, and less in riskier investments, like stocks.

- **Consider any workplace benefits:** Did a previous or current job offer a pension or other benefit, like a health insurance program? While pensions are rare these days, some employers still offer them, providing you with income in retirement based on a certain number of years' service. Some government jobs in particular may offer benefits that can significantly decrease your cost of living in retirement, like healthcare. Lastly, if you're open to working part-time, some employers provide benefits even to part-time employees, such as Starbucks, Amazon, and Walmart, to name a few.

- **Wait on your Social Security:** You're able to withdraw your Social Security at age 62, but that doesn't mean you should. Mandatory withdrawals don't start until age 72, and if you wait until 70, your benefit increases, so you might want to work a bit longer while you can and hold out for the larger benefit in retirement.

Update Your Investment Goals

If you haven't already, now is a good time to revisit your budget to see what you may be able to fit into your investing goals alongside your fixed and variable expenses. Don't worry if you can't contribute your ideal amount right away. Just getting in the habit of investing is a great start, and you can play catch-up as your income grows, you pay off your debt, and so on.

Keep in mind that any pre-tax contributions may be withdrawn in the form of salary deferrals, meaning they may be taken out of your paycheck before you even see it. This is common with 401(k)s and employer-sponsored retirement accounts. If they are post-tax contributions or will be directed to an investment account after you receive your paycheck, make sure to automate those transfers as well. Put any post-tax investments in the Goals section of your budget and automate those transfers early in the month (or soon after you're paid) so it's easier to track what's left in your spending cap. Remember, you may need to adjust your budget if you've changed any goals since you drafted it initially.

As a reminder, here is the calculation for your variable spending cap:

Monthly take-home pay − Fixed expenses − Goals = Monthly variable spending

Monthly variable spending ÷ 4.3 = Weekly spending cap

Lastly, here are a few things to keep in mind as you determine how much you'd like to invest:

- Strive to meet your employer match top to take advantage of that free money! If you're self-employed or don't have an employer match, I'll cover your options for using an IRA in the next chapter.

- If you have any high-interest debt (above 7 or 8%), you'll want to focus on paying this off before investing beyond your employer match.

- If you have debt that's not high interest, continue making the minimum payments and put whatever else you can toward your investments – whatever you can contribute, even if it's only $10 to $25 a month to start, it's better than nothing.

Note: Do not continue until you've calculated how much you can afford to invest right now based on your budget.

Enter your pre-tax contributions/salary deferral	$_____
Enter your employer match, if any	$_____
Enter your post-tax contributions	$_____
Total amount to be invested per month	$_____

Summary

In this chapter, you learned a few different ways to estimate how much you should be investing for retirement, like the 25× rule, the 4% rule, and what assumptions they're based on so you can adjust accordingly. Even more importantly, however, I hope you learned through Tanya's story just how important it is to start investing as much and as often as you can. Remember: Even one year can make a big difference over time!

Now that you understand the benefit of investing early and have a ballpark of how much you'd like to invest on a monthly basis, your next question is probably, "What should I invest in?"

The answer to your question depends on whether you're asking about the type of account to put your investments in, or the investments themselves, but either way – what a time to be alive, money maker. There are so many options! And it's never been easier to invest thanks to some serious advancements in technology over the years. In the next chapter, I'm going to cover the different types of investment accounts you should consider to keep more of your wealth, and the investments you might want to make within those accounts to give yourself the best chance for high growth over time.

Notes

1. Measured by the S&P 500.
2. Assuming a 7% average rate of return.
3. Social Security Board of Trustees, "Outlook of Combined Trust Improves," press release, Social Security Administration, June 2, 2022, https://www.ssa.gov/news/press/releases/2022/#6-2022-1.

Chapter 8

Investing 101

*I*n the previous chapter, we focused on Tanya started investing as soon as she learned how important it was to start early, but now she's ready to go all in. She has a few options to level up her investing game but doesn't know where to start. Tanya recently paid off all of her student loans using the avalanche method and was able to build her emergency savings back up after a setback last year. She knows she can increase her 401(k) contribution, but thinks it could also be fun to open up an account of her own – but which kind? She's also not sure what types of investments to make or how any additional contributions might impact some of her other goals. For example, she'd like to save up for a home one day.

Tanya's salary has also increased since she was 28 – she now makes $100,000 a year. With her loans paid off, this gives her tons of room to increase her investments or level up her lifestyle.

Let's take a look at Tanya's current expenses:

Tanya, 34	Monthly Expenses
Chicago, IL, $100,000 salary Sufficient emergency savings	6% to 401(k) (pre-tax) = $500 Employer match = $333
Take-home pay	$5,477
Fixed expenses: • Rent: $1,600 • Utilities: $100 • Phone bill: $45 • Subscriptions: $120 • Metro pass: $75 • Pet insurance: $75	$2,015

(Continued)

(Continued)

Tanya, 34	Monthly Expenses
Goals	$2,063
• Vacation fund: $350	
• Pet sitting fund: $100	
Note: $1,613 to be redistributed, formerly going toward her student loans and emergency fund.	

$5,477 – $2,015 – $2,063 = $1,399 remaining for variable expenses

Variable spending cap: $1,399	$1,399 = variable spending cap
$1,399 ÷ 4.3 = $325 weekly	$1,399 ÷ 4.3 = $325 weekly
• Groceries: $300	
• Dining/drinks: $300	
• Other transport: $150	
• Entertainment: $200	
• Fitness: $99	
• Shopping: $200	
• Personal care: $150	
Total Budget:	$5,477

Let's go, money makers! I'm pumped for Tanya – all these options are so exciting! We'll continue to follow her story as she figures out her next move, noting the different types of accounts and investments she could build wealth with over time.

Apart from Tanya, I'm also pumped for you because this is where you start learning all the tips and tricks financial advisors know, and I can't wait for you to take advantage of them! In this chapter, I'll detail the different types of accounts and investments you should consider to make the most of your money while building wealth. Specifically, you'll learn the following:

- Which tax-advantaged accounts can save you hundreds of thousands of dollars over time – that's a lot of money!

- How much you're allowed to contribute to each type of account. Pssttt, when the IRS limits how much you can contribute to an account, you know it's something good!

- What types of investments to consider (e.g., individual company stocks, index funds, mutual funds, exchange-traded funds (ETFs), bonds, and annuities).

- What to look out for when making investments, like expense ratios and administration fees, so you don't spend more money than you have to.

Then, in Chapter 9. Beyond the Basics, I'll get a little more advanced, covering investment strategies used by the pros, completely legal loopholes, and alternative investments. I'll also provide a step-by-step process for opening an investment account of your own.

Cool? Cool . . . let's get you on your merry, money-making way!

The Magic of Tax-Advantaged Accounts

Oh, the beauty of the most boring-sounding thing ever: tax-advantaged accounts! I know you might be fighting the urge to fall asleep right now, but trust me, you'll want to pay attention here. The differences between a tax-advantaged account, like a 401(k) or IRA, and a taxable brokerage account are key to building wealth. So tape your eyelids open, whatever you have to do; you'll want to know what's in this chapter.

The reason tax-advantaged accounts are so amazing is they save you a ton of money in taxes, either when you invest, while your investments grow, or when you withdraw funds in retirement. This is very different from a taxable brokerage account, where your investments are taxed at three levels:

1. As you make investment contributions (you pay income tax on the money you use to invest in a standard taxable brokerage account).

2. In the year you receive a dividend (in most cases you'll pay *capital gains* tax, which I'll cover in detail in this chapter).

3. When you *realize* any capital gains – or the amount by which your share(s) have grown when you sell or withdraw.

Essentially, you're taxed two to three separate times when you invest in standard brokerage accounts, as opposed to a tax-advantaged account. By using tax-advantaged accounts, you can avoid or defer taxes in one or multiple stages:

1. You can defer income tax on contributions if using a tax-deferred account, like a Traditional 401(k).

2. Your money grows tax-free – this is the biggest benefit! – deferring or avoiding what would otherwise be capital gains tax in a taxable brokerage account.

3. Your contributions and earnings can be tax-exempt if using a post-tax account like a Roth IRA.

In other words, tax-advantaged = tax savings = more wealth.

I love when that happens!

Table 8.1 shows the various types of tax-advantaged accounts I'll cover in this chapter. They include investment accounts offered by employers, which I'll refer to as employer-sponsored retirement accounts, as well as a few you might use separately or in addition to your employer-sponsored retirement plan. Some of them may sound familiar to you, but keep in mind that you can likely take advantage of more than one! I'll talk about this in just a bit.

Table 8.1 Common Tax-Advantaged Investment Accounts

Type of Account	Employer, Individual, or Business Owner	Pre-tax	Post-tax	Annual Max. Employee Contribution Limit (2022)	Annual Max. Income Limit	Penalty for Early Withdrawal of Contributions
Traditional 401(k), 403(b), or 457(b)	Employer-sponsored retirement plan	Yes	No	$20,500	None	Y, except 457(b)
Roth 401(k), 403(b), or 457(b)		No	Yes	$20,500	Yes*	No, so long as you've held the account for at least five years
Thrift Savings Plan (TSP)		No	Yes	$20,500	None	Yes
Traditional IRA	Individual	Yes	No	$6,000	None	Yes
Roth IRA		No	Yes	$6,000	Yes*	No
Health Savings Account (HSA)	Individual or Employer	Yes	Yes	$3,650	None	No, so long as they're for qualified medical expenses
Solo 401(k)	Solopreneur/ Business Owner	Yes	No	See Table 8.6 for details		
SEP IRA		Yes	No			
SIMPLE IRA		Yes	No			

Note: current as of 2022. Keep in mind contribution limits are likely to change in 2023. Check the IRS website for the latest.

*For 2022, you can make the full contribution so long as you make less than $129,000 if single, head of household or married filing separately ($204,000 if married filing jointly). Above that, and you face reduced contributions up to $144,000 if single (or $214,000 if married filing jointly), at which point you are no longer eligible.

Before we get into the pros and cons of each of these accounts, here are a few important terms you should know:

- **Traditional versus Roth:** The major difference between a Traditional and Roth account is whether your contributions are taxed later (making them *pre-tax contributions* in a Traditional account) or taxed now (making them *post-tax contributions* in a Roth account). It's worth noting that depending on your income, you may also receive a tax deduction for contribution to a Traditional IRA but not a Roth IRA. Whether you receive a deduction depends on your income and whether you also have an employer-sponsored retirement plan; but either way, you'll still benefit from *tax-deferred* growth![1]

- **Tax-deferred:** You don't pay taxes on any earnings as your investments grow now, but you *will* pay when you withdraw in retirement. In some cases, your contributions may also be tax-deferred, making it less expensive for you to invest now, as opposed to paying tax on that money and investing what's left. Any type of 401(k), 403(b), 457(b), TSP, or IRA with the word "Traditional" in front of it (e.g., Traditional IRA) uses *pre-tax contributions* that are taxed in retirement. This is opposed to a "Roth" version of those accounts (e.g., a Roth IRA), which use *post-tax* contributions.

- **Tax-exempt:** You don't pay taxes on your investment, such as contributions to or distributions from a Health Savings Account (HSA). Any earnings made in a Roth version of a 401(k), 403(b), 457(b), TSP, or IRA (separate from your contributions) are also tax-exempt when withdrawing after age 59½. This can be a big incentive, especially if you expect to spend more in retirement and will therefore be taxed at a higher rate.

- **Maximum employee contribution limit:** This is the maximum amount you can contribute as an employee to an employer-sponsored retirement plan for the year, depending on the type of account – Traditional accounts follow the calendar year, Roth accounts follow the tax year. Remember, the employee contribution limit is different from the *total contribution limit*, which includes contributions from you and your employer.

- **Maximum income limit:** This is the maximum income you can have and still be eligible to contribute to that type of account, based on your Modified Adjusted Gross Income (MAGI). Luckily, your MAGI will never be higher than your gross income by definition, so you really only need to figure out your MAGI if you think it might change your eligibility for a particular investment account. If that's you, and you want to get super accurate, check out the text box below. If you're fine using your gross income, skip it.

How to calculate your MAGI

Your MAGI is calculated by taking your adjusted gross income (AGI) and adding back in certain deductions you may have taken in doing your taxes, like a student loan interest deduction, for example.

Your AGI is simply your gross income, less any deductible expenses, like pre-tax contributions to your IRA, student loan interest, and so. You can find the full list of adjustments on IRS Form 1040, Schedule 1. Your MAGI then takes your AGI and adds certain deductions back in to account for tax-exempt interest, foreign income, and social security benefits. Your MAGI will either be the same or higher than your AGI, but always less than your total gross income.

(Continued)

(*Continued*)

> Unfortunately, you can't find your MAGI on your tax return, but you can estimate it.
>
> You: This is *really* confusing.
>
> Me: I know. The IRS is ridiculous. If you think your MAGI could change your eligibility for a particular account, I've included a simplified example below and recommend speaking with a tax professional.
>
> *Figures are illustrative and have been simplified for this example.*

Total gross income: • Salary / wages (W-2) • Rental income • Other income	$78,000
Less certain adjustments: • Student loan interest • Traditional and self-employed IRA contributions • HSA contributions • Self-employed health insurance • Other adjustments per IRS Form 1040, Schedule 1	- $6,000
AGI (line 11 of IRS Form 1040)	= $72,000
Plus certain "add-back" deductions: • Student loan interest • Traditional and self-employed IRA contributions • Other specific deductions	+ $5,000
MAGI	= $77,000

Just *one last thing* (I promise!) before we move on.

No one likes a penalty, especially when it costs you money, so it's important to know that most tax-advantaged accounts come with one if you withdraw before age 59½ – usually around 10% of your withdrawal. These tax-advantaged accounts were designed to save for retirement, so there's an incentive to wait until retirement age – which I guess the IRS decided was 59½. There are exceptions to this, for example, if you want to withdraw up to $10,000 for your first home or you've invested in a Roth IRA (more on this later), but generally, it's in your best interest to keep your money in these accounts as long as possible, especially if you're building wealth.

If you're considering early retirement and wondering what your options are here, I'll cover some advanced tactics in Chapter 9. Beyond the Basics.

Now that we've gotten that over with, let's break down the different types of tax-advantaged accounts. First, I'll cover capital gains tax, which is applied to investments in taxable brokerage accounts and is crucial to understanding what makes tax-advantaged accounts so amazing! Then, I'll break down the different types of accounts to help you build wealth fast.

Capital Gains Tax

Capital gains tax is the tax you have to pay when you *realize* gains on an investment in a taxable brokerage account, meaning you sell an investment that grew or the year in which a dividend was paid. If you own a stock and it grows inside of an investment account, you don't pay any gains tax on that growth until you sell it, at which point you're taxed based on how much growth you've had and how long you held that particular asset. If your stock pays a dividend, you'll be taxed the same year in which the dividend was earned unless it's kept in a tax-deferred account.

- *Short-term gains* are applied if you've held an investment for less than a year, taxed as regular income (your income bracket), ranging from 10 to 37%.

- *Long-term capital gains* are applied if you've held an investment for more than a year, at 0%, 15%, or 20%, depending on your income and filing status.

187

- The long-term gains tax is almost always lower than the short-term gains tax, incentivizing most investors to hold assets for at least a year. Tables 8.2 and 8.3 show the different tax rates for short- and long-term capital gains.

Table 8.2 2022 Short-Term Capital Gains / Income Tax Rates for Single Filers and Married Couples Filing Jointly

Tax Rate	Taxable Income			
	Single	(Married Filing Jointly)	Married Filing Separately	Head of Household
10%	Up to $10,275	Up to $20,550	Up to $10,275	Up to $14,650
12%	$10,276 to $41,775	$20,551 to $83,550	$10,276 to $41,775	$14,651 to $55,900
22%	$41,776 to $89,075	$83,551 to $178,150	$41,776 to $89,075	$55,9091 to $89,050
24%	$89,076 to $170,050	$178,151 to $340,100	$89,076 to $170,050	$ 89,051 to $170,050
32%	$170,051 to $215,950	$340,101 to $431,900	$170,051 to $215,950	$170,051 to $215,950
35%	$215,951 to $539,900	$431,901 to $647,850	$215,951 to $323,925	$215,951 to $539,900
37%	Over $539,900	Over $647,850	$323,926 or more	$539.901 or more

Source: IRS Revenue Procedure 2021-45, https://www.irs.gov/pub/irs-drop/rp-21-45.pdf.

Table 8.3 2022 Long-Term Capital Gains Tax

Tax Rate	Taxable Income			
	Single	Married Filing Jointly	Married Filing Separately	Head of Household
0%	Up to $41,675	Up to $83,350	Up to $41,675	Up to $55,800
15%	$41,676 to $459,750	$83,351 to $517,200	$41,676 to $258,600	$55,801 to $488,500
20%	Over $459,750	Over $517,200	Over $258,600	Over $488,500

Source: IRS Revenue Procedure 2021-45, https://www.irs.gov/pub/irs-drop/rp-21-45.pdf.

Ideally, in addition to holding an investment until it meets the requirement for long-term capital gains, you could also use a tax-advantaged account to defer this tax, allowing more of your wealth to compound, which is *exactly* what you want when investing.

To see the difference, let's take an example of what a $2,400 annual investment starting at age 35, for 30 years, would come out to after taxes, using a fully taxable account versus a tax-advantaged account (e.g., a Roth IRA). Assume an 8% rate of return on both accounts where the investments themselves are exactly the same (see Table 8.4).

Table 8.4   Taxable versus Tax-Deferred Investment Vehicle

Summary	Fully Taxable	Tax-Deferred	Tax-Free
Current investment balance	$0	$0	$0
Annual contributions	$2,400	$2,400	$2,400
Number of years to invest	30	30	30
Before-tax return	8.0%	8.0%	8.0%
Marginal tax bracket	24%	24%	24%
After-tax return	6.1%	8.0%	8.0%
Future account value *	$192,433	$271,880	$271,880
Future account value (after-tax)	$192,433	$223,909	$271,880

Lump sum after taxes is based on 24% tax rate.

To keep things simple, for the taxable account in the example in Table 8.4, we assume taxes are paid on any investment growth annually. On the tax-deferred account, we assume taxes are paid on the lump sum of all growth at age 65 – although in practice, you would likely withdraw what you need in retirement as I covered in Chapter 7.

The result? A $31,476 difference *after taxes* from simply using a tax-deferred account – and that's with a relatively small contribution averaging $200/month. At $1,000 a month, or $12,000 per year, that difference grows to $157,379. The larger the growth, the larger the impact.

From this example, you can see how much faster the tax-advantaged account grew because the individual didn't have to pay capital gains as the investments grew. That's the power of using tax-advantaged accounts, although there are some major differences between them that I'll cover now.

Employer-Sponsored Accounts

Employer-sponsored retirement plans are tax-advantaged accounts offered by your employer. For starters, the Traditional 401(k), 403(b), 457(b), and Thrift Savings Plan are all more or less the same type of account, simply offered by different types of employers:

- 401(k): private companies
- 403(b) or 403(f): state/local government or nonprofit organizations, respectively
- 457(b): the federal government and some nonprofit organizations
- Thrift Savings Plan (TSP): civilian employees of the federal government

Note: Independent contractors may also be able to participate in 457(b) plans. I'll cover this in just a bit.

The first thing you might notice about these accounts is that most of them use seemingly random numbers like 401, 403, and so on.

Annoyingly, these just refer to different sections of the U.S. tax code, not that any money maker would ever want to read it! So I'm just going to cover the stuff you actually want to know.

At a high level, all of these accounts have the same maximum contribution limit, no income limits (meaning you can contribute regardless of your salary), and the same penalty of 10% if you withdraw before age 59½.

The major benefit of employer-sponsored retirement accounts compared to other tax-advantaged accounts like an IRA, is that they have a significantly higher annual contribution limit, meaning you can invest more money to build wealth faster. In 2022, the maximum contribution limit was $20,500 for the calendar year compared to a $6,000 limit on a Traditional or Roth IRA; and that's just the employee contribution, not including any employer contribution. Now, keep in mind this isn't an either/or scenario. You can take advantage of an employer-sponsored plan *and* an IRA, so long as you stay within the income and contribution limits for each.

> Note: The rules on contribution limits across multiple accounts change with other types of 401(k)s and IRAs, which I'll cover in a section intended for solopreneurs and small business owners. For Traditional and Roth IRAs, you don't need to worry about this.

For example, let's say you have a Traditional 401(k) and also want to invest in an IRA. You could, if you had the savings, invest $20,500 pre-tax into your 401(k) in 2022, and another $6,000 pre-tax in your IRA for double the tax savings. It's a beautiful thing!

But this isn't even the biggest benefit of an employer-sponsored retirement plan. The biggest benefit in my opinion is an employer match! Now, I already covered the employer match in Chapter 7, but I want to underscore how amazing they are just one more time.

You *know* I'm not about to pass up free money on the table, and you shouldn't either. If you're not sure whether your employer offers a match or if you're meeting the requirements to get it, you should ask your HR department about it *right now*. Here's an email script you can use to make it easy. This book will still be here when you get back.

Hello HR representative,
Hope all is well, I have two quick questions:

1. Can you remind me whether [insert your employer] offers an employer match to our retirement program and if so, what it is?
2. Please confirm whether I'm currently enrolled and contributing what I need to do to get the full employer match? If not, how much more do I need to contribute per paycheck?

Thanks for the help!
[Your name]

And if you're not enrolled in your plan, you'll want to do that ASAP. You can easily enroll in a *target-date retirement fund*, which is based on your age and is a totally acceptable option for investing. There are lots of great things about a target-date fund that I'll dive into in the Average Money Maker's Guide to Investing section.

Learn from my mistake!

In my early 20s, I thought I was okay investing with just what I needed to meet my employer match in my 401(k) – in my case, 4% of my income. In reality, my contribution limit was significantly higher, and I should have pushed to invest more from the get-go. Instead, I have to invest that much more aggressively now to play catch-up. I hope you'll learn from my mistake!

Reminder: We're only covering the types of accounts right now, specifically, tax-advantaged accounts. These hold your investments, but you'll still need to choose which investments to buy within those accounts (e.g., which stocks, funds, bonds, etc.). It's like how you can take your money to your favorite restaurant and sit inside it, but you haven't bought anything of value until you actually order something to eat – your money is just sitting there. You want to make sure you place an order. More on this in just a bit.

A Health Savings Account (HSA): more than just health insurance

There's one more type of account you might encounter as part of your work benefits that actually has 3× the tax savings, and that's an HSA. While most people associate their HSA with health insurance, it's also a badass investment vehicle! Compared to a 401(k) or IRA, an HSA actually has 3× the tax advantages because (1) it uses tax-free contributions, (2) the earnings grow tax-free, and (3) you can use the withdrawals, also tax-free, for qualified medical expenses,

(Continued)

193

(Continued)

which include everything from doctors visits to hundreds of items at your local pharmacy. Further, unlike a Flexible Savings Account (FSA), any unused funds do roll over to the following year. The only catch is that an HSA requires a high-deductible health plan, which may not be great for money makers who find themselves at the doctor's frequently – depending on the deductible, it may not be worth it. That said, if you don't go to the doctor too often, then it can be a great option to invest and cover your healthcare expenses at the same time! The maximum annual contribution limit from both the employee and employer is $3,625 as of 2022.

So here's what we've covered so far:

- Why tax-advantaged accounts are so great.
- The difference between pre- and post-tax contributions.
- The difference between tax-deferred and tax-exempt.
- The differences between a Traditional and a Roth account.
- What your MAGI is and why it's important.
- The common types of employer-sponsored accounts.

But what if you don't have an employer or want to take advantage of more than one type of tax-advantaged account? Enter the IRA. Spoiler alert: There are several different kinds.

Individual Retirement Accounts (IRAs)

Note: For the purpose of comparison, when I refer to 401(k)s in this section, that also includes 403(b), 457(b), and TSP accounts.

The money maker. The side hustler. The Uber driver. The business owner.

The IRA was made for money makers like you!

There are several benefits to an IRA:

1. You can have one without or in addition to a 401(k). This means you can benefit from even more tax savings to build wealth even faster!

2. You can choose your financial institution instead of whatever your employer picks, giving you more control over the types of investments available to you.

3. Any growth in an IRA is still tax-deferred like a 401(k), and in some cases tax-exempt – for example, in a Roth IRA.

4. With a Traditional IRA, depending on your income level and whether you already have an employer-sponsored plan or not, you may be eligible for a tax deduction.

5. With a Roth IRA, you can withdraw your contributions (but not earnings) before age 59½ without facing any penalty.

All of these, plus the fact that you can have both a 401(k) and an IRA at the same time, make using an IRA something you should definitely consider. The only downsides to IRAs are that most have significantly lower contribution limits, and some of them – for example, a Roth IRA – have income limits as well. That said, if you're under the maximum income limit, you can use whichever you prefer.

For example, at a salary of $100,000 a year, Tanya is well below the maximum income limit of $144,000 for a Roth IRA (refer to Table 8.1). This means that Tanya could invest in her 401(k) and/or an IRA of her choice – a Traditional or Roth IRA – but which kind should she go with?

By now, you're probably wondering, *"How many different types of IRAs are there?"* I'll cover four in total, the first two being the most common – a Traditional IRA and a Roth IRA. These are for the everyday money maker, whether you have a standard 9-to-5 job or not, and do not require you to own a business.

Then, I'll cover two IRAs specific to business owners: the SEP IRA (Simple Employee Pension) and the SIMPLE IRA (Savings Incentive Match Plan for Employees) IRA. I'll also cover the Solo 401(k), unique to business owners as well – all of which were included in Table 8.1.

The Traditional versus Roth IRA

A Traditional and Roth IRA both allow your investments to grow tax-deferred, with the major difference being that with a Roth account you pay taxes on contributions now (but not on contributions or earnings later), and in a Traditional account, you don't pay taxes now, but you pay on your contributions and earnings when you withdraw in retirement. In general, if you think you'll make more in retirement than you do now, you probably want to go with a Roth IRA, so you pay taxes on your contributions now and avoid them in retirement. If you think you'll make less in retirement than you do now, you're good to go with the Traditional version.

Note: If you're thinking "Of course I'll make less in retirement, I won't be working!" keep in mind that withdrawing (read: selling) any investments from a Traditional 401k or Traditional IRA in retirement will be taxed as income, unless it's from a Roth account. As such, it may be easier to think of it as how much you'll want to withdraw in retirement, rather than how much you'll be "making."

Both Traditional and Roth IRAs have key differences from a 401(k):

- You don't need an employer to invest in either IRA.
- There is no employer match.
- The contribution limits are significantly lower in a Traditional or Roth IRA than a 401(k) – $20,500 vs. $6,000 in 2022, although these numbers may increase in 2023 to adjust for inflation.
- There is no income limits on a 401(k), but there is one for a Roth IRA (but not a Traditional IRA).

Now, if you already have a 401(k) with an employer match, there'd be little reason to contribute to an IRA before meeting your employer match. That said, if you're able to take advantage of both a 401(k) and IRA at the same time, then that's the way you want to go. Strive to include both in your budget if you can.

So which IRA should you choose? Ask yourself two questions:

1. Do you think you'll make (or need) more or less income in retirement than you do now?
    a. If you think you'll have a lower income in retirement than you do now, then you'll want to consider a Traditional IRA so you pay taxes when you're in a lower tax bracket.

b. If you think you'll have higher income in retirement and be in a higher tax bracket, you'll likely want to consider a Roth account because you'll pay income taxes on your contributions now but won't have to worry about them later.

2. Might you want to withdraw any of your contributions before age 59½?

a. If the answer is maybe or yes, then you might reconsider a Roth IRA regardless of your answer to Question 1. Roth IRAs are one of my favorite investment vehicles because they allow for penalty and tax-free withdrawals of your investments before age 59½, so long as you've had the Roth for at least five years. This makes it sort of like an awesome savings account that allows for growth – although it will always be an investment vehicle and therefore, always involves some risk. Now, if your income is too high to contribute directly to a Roth IRA, there's a strategy I'll cover in Chapter 9, Beyond the Basics called a *backdoor Roth IRA*. For now, all you need to know is that you can withdraw any and all of your contributions without taxes or early withdrawal penalty, so long as your account has been open for five years.

b. If the answer is no, then you can go with either the Traditional or Roth. You won't face penalties on either after age 59½.

Based on the questions above, which IRA would you choose?

Going back to Tanya's story, given she's still eligible based on her income for a Roth IRA, she ultimately goes with that over a Traditional IRA just in case she ever needs access to her contributions before age 59½. It feels more comfortable to her than a Traditional IRA and she likes the idea of her earnings growing tax-free.

Now that you've determined which IRA works best for you, you might have a few questions.

Q: Can I contribute to a Traditional and Roth IRA at the same time?

A: Yes, but you cannot go above the yearly contribution limit across both. So, if you put $2,500 in a Roth IRA in one year (2022), you can only contribute up to $3,500 to a Traditional IRA, though the only reason you might do that is if you had a major income increase within the same year and were concerned you might no longer qualify for a Roth IRA.

Q: But I can contribute to a 401(k) and an IRA, up to both contribution limits?

A: You got it! You can contribute up to $20,500 to a 401(k) as of 2022, plus an additional $6,000 to either a Traditional or Roth IRA in the same year.

To make it crystal clear, here's the order of operations I recommend if you have an employer-sponsored plan and an IRA (see Figure 8.1). This ladder assumes you already have at least $1,000 in emergency savings per the Goals Flowchart in Chapter 4.

1. Contribute to your 401(k) up to your employer match.

2. Depending on the deductible, you might consider an HSA if your employer offers one in combination with a high-deductible health plan. This is because it offers 3× the tax benefits when used for medical expenses that you're very likely to have in retirement. You can invest whatever you don't use, with a maximum contribution of $3,650 in 2022 for an individual or $7,300 for families. If you are age 55 or over, you can contribute an additional $1,000.

3. Contribute to the IRA of your choice, up to the maximum contribution limit ($6,000 in 2022, plus $1,000 if age 50 or over).

4. Return back to your 401(k), contribute up to the max contribution limit for even more tax-deferred growth (up to $20,500 in 2022, plus $6,500 if 50 or over).

5. If you max out both your accounts, a total of $26,500 in the same year, *then* move onto a taxable brokerage account, which I cover in Chapter 9. Beyond the Basics. If for some reason you open up a taxable account before then, just know you're not benefiting from that magical tax-deferred growth.

Figure 8.1   Tax-Advantaged Ladder

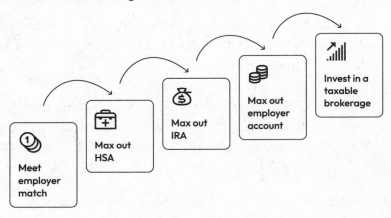

Given that Tanya is already meeting her employer match, she decides to open a Roth IRA to accelerate her investment goals. At first, she starts with $20 just to see how it works before quickly increasing her automatic transfer to $500 per month. That will bring her to the maximum contribution limit of $6,000 per year. If she keeps with it, her $186,000 investment over time will grow to $612,438 by the time she's 65, making a $426,438 profit. This is in addition to the money she'll have separately in her 401(k).

Note: Curious how Tanya opened her Roth IRA? In Chapter 9, Beyond the Basics, I'll cover all the steps you need to open up your own investment account.

After opening up her Roth IRA, Tanya takes another look at her budget. She still has a good amount of money left to play with since the IRA only took up a portion of what she was used to paying on her student loans. Shifting to her other goals, she decides to start a separate high-yield savings account to save for a down payment on a home, with another automatic transfer of $675/month. As a last step to try and build wealth, Tanya is comfortable with her current spending, so she sticks everything else in her 401(k) with a small reduction to her fixed expenses. This increases her monthly pre-tax contribution from $500 to $1,200 per month, not including her employer match. She's not maxing out that account yet, but she's pretty damn close! In total, she increased her monthly investment contributions by more than 3× across her 401(k) and IRA, not including any employer contributions.

In other words, Tanya is *killing* the money game. Let's take a look at what her budget looks like with these changes (see Table 8.5).

Table 8.5   Tanya's Money Moves

Before Changes	After Changes
$100,000/year	$100,000/year (no change)
6% to 401(k) (pre-tax) = $500 Employer match = $333	401(k) (pre-tax) = $1,200 Employer match = $333 (no change)
Take-home pay: $5,477	Take-home pay: $4,970 (decrease)

Fixed expenses: $2,015 total
• Rent: $1,600
• Utilities: $100
• Phone bill: $45
• Subscriptions: $120
• Metro pass: $75
• Pet insurance: $75
	Fixed expenses: $1,946 total (decrease)
	    Slight change to utilities (reduced to $70)
	    and subscriptions (reduced to $81)

(Continued)

Table 8.5   (Continued)

Before Changes	After Changes
Goals: $450 total • Vacation fund: $350 • Pet sitting fund: $100 *Note: $1,613 to be redistributed,* *formerly going to student loans and* *emergency fund.*	Goals: $1,625 total (increase) Addition of $500 toward Roth IRA and $675 toward saving for a down payment on a future home.
$4,970 − 1,946 − $1,625 = $1,399	
Variable spending cap: $1,399 $1,399 ÷ 4.3 = $325 weekly • Groceries: $300 • Dining/drinks: $300 • Other transport: $150 • Entertainment: $200 • Fitness: $99 • Shopping: $200 • Personal care: $150	Variable spending cap: $1,399 No change
Total budget: $5,477	Total budget: $4,970

With these changes, Tanya saves $16,200 for a down payment with her fiancé in two years, plus another $12,000 in her Roth IRA that she could also use toward her first home if she wanted. With a little adjusting, Tanya *could* max out her 401(k), exhausting all tax-advantaged options before opening a taxable brokerage account. This would really help her build wealth faster, especially if she might want to retire early. If she sticks to her new contribution of $2,033 per year (401(k), match, and Roth IRA) on top of the $51,215 in her existing 401(k), even if she never increased her contributions again, she'd have $2.9 million by age 65.[2]

I'll revisit Tanya's options for retiring early in the next chapter.

■ ■ ◤

This next section will cover three additional tax-advantaged vehicles for entrepreneurs, independent contractors, and small business owners. If you're not self-employed and don't own a business, feel free to skip ahead to the Average Money Makers Guide to Investments section.

Options for the Self-Employed

If you're self-employed, an independent contractor, or a small business owner, there are two more IRAs and a unique 401(k) to consider for additional tax savings as you build wealth. Also, major props to you! Starting a business is no easy task, but it can be extremely rewarding and play a big role in building wealth if you're successful.

The last three tax-advantaged vehicles I'll cover include:

1. **The Solo 401(k):** You don't hear about this type of 401(k) often because it's only for business owners or independent contractors where you are the only employee. That said, with a seriously high contribution limit of $61,000 in 2022 (plus $6,500 if you're 50 or older), this can mean huge tax savings if you're eligible!

2. **The SEP IRA:** A bit different from other retirement accounts, a SEP IRA is essentially a profit-sharing plan that allows the employer to contribute to employee retirement. If you're the only employee of your company, this is pretty simple. If you have other employees, the plan will require you to contribute to their accounts, too, so that's important to keep in mind. Note that employees, including yourself, do NOT make any contributions, only the employer.

3. **The SIMPLE IRA:** A SIMPLE IRA is more similar to the other retirement accounts you've been learning about. Both the employee and the employer can contribute, except employer contributions are required, though they can be less intimidating than the required contributions of SEP IRA.

All three accounts allow your investments to grow tax-deferred, with the Solo 401(k) offering both a Traditional and Roth version for pre- or post-tax contributions. The SEP and SIMPLE IRA are both post-tax accounts.

One of the biggest differences between these accounts is that both the SEP and SIMPLE IRA can be used if you have more than one employee, while the Solo 401(k) can only be used if you're the only employee. That said, if you're considering setting up one of these accounts for your business, I strongly recommend you speak to a tax professional, especially if you have other employees to consider.

In the meantime, Table 8.6 maps out some of the pros and cons across all three types of accounts. I'll also go through an example if you started a side business and wanted to pick between one of these.

Table 8.6 Retirement Account Options for Solopreneurs and Small Business Owners

Descriptor	Solo 401(k)	SEP IRA	SIMPLE IRA
Max. employee contribution	Up to 100% of income up to $20,500	$0 (employees do not contribute)	Up to $14,000
Max. employer contribution	Up to 25% of your salary (20% if sole proprietorship or single member LLC) up to $61,000 total (employee and employer combined)	The lesser of up to 25% of the employee's compensation or up to $61,000 in 2022 Must contribute the same percentage to all employees	Employers must contribute either an employer match between 1% and 3% compensation or 2% for each eligible employee up to $305,000 of their salary
Traditional or Roth?	Traditional or Roth	Traditional	Traditional
Pros	High contribution limit Traditional or Roth	High contribution limit	If more than one employee, less intimidating contribution guidelines

Descriptor	Solo 401(k)	SEP IRA	SIMPLE IRA
Cons	Cannot use if more than one employee (excluding spouse)	Contribution is limited to percentage of employee compensation. Requires contribution to all employees same as yourself (although you may skip years)	Lower total contribution limit than Solo 401(k) or SEP IRA
Max income limit?	None	None	None
Employer vs. employee contributions	Employer and employee	Employer only	Employer and employee
Okay even if you have another employer-sponsored plan?	Yes	Yes	Yes
Limitations	Cannot have any additional full-time employees except a spouse	Any business size	Must have 100 or fewer employees
Other comments			25% penalty tax if the account is less than two years old

*All limits are as of 2022. Check the IRS website for the latest.
Sources: IRS, "One-Participant 401(k) Plans," https://www.irs.gov/retirement-plans/one-participant-401k-plans; IRS, "SEP IRA," https://www.irs.gov/retirement-plans/plan-sponsor/simplified-employee-pension-plan-sep; IRS, "Simple IRA Contribution Limits," https://www.irs.gov/retirement-plans/plan-participant-employee/retirement-topics-simple-ira-contribution-limits.*

Based on these options, let's pretend you wanted to start an online business. You have no other employees. As an employee and employer of 1, you could go with any of the above options to maximize your tax benefits. You could also contribute to these in addition to a 401(k) – nice! But which type of account would you choose?

Here are some more (hypothetical) assumptions:

- Based on your current income, you think you might spend more in retirement. While this isn't the case for everyone, you want to live a more comfortable lifestyle in retirement and plan on supporting some family.
- You have no other employees.
- Your side hustle makes $20,000 in the first year.
- You already have a 401(k) and a Roth IRA.

Based on these assumptions, my recommendation would be the Solo 401(k). Why?

- You're eligible for a Solo 401(k) as an employee and employer of 1.
- You can contribute up to 100% of compensation for a higher contribution limit than the SEP or SIMPLE IRA in this example.
- You can decide between a Roth or Traditional version.

Now, if you had additional employees, you wouldn't be able to use the Solo 401(k). In this case, I might recommend a SIMPLE IRA over a SEP IRA because the SEP IRA requires you to make the same percentage contribution across all employees as you do yourself. As the owner, that can be a bit scary when you're first starting out!

With a SIMPLE IRA, you have more flexibility, contributing between 1 and 3% of an employee's salary as a match, or 2% to all eligible employees, and could still contribute more if you wanted as the *employee* contribution to the SIMPLE IRA (separate from your contribution as the *employer)*. In my opinion this makes it a less intimidating and more flexible option than the SEP IRA.

Ultimately, if you're considering one of these plans, I strongly recommend speaking to a Certified Public Accountant (CPA) or tax professional. That said, I hope this rundown is helpful in thinking through your options and preparing for any discussion with a tax pro.

Contribution Limits across Multiple Accounts

If you work two jobs and therefore have access to both an employer-sponsored retirement plan and a separate plan through your business, your total *employee* contribution cannot exceed the maximum employee contribution of $20,500 across these plans (in 2022):

- Any 401(k) or 403(b) (but not 457(b))
- SIMPLE IRA (although SIMPLE IRA contributions cannot exceed $14,000)
- SARSEP (a SEP IRA set up before 1997)

> Note: A 457(b) is not included in this list; its deferral is counted separately.

This means that if you have one or more of the above plans, then your individual or employee contribution limit is capped at $20,500 in 2022 across your accounts. However, the *total* contribution limit, which includes both employer and employer contributions, is considered individually for each employer (at $61,000 per employer in 2022). This means, for example, that if you had a Traditional 401(k) from your main job and a Solo 401(k) for your side hustle, you could – in theory – take advantage of the full $20,500 employee contribution, plus up to $61,000 in employer contributions *per employer* (with your company being the second employer).

Do you see what happened there? So long as your business was successful and you stayed within the terms of your chosen retirement plan, you could take advantage of some serious tax savings – an additional $61,000 to be specific! Remember, I want you to dream big here – while a salary or contribution that high might seem impossible now, it's still good to be informed as your income and financial trajectory change – especially if you're hoping to grow your business over time.

Where to Open a Solo 401(k), SEP IRA, or SIMPLE IRA?

While the above considerations might feel a complicated, opening an account is actually super easy. I'm a big fan of Vanguard as the O.G. brokerage of index funds (you'll learn all about these in just a bit). Vanguard also offers all three types of accounts, but there are other options, too. You can open a Solo 401(k) with Fidelity or a SEP IRA with Ally or Betterment, among others. I've used Ally for years, so they get a personal recommendation from me for incredible customer service and a great online interface.

The Average Money Maker's Guide to Investments

Now that you have an idea of how much you want to invest and the types of tax-advantaged accounts you might utilize, your next question is probably what you should invest in. Now, I legally can't give you specific investment advice, but I can definitely help you understand the pros and cons of different options you might consider. Ultimately, the final decision is yours. This should not be taken as investment advice, only the education you need to inform your decision.

Some investments I'll cover in this chapter include:

- **Mutual funds:** These are usually actively managed funds that try to beat the performance of the market, and are traded and priced each day after the market closes. The exception to this is mutual index funds, which are passively managed.

- **Exchange-traded funds (ETFs):** Most of these are *index funds*, meaning they passively track a particular stock market index, mimicking the market instead of trying to beat it. They are traded during market hours, and prices change throughout the day, similar to a stock.

- **Index funds:** A mutual fund or ETF that tracks a particular stock market index, like the S&P 500 Index, mimicking the market instead of trying to beat it. They are known to have much lower fees than other types of funds and are extremely popular in the personal finance community.

- **Target-date funds:** A specific type of mutual fund structured around the particular year an investor or investors anticipate retiring. Target date funds are great because they automatically rebalance themselves, which helps mitigate risk.

- **Bonds:** Often sold by municipalities and governments, a debt security that pays interest or dividends as the bond matures.

- **Annuities:** An insurance contract where an insurance company agrees to pay you interest in exchange for your investment.

Wondering why I don't mention individual company stocks on this list? It's because I'll never recommend investing in a specific company over a fund that includes a much broader set of investments and is safer for your money.

Individual stocks are super risky, money makers!

Yes, picking individual stocks can make for higher returns *sometimes*, but there's a ton of analysis that goes into picking them, and even the pros get it wrong on occasion – so I'll focus mostly on the different types of funds and investments listed above.

As you may recall from Chapter 7, an investment fund allows investors to pool their money and invest in a particular group of investments that might include various stocks, bonds, or even funds within a fund. The greatest benefit of investing in a fund is that because it's made up of multiple investments, even one share is pretty diverse. Diversification, at a basic level, is essentially how many different types of investments you have in your portfolio, with the goal of spreading out your risk. You can diversify at many different levels – the types of investments (e.g., stocks vs. bonds), the sizes of companies (e.g., large-cap vs. small-cap), the industries of those investments (e.g., are they all in tech, or maybe some in tech, healthcare, retail, etc.).

Think of diversification as going to a new Mexican restaurant. You have $50 to spend, and you could just get chicken tacos, but what if those tacos weren't the best? Then you spent $50 and didn't get anything that great. But what if that $50 went to a chicken taco, a burrito, and some huevos rancheros – chances are, you'll probably like something. If the taco is bad, but the burrito is awesome, that's a much better return on your investment. Even more diversified is if you spend $25 at the Mexican restaurant and $25 at the burger joint down the street.

Funds can be structured around several factors, including a particular industry, the size of a company, and the performance of a stock market index, among other factors. Ultimately, because funds are more diversified than an individual stock or bond, they lower your risk – which is a good thing, regardless of what's known as your *risk tolerance*.

What's Your Risk Tolerance?

"What's your risk tolerance?" is a fancy way of asking how much risk (or how big a drop) you could handle when it comes to your investments. For example, would you prefer to take on more risk, with potential for higher return, or prefer slower-growth investments that are more predictable? Would you be okay if you lost 10% of your portfolio's value in a day? What about 20% in a year? Would you keep your cool if the market entered a recession, or feel pressured to sell? Essentially, how would you react or feel in a not-so-great situation? Only you will know the answers to these questions.

If you have a high risk tolerance, that means you're willing to tolerate the ups and downs for a higher potential return over time. The lower your risk tolerance, the more conservative you want your portfolio to be. If you feel you can handle more risk, you might be more of an aggressive investor, and choose more high-growth stocks over index funds or bonds, for example. If you're more conservative, you might choose index funds, which are more predictable over the long run, and bonds as opposed to more volatile investments, despite higher potential returns.

Reminder: investing is a long game

Even if your portfolio is relatively predictable, you'll still want to invest for the long term (at least 5–10 years, ideally 10–20) to build wealth and recover from any dips your portfolio might experience along the way.

Ultimately, your risk tolerance will inform your *asset allocation*, or the portion of your portfolio that's composed of stocks versus bonds, which also plays a role here – the more aggressive you are, the higher proportion of stocks you'll have. The less aggressive, the more bonds and other types of stable securities you'll want.

Regardless of your risk tolerance as you get closer to retirement, the less risky you want to be. To be clear, no one *wants* more risk, but it's especially important to keep it low as you near retirement because if the market does go down, you'll have less time to recover – you might need that income that year or the next. Personally, my portfolio is almost all stocks (via index funds) because I still have a long time for the market to recover if it tanks. Within those stocks, I tend to play it conservative, with the vast majority of my investments in index funds.

What's Asset Allocation?

Asset allocation is a pretty boring but really important part of any investor's portfolio. Essentially, it's the split of stocks versus bonds versus cash you have across all the investments in your portfolio. The younger you are, the more risk you can afford to take on, which would lean heavier toward stocks. The older you are, the more conservative you probably want to be, with less stocks. For example, let's say you have a $100,000 portfolio. If you had $65,000 invested in stocks, $30,000 invested in bonds, and $5,000 in cash, that would be a 65/30/5 split. The reason you want a spread is to lower your risk . . . but how do you know if your current allocation is good or bad?

Luckily, there's an easy rule of thumb for this called the *120 rule*. Simply take your age and subtract it from 120, and that's the percentage you want to invest in stocks versus bonds. So, if you're 30 years old, 120 − 30 = 90, you want 90% of your portfolio invested in stocks versus 10% in bonds. If you're 35, that would be 85% in stocks and 15% in bonds.

Pretty easy, right?

While advisors previously used a 100 rule instead of 120, I prefer using the updated guidance of 120, as life expectancy has risen along the way. If you want to be a bit more aggressive with your investments, you can pretend you're five years younger; more conservative, tack on another five years. Unless you're using a target-date fund, which you'll learn about in just a bit, you'll want to check your asset allocation at least once a year to see if it needs to be rebalanced – though I wouldn't do it more than twice a year, and especially not in a down market. Some 401(k) providers can also set this up automatically, so check with the program administrator if you're unclear.

You: This sounds like a lot of research and math . . .

Not gonna lie, sometimes, it is – luckily, there's a tool for this! Visit www.wealthonadime.com/resources to check out Blooom, a company that will automatically check and rebalance your 401(k) or IRA for you, completely free. This way, you know *exactly* what your asset allocation is and can adjust based on your risk tolerance accordingly.

Mutual Funds versus ETFs

Mutual funds and ETFs allow investors to buy into a basket of various investments that will vary from fund to fund and ETF to ETF. This is great for investors because both ETFs and mutual funds are diversified, which helps keep their risk low. That said, there are some major differences between them.

- **How they're managed:** Most ETFs track a stock market index, meaning they are *passively managed* and do not require active trading, as opposed to mutual funds, most of which are *actively managed* in an attempt to beat the market – unless it's a mutual index fund. Because index funds are a personal favorite of mine, I've included an entire section on them below.

- **Fees:** Because most ETFs track an index, they're considered to be *passively managed* investments. This significantly lowers the fees on ETFs compared to most mutual funds.

- **Upfront investment:** Most financial institutions do not require a minimum investment amount for ETFs so long as you can afford the price of one share, while mutual funds usually have a minimum investment amount that can range from $100 to $3,000 for passively managed mutual funds, to $50,000 for actively managed mutual funds.

- **How they're purchased:** ETFs require you to purchase a full share (unless the brokerage allows for fractional investing) as opposed to mutual funds, where you can invest any dollar amount so long as you've met the initial minimum.

- **When they're traded:** Mutual funds can only be traded once per day, after the market closes, while ETFs can be traded throughout the day (and their price per share fluctuates with it). (See Figure 8.2.)

Figure 8.2   Share versus ETF versus Mutual Fund

	Mutual Fund	ETF
Trading Hours	Usually 4–6pm ET	Usually 9:30am–4pm ET
Minimum Initial Investment		
How They're Purchased		
Passively vs. Actively Managed		

Target-Date Funds

While there are several types of mutual funds – those consisting of just stocks, just bonds, or focused on a particular interest, like technology – the most common mutual fund you may have heard of is a *target-date fund.* It's usually the first thing you see in an employer-sponsored retirement plan, like a 401(k). This is a type of mutual fund, based on the target date you plan to retire, and is pre-diversified and allocated according to when you plan to retire.

While people talk about getting fancy with their individual stock picks all day, know that a target-date fund is a totally solid and safe option – and safe is a fantastic thing when it comes to your investments! Living on the edge and want to make a few individual stock picks of your own? Save that for a very small portion of your portfolio once you've maxed out your tax-advantaged accounts. For now, a target-date fund is a great way to go. The best part? As you get older, target-date funds will automatically be rebalanced using what's called a *glide path*, so you never have to revisit it if you don't want to.

Want to adjust your target-date plan a little bit? Simply add five years to your target date for a more aggressive portfolio or subtract five years for a more conservative play.

If you do nothing else from this book except start or increase your automatic contribution to a target-date fund, in a tax-advantaged account, that would be a win for your financial future – there's no doubt.

Note: Target-date funds are offered by most financial institutions, including but not limited to 401(k)s and IRAs.

Index Funds

Next, onto my personal favorite, *index funds*. A stock market *index* measures how the total stock market, or a portion of the stock market, is performing using price data across a set of companies that make up a respective index. Indexes can vary in size and purpose, for example, the S&P 500 tracks the top 500 companies in the United States while the Nasdaq index focuses on top technology stocks. There are thousands of indexes in the U.S. stock market, and an index fund can be built to track any of them.

Index funds "track" an index by investing in the same companies in the same proportions that make up a given index. Essentially, they copy that same index, and do not intend to beat that index but perform alongside it. Because of this, they're considered *passively managed* as opposed to an *actively managed* investment that requires much more active trading in an attempt to beat the market. While it can be easy to assume that the more work, the better, passively managed index funds are actually an investor favorite because they are more predictable than other funds and have very low *expense ratios*.

Expense ratios reflect the cost of doing business with the investment fund, measured as a percentage of total costs over total assets. Costs can include management fees, operating expenses, and administrative costs, and ideally, you want your investments to have as low an expense ratio as possible. Generally anything below 0.2% is considered pretty good, and anything over 1% is higher than you want to be paying. While 1% may not sound like much, even a 1% expense ratio can save (or cost) you hundreds of thousands of dollars over time. If you're not sure of what the expense ratio of a particular investment is, you can ask to see them in what's called an *investment prospectus*. Financial institutions should make this readily available; if not, it could be a red flag, so don't be afraid to do a little digging.

While some index funds are more popular than others, like the Vanguard Total Stock Market Index Fund (ticker symbol: VTSAX), there are almost 2,000 different index funds to choose from. You can also buy them in mutual fund or ETF form, depending on your preference. For example, Vanguard offers two major funds that track the total U.S. stock market via the same index – VTSAX mutual fund and the VTI ETF (see Table 8.6)

Table 8.6   Mutual Fund versus ETF Example

Fund	VTSAX Mutual Index Fund	VTI ETF
Expense ratio	0.04%	0.03%
Index tracked	CRSP U.S. Total Market Index	
Number of companies in fund	4,112 as of July 2022	
Minimum investment	$3,000	No minimum
Example price of share	$100.39	$206.25
When shares can be traded	End of trading hours	During trading hours

So, which one would I pick in this scenario? It depends. Because the index mutual fund is cheaper per share, I'd likely go with (VTSAX) even with the $3,000 required minimum investment – plus, any investment beyond that $3,000 can be as low as $1 moving forward, meaning you could invest another $30 in the same fund next time. This doesn't mean it's the right fund for you! You might prefer to go with the ETF because it has a lower expense ratio, even though you'll need to pay the full price of the share moving forward to invest more. A share in either will grow or decline at the same rate, because they're both tracking the same index – and most importantly, they both have ridiculously low expense ratios!

Fractional shares

Let's say, for example, a single share of Tesla is $270.21 and that's more than you'd like to pay. Instead of buying an entire share, fractional investing allows you to buy a portion of that share, for example, $50 or 18.5% of a single share. As the value of that stock increases or decreases, your $50 investment will also increase (or decrease) at the same rate. For those looking to start small – $5 here, $20 there – this can be a great option, allowing you to invest and diversify using smaller amounts. Further, while usually reserved for individual company stocks, some companies are starting to offer fractional shares of ETFs, including Fidelity and Robinhood.

All right, money maker! So far, we've covered the following types of funds:

- Mutual funds
- ETFs
- Target date funds
- Index funds

In addition to these different funds, you might also be curious about two other types of potential investments: *bonds* and *annuities*. While these aren't my personal favorites – they usually make lower returns – they're still worth mentioning as a reliable investment, especially if you're a more conservative investor. Bonds and annuities are generally known to be more predictable than mutual funds and ETFs but not without their considerations as well.

You can think of a *bond* as an I.O.U. – usually from a municipality or government – that provides a certain rate of return for a distinct period of time as that bond matures. It's not dissimilar to how you pay interest on a loan to a financial institution for letting you borrow money, except in this case, the money is going back to you!

That's way better :)

- Pros: Compared to a stock, mutual fund, or ETF, bonds are much more predictable and less risky.

- Cons: Lower returns and interest income generated from a bond is only guaranteed for a particular period of time. Further, you may only be able to cash out a bond after a certain holding period. For example, U.S. Savings Bonds require you to keep the bond invested for at least 12 months – after that and before five years, you'll lose three months of interest – but after the five years, you can cash them in, or hold onto them to gain interest for another 25 years.

In my opinion, while bonds are going to be way less exciting (read: more predictable) than a fund or ETF in the long run, they are a key part of an investor's portfolio when thinking about asset allocation and how to protect your portfolio in the long run.

Lastly, an *annuity* is a contract you buy into, between yourself and an insurance company, that guarantees a certain return on your investment no matter how long you live – sounds like a pretty good deal right?

I actually have a pretty firm stance against mixing insurance (especially whole life insurance) and investments for a few reasons:

1. Generally, I just don't like the idea of insurance companies selling anything to do with an investment. I'm simply not comfortable with a business model that bets on how long I'm going to live or be healthy – maybe that's just me.

2. The commissions and fees are usually pretty ridiculous and never easy to find. To be clear, an annuity is different from the

cash value offered by a whole life insurance policy. The problem is, they both have high fees and commissions.

All that said, while annuities do provide a reliable, predictable source of income, I wouldn't recommend them to the average investor or to a friend. There are other, less expensive, higher-reward options you can consider, like the index funds discussed earlier – they may not provide you with income for life, but you'll hopefully have more of it by skipping the annuity commission and fee structures.

Beware of Scams

Please be careful when considering investment options being sold by an insurance agent or insurance company. While annuities, for example, *can* be a legitimate investment, there are plenty of scammers out there talking new investors and senior citizens into annuities investments that ultimately benefit the insurance company, as opposed to the investor. This is also common with whole life insurance, where agents will often advertise a guaranteed cash value. It can be easy to talk young investors into whole life insurance policies because they get more expensive as they get older (and, likely, less healthy) – but the fees can be out of control. Trust me, I almost fell for this in my early 20s! Instead of whole life, consider a term life policy, which is much less expensive and will still provide for your loved ones in the event of your passing (the intended benefit), without the high fees.

Summary

All right, money maker, you're really covering some ground here! Let's keep this wealth train moving.

We covered A LOT this chapter, including the following:

- Why tax-advantaged accounts are the best.
- Why I love Roth IRAs.
- How to determine your asset allocation.
- How to determine your risk tolerance.
- The types of investments you might consider like target date funds, mutual funds, and ETFs.
- The benefits of index funds.

If you walk away with one thing from this chapter, let it be this: Generally speaking, you want to make the maximum contribution allowed by the IRS to your tax-advantaged accounts, all of them, before investing in a standard brokerage account. The maximum employee contribution differs depending on the type of account, is **not** inclusive of an employer match (except in the case of an HSA), and is separate from a *total contribution limit*, which includes both both employee and the employer contributions.

In Chapter 9. Beyond the Basics, I'll talk about what Tanya could accomplish if she decides to make some major changes to her money, going beyond her retirement accounts, to open a taxable brokerage of her own. She's not super confident in her finances yet because she doesn't know exactly what steps to take, but she'll get there.

And so will you.

Let's follow Tanya's story as she figures out her next steps.

Notes

1. You can find where these deductions start at https://www.irs.gov/retirement-plans/ira-deduction-limits.
2. Assuming an average 7% annual rate of return.

Worksheet: Investing 101

Below is an example you can follow to estimate your MAGI if you feel it may put you just over or under the maximum income requirements for a particular type of account.

*Figures are illustrative and have been simplified for this example

Total gross income: • Salary/wages (W-2) • Rental income • Other income	
Less certain adjustments: • Student loan interest • Traditional and self-employed IRA contributions • HSA contributions • Self-employed health insurance • Other adjustments per IRS Form 1040, Schedule 1	
AGI (line 11 of IRS Form 1040)	
Plus certain "add-back" deductions: • Student loan interest • Traditional and self-employed IRA contributions • Other specific deductions	
MAGI	

Below are some common types of income, adjustments, and deductions you might add back in when estimating your MAGI to determine eligibility for different investment accounts.

Income Sources	Common Adjustments	Common "Add-Back" Deductions
• Salary / wages • Business income • Capital gains • Dividends • Interest Income • Rental Income • Taxable interest	• Student loan interest • Traditional and self-employed IRA deduction • Alimony payments • HSA contributions • Moving expenses for military • Self-employed health insurance • Jury duty pay • 50% of self-employment tax • Educator expenses	• Student loan interest • Traditional and self-employed IRA deductions • Passive income or losses • Excluded foreign income interest • Rental losses (if landlord) • Half of self-employment tax

For a full list of adjustments see IRS Form 1040. Keep in mind that pre-tax 401k contributions/deferrals and most social security benefits are not included in gross income.

Chapter 9

Beyond the Basics

*C*ontinuing *with Tanya's story, she recently adjusted her budget, opened up an IRA, and is very close to maxing out her 401(k). She's also in a really comfortable place with her spending – certainly more than she ever thought she'd be able to afford or justify on certain things like restaurants and shopping. She knows she could cut back if she wanted to, but there are so many good places to eat in Chicago!*

Tanya recently heard about the financial independence, retire early (FIRE) community on a podcast, where people invest as much and as early as they can to be "work optional" as soon as possible – she wonders if she can do it, too. Even though she likes her job, she'd love the flexibility of only working when she wants to, or maybe not at all! She's just not sure how it works or if she can do it. She'd also like to do what she can to help out her family. Whether that's increasing her wealth so she can pass it down later or setting up her nieces and nephews for success, she's all for it.

Tanya is starting to dream bigger than she thought she could. Amazing!

With a six-figure salary and some "nice-to-have" things in her budget, Tanya has a few ways she could switch things up if she wants. If she was willing to reduce her spending or find a way to generate additional income, she could increase her 401(k) contribution, but if she retires early, she'll face a penalty on any withdrawals before age 59½. Alternatively, or in addition, she could open up a standard brokerage account to build wealth for retirement or other financial goals, though it wouldn't have the same benefits as her 401(k). For every decision Tanya makes, there's an opportunity cost for not doing something else – but that doesn't mean she can't tackle more than one goal at the same time.

In this chapter, you'll learn all about the different considerations Tanya makes to come up with a new financial plan. These include things like when she'll plan to withdraw her investments, how comfortable she is with technology, and how hands on (or not) she wants to be in managing her portfolio. Unlike the previous chapter, which focused on tax-advantaged accounts, this chapter goes beyond the basics of your 401(k) or IRA. To be clear, those are important accounts that I recommend you use before any taxable brokerage account, but for those who are close to hitting the contribution limits or want to retire early, you'll need some more advanced strategies. Here's what I'll cover:

- What the FIRE community is all about.
- How to open your own brokerage account, whether that's a tax-advantaged account or taxable brokerage.
- A completely legal loophole to using a Roth IRA, even if your income makes you ineligible to contribute directly.
- Advanced investment strategies, like how to implement a *Roth conversion ladder* if you want penalty-free access to investments before age 59½.
- What you can do to build generational wealth in your family.

By the time you finish, you should have a ton of knowledge and options at your fingertips to build wealth like the pros.

Tanya's Next Steps

Tanya is looking to switch up her investment strategy and is completely debt-free for the first time in years. She already has a high-yield savings account set up for a future down payment that she plans on using in the future. Now, if Tanya had a high risk tolerance and a few more years to save up for a home, she might have used a Roth IRA or a taxable investment account to grow those savings – but she's not comfortable with that. While the market is predictable in the long run, it's unlikely that five years would be enough time for the market to recover if her investments were to take a dip. Similarly, if you have a specific goal you want to reach in just a few years, a high-yield savings account is usually a better (and safer) way to go.

Home down payment goal, check! Or at least in progress.

The next thing on Tanya's priority list is to increase her investments so she might have a shot at retiring early. She may not be able to retire at 35 or 40 – she's too late to the game – but wonders if retirement at 50 might be a possibility for her.

The FIRE community

A member of the FIRE community is someone who aims to invest as early and as aggressively as they can to reach a point where they can retire early, knowing their investments will generate sufficient returns to cover their annual expenses. In reality, many people in the FIRE community have passive income streams separate from their investment accounts, such as rental income or digital products – but the premise is the same. By investing early, you can reach a point where the annual return on your investments replaces the

(Continued)

(*Continued*)

income from your employer. While most people might think of retirement as a particular age, it's actually a value at which point you can afford not to work anymore – and that's determined by the growth of your investments.

Within the FIRE community, you'll hear about reaching FIRE, which is the point at which you can replace 25× your income. However, as I discussed in Chapter 7, more recent studies show that this isn't enough because it's based on the 4% rule that assumes a 30-year retirement. If you plan for a longer retirement, like 40 or 50 years, you'll likely want to save closer to 30× or 33× your annual expenses, withdrawing 3.3% or 3% of your income, respectively. All this said, depending on how early and/or aggressively you're willing to invest, early retirement may be a realistic possibility. And while starting early definitely helps, you can certainly reach FIRE later in life, too. It's not how much you make, but how much you invest, and there are multiple ways you can support that goal through a side hustle, part-time job, etc.

Looking at her budget, Tanya thinks $4,000 per month would give her enough wiggle room for her to live off in retirement, or $48,000 per year. It's higher than the retirement earlier we calculated in Chapter 7 because she anticipates she'll still have a mortgage if she retires early. Adjusted for inflation at a rate of 2% per year and that $48,000 would be $65,894 by the time she's 50. Multiplied by 30 – higher than the 25× rule because she'll be in retirement for more than 30 years – and Tanya's FIRE number is $1.97 million.

Keep in mind this does not account for any additional income Tanya may receive from Social Security.

We know from Chapter 8 that Tanya is already set to reach $2.9 million by the time she's 65, based on her IRA and current 401(k) contribution of $1,200 per month. She'd hit $1.9 million at 60. That said, it's important to remember just how much of an impact time can have on compound growth. Even though 60 would technically be an early retirement, Tanya's hoping to build wealth faster than that.

She'll have to work harder – or rather, her money will.

To increase her chances, Tanya needs to invest a lot more upfront than she would have if she didn't want to retire early. She'll also need to be mindful of when she needs access to those investments due to tax and penalty implications of withdrawing from tax-advantaged accounts. That said, even though her 401(k) comes with a 10% penalty on withdrawals before age $59^1/_2$, she'll still want to max it out because the tax-deferred growth will help her build wealth faster. Then, she can use what's called a *Roth conversion ladder* when she's closer to retirement to tap into those contributions early and penalty-free, which I'll cover later in this chapter.

Investing with an average income

You might be reading this thinking that it's easy to become a millionaire when you make six figures – and it certainly is, I'll give you that – but it's not impossible at lower incomes either. At an average annual return of 7%, it takes an investment of $819.69 per month to reach $1 million in 30 years. Keep in mind your employer match can drastically reduce the amount you need to contribute, and the sooner you start, the less you'll have to invest to get there.

In the meantime, the first thing Tanya does is cut back on her variable spending to increase her 401(k) contribution from $1,200 per month to $1,500 while she continues to save for her down payment. This requires cutting $219 from her monthly variable spend – she'll cut back on dining out and shopping. Once she's finished saving up her down payment (at age 36), she'll reallocate her savings of $675 to (a) max out her 401(k) at $1,708 per month, (b) add $100 per month to her vacation fund, and (c) open a taxable brokerage account with a $499 monthly contribution. Any pay increases she receives between now and then can also be used to give her a bit more wiggle room in her variable spend.

Table 9.1 is what Tanya's budget looks like before and after the shift.

Table 9.1   Tanya's Money Moves

Before changes	After changes
$100,000 salary (age 34)	$104,040 salary (age 36)
401(k) (pre-tax) = $1,200 4% employer match = $333	401(k) (pre-tax) = $1,708 4% employer match = $347
Take-home pay: $4,970	Take-home pay: $4,820 (decrease)
Fixed expenses: $1,946 total • Rent: $1,600 • Utilities: $70 • Phone bill: $45 • Subscriptions: $81 • Metro pass: $75 • Pet insurance: $75	Fixed expenses: $2,091 (increase) • Rent: $1,700 • Utilities: $100 • Phone bill: $60 • Subscriptions: $81 • Metro pas: $75 • Pet insurance: $75
Goals: $1,625 total • Vacation fund: $350 • Pet sitting fund: $100 • IRA: $500 • Down payment: $675	Goals: $1,549 (increase) • Vacation fund: $450 • Pet sitting fund: $100 • IRA: $500 • Taxable brokerage: $499
Variable spending cap: $1,399 $1,399 ÷ 4.3 = $325 • Groceries: $300 • Dining/drinks: $300 • Other transport: $150 • Entertainment: $200 • Fitness: $99 • Shopping: $200 • Personal care: $150	Variable spending cap: $1,180 (decrease) $1,180 ÷ 4.3 = $274 • Groceries: $300 • Dining/drinks: $200 • Other transport: $131 • Entertainment: $200 • Fitness: $99 • Shopping: $150 • Personal care: $100
Total budget: $4,970	Total budget: $4,820

Increased investments, check.

Using this strategy, Tanya saves $16,200 for her down payment, and her portfolio grows at a 7% rate of return from $51,215 to $117,436 in two years with her increased contributions. Once she's done saving for her down payment, she reallocates that savings transfer to max out her 401(k) and opens a taxable account with a $499 monthly contribution. Her total investment rate, including her employer match, is an impressive 35% of her gross income. If she continues on this path, she'll reach FIRE by age 55 with over $1.9 million across her accounts (see Figure 9.1). This is separate from any income she may expect to receive from Social Security.

So, is Tanya able to retire by 50? No, she's not. But the option to retire at 55 is close enough for Tanya :) combined with Social Security benefits starting at age 62, and she'll have more than enough to pass down to her family, too.

Figure 9.1   Tanya's Path to Wealth

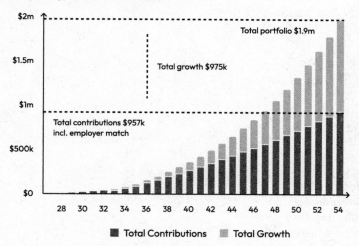

In the next few sections, I'll cover how you could follow the same steps Tanya took to open her own investment accounts – a

Roth IRA and taxable brokerage account. So far, I've been pretty adamant about maxing out any and all tax-advantaged accounts if you want to build wealth fast, but especially for those looking to retire early, you'll want to take advantage of a Roth IRA (if eligible) before a maxing out any pre-tax account to avoid the 10% penalty.

If your income is too high to contribute to a Roth IRA directly (because you're ineligible), you could get around this using what's called a *backdoor Roth IRA*. I'll cover this in just a bit.

Want to know if you might be able to retire early? Use the NerdWallet calculator on my website at www.wealthonadime.com/resources.

How to Open a Brokerage Account

There are six steps you'll take when you open a brokerage account:

1. Decide if you want a person or a robot.
2. Select the type of account you want.
3. Select your brokerage company.
4. Create an account and add your bank information.
5. Pick your investments.
6. Automate your investments.

Step 1: Decide If You Want a Person or Tech

Thanks to some serious advancements in technology, even beginner investors have a variety of ways they can choose to pick and/or manage their investments. But it also means, out the gate, you'll want to decide whether or not you're comfortable using technology or prefer a real person to manage your investments. To help you make that decision, here's the rundown of your options.

Option 1: Financial Advisor

If you want an actual person to advise and/or manage your investments, you'll want a financial advisor – specifically, a Certified Financial Professional (CFP) because they're required to act as a *fiduciary*. Being a fiduciary means that they're legally and ethically required to act in your best interest (read: won't invest in anything risky with your money in an attempt to make themselves more money). Financial advisors usually charge clients in one of two ways: a percentage of their portfolio or *fee-based* using a retainer or other type of annual fee. If you go with a percentage-based advisor, the running rate is usually around 1% of assets under management or less – anything above that, and I'd walk the other way.

FYI, some companies may require a significant amount of *assets under management (AUM),* or the value of your investment portfolio before working with you, but you can find companies willing to work with those that have less or even $0 to start. In addition to managing your investments, most can also set you up with a general financial plan – but they are more expensive in most cases than a robo-advisor or managing your own.

> Note: If you need a CFP, financial advisor, or coach for planning purposes (as opposed to management of your investments) I generally suggest going with a fee-based service, simply because they're more predictable.

Option 2: Robo-Advisor

If you want to go with a low or no fee (or just think technology is awesome), then you might consider what's known as a *robo-advisor*. Robo-advisors include companies like Wealthfront or Betterment that use an algorithm to recommend, pick, and manage your investment accounts. While it may sound risky to rely on a computer to do the work for you, research has shown that robo-advisors can match the returns, if not do better than financial advisors over time. When you sign up for a robo-advisor, after selecting your type of account, you'll likely take a quick quiz to determine your risk tolerance, select any specific industries or preferences you may have, and the robo-advisor will take it from there. If you're not comfortable with technology, this wouldn't be the right option for you – but I've used robo-advisors since I first started investing in 2016. It was helpful because I didn't have to worry about picking anything myself or making sure my portfolio was properly diversified.

Lazy *and* profitable investing will always be my favorite.

Option 3: Manage Your Own Investments

Want to manage your own investments? I love the confidence! But there are also some serious drawbacks to be aware of.

Managing your own investments does come with its benefits – mainly, no fees – but in my experience, unless you're going with a pretty passive portfolio like a target-date fund or a mix of ETFs, it can get a bit complicated to stay on top of those accounts over time. Reviewing your asset allocation, rebalancing your accounts, etc. While there are apps that help you see that information, it's still more work than it's worth, in my opinion. Do I manage my own investments? Yes, but only a small fraction of my portfolio are individual company stocks – the majority are index funds I don't have to worry about because I know they'll go up over time. If you're going to pick your individual stocks, I caution you against managing your own portfolio until you're more advanced. Instead, I'd pay the 0–0.3% fee for a robo-advisor and call it a day. If you do pick your own stocks, I recommend only doing so after you max out all of your tax-advantaged accounts and with a small portion of your total portfolio – like 5% or less.

Step 2: Select the Type of Account You Want

Are you opening a Traditional IRA, Roth IRA, or taxable brokerage account? If it doesn't say "IRA" in the name, then it's likely a taxable account. If you're unsure, take the time to call the company – this is an important step you want to get right.

A reminder for taxable brokerage accounts

Keep in mind that investing in taxable brokerage accounts means you'll be required to pay capital gains tax on any qualified dividends paid in the tax year they were received, regardless of whether you sell the stock or reinvest those dividends. So, if you receive $1,000 in dividends in 2023, you'll have to pay capital gains tax on $1,000. How much tax you'll pay will depend on whether the dividend is considered a *qualified dividend* or not, your income level, and how long you've held the investment.

Step 3: Select Your Brokerage Company

There are four factors you'll want to consider when choosing a brokerage:

1. **How cool are you with tech?** If you like technology or want the ability to check your investments on an app, I recommend checking out some of the fintech companies out there, like Wealthfront, Betterment, or Ally – all with manual and robo-advisor options.

2. **What do you want to invest in?** Most brokerages will give you the ability to buy individual stocks and/or funds, but if you're looking for a specific fund or ETF, you'll want to check what the brokerage offers before setting up your account. Keep in mind they may have a similar fund to the index fund or ETF you're looking for. For example, Fidelity's Zero Total Market Index (FZROX) closely mirrors Vanguard's VTSAX. Still, there are some key differences – mainly that FZROX has a 0% expense ratio and tracks a smaller portion of the stock market than VTSAX. Because they track a different mix of stocks, their returns will be different. Generally speaking, I'm a big fan of the brokerage company Vanguard because they literally invented the index fund, but the choice is yours.

3. **Have you compared expense ratios?** Once you know the investments you want to make, take a few minutes to compare the expense ratios of similar investments between brokerages, which will include any management or administration costs. It's in your best interest to keep the expense ratio as low as possible. As a reminder from Chapter 8, anything under 0.2% is pretty good, and anything over 1% is high.

4. **What type of account are you opening?** Any brokerage will have a taxable brokerage account, most will have Traditional and Roth IRAs, but the other accounts (SEP IRA, SIMPLE IRA, etc.) are not offered as frequently. You'll want to be clear on the type of account (or multiple accounts) you want before deciding.

Roundup investing

If you want to invest little by little, you might be interested in a brokerage company or app that offers investing in fractional shares like Fidelity or Charles Schwab (the O.G. brokerages) or mobile apps like Acorns, Public, and Robinhood. Among these, Acorns and Stash are popular for their ability to round up your debit or credit card transactions to the nearest dollar and invest the difference using fractional shares. Personally, I'd rather you decide what you're willing to invest on a monthly basis and automate that transfer, but every dollar counts!

Wondering what my recommendations are? You can find all of my personal favorites for brokerages, robo-advisor, and fintech companies at www.wealthonadime.com/resources. Table 9.2 also provides a rundown of some of the popular companies at the time of this writing.

Table 9.2   Different Brokerage Companies and Investment Platforms

Brokerage	Manage Your Own	Robo-Advisor	Financial Advisor	
			AUM	Fee-based
Vanguard*	X	X	X	
Fidelity	X	X	X	
Ally Invest*	X	X	X	
TD Ameritrade	X	Offered via affiliate relationship with Schwab		
Morgan Stanley	X	X	X	

(Continued)

Table 9.2 (Continued)

Brokerage	Manage Your Own	Robo-Advisor	Financial Advisor	
			AUM	Fee-based
Charles Schwab		X	X	
Wealthfront*		X		
Betterment		X		
Robinhood	X			
Acorns		X		
Public*	X			
Facet Wealth	More financial planning than a brokerage, with advisors who can manage assets directly		X	

*Indicates personal recommendation based on my own experience.

Step 4: Input Your Bank Account Info

Once you've picked a brokerage, you'll be asked to select what type of account you'd like to open and link a bank account you'll use to transfer money from that account to your new investment account. You'll need your routing number and account number ready to go. It may take a few days for the brokerage to verify your bank account before you can make your first transfer.

Step 5: Pick Your Investments

This is where the fun starts! I can't tell you which investments to buy, but remember what you learned earlier about target-date funds, mutual funds, and ETFs. Remember to consider the expense ratio and any other management or administration fees, as well as the historical rate of return, usually broken out by years (like 1, 5, and 10 years). You can find all this information in the *investment prospectus* for each fund or ETF.

Step 6: Automate Your Investments

If you've completed the steps outlined earlier in this book, then you already know how much you want to invest every month – I recommend you automate as much of your investments as possible. If you're not asked about this when linking your account or picking your investments contact the support team at your brokerage for help. If you're not comfortable setting up an automatic transfer, then set up a monthly calendar reminder on your phone to make you don't forget.

Reminder: Make sure your automatic transfer is set up to purchase the investments you select as soon as the money hits your account, which will likely be a money market account until it's invested (see Figure 9.2). I strongly recommend you double check that this is happening after your first transfer. Set a calendar reminder so you don't forget! If not, this means your money is just sitting there and not growing at all, which would be the worst thing to find out 5, 10, or 15 years from now.

Figure 9.2   Don't Forget to Pick Your Investments within Your Accounts!

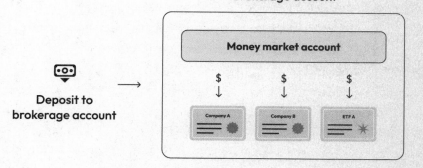

For High Income Earners: Consider a Backdoor Roth

Remember this term from earlier in Chapter 8? I know . . . it sounds sketchy, but it is actually completely legal, allowing you to take advantage of a Roth IRA *even* if your income level makes you ineligible to directly contribute to one.

So here's how it works . . . it's really a method and not a type of account.

First, you'll contribute money to a Traditional IRA that you're eligible for no matter your income – but don't select which investments just yet! Then, you'll *roll over* (read: convert) your Traditional IRA funds to a Roth IRA. This is completely legal per the IRS, and people do it all the time.

Money tip: Roll over your Traditional IRA as soon as possible.

While you can roll over a Traditional IRA to a Roth IRA anytime, you're better off contributing to your Traditional IRA, and rolling over those funds before you invest them. Remember, an IRA is just a type of account to hold your investment; you still need to select them – otherwise, your money can just sit there. Generally,, this would be horrible because you want those funds to grow! But if you're planning to do a backdoor Roth IRA, by converting before you invest, you avoid paying taxes on any earnings you may have made when you made the initial investment and converted to the Roth.

The key benefit here is twofold: (1) your earnings will grow tax free, and (2) you'll have penalty-free and tax-free access to any contributions (but not earnings) before you turn 59½ so long as your

Roth has been open for at least five years. You wouldn't be able to do that with a Traditional IRA. This also gives some people a sense of security, knowing they have access to their contributions without penalty, if they need it.

The downside is that because Traditional IRAs are pre-tax accounts and any contributions are tax-deferred, converting to a back-door Roth IRA means you'll pay taxes on those contributions and any growth up until that point. That said, if you prefer not to worry about paying taxes in retirement, or you think you'll be taxed at a higher rate in retirement, a backdoor Roth might be something to consider.

Get Penalty-Free Access to Your Investments? Using a Roth Ladder

A Roth ladder is an advanced but simple strategy for those looking to access their investments tax- and penalty-free before age 59½ while still enabling the rest of their investments to grow. Unlike the backdoor Roth IRA, which focuses on how you make contributions or put money into an account, a Roth ladder focuses on *distributions* or taking money out. It's best used for those who know they'll want access to some of those funds before age 59½, making them popular with the FIRE community for funds that otherwise might have been in pre-tax investment accounts with penalty clauses.

Similar to a backdoor Roth IRA, a Roth conversion ladder converts a series of annual transfers to a Roth IRA across a five-year period. At the end of those first five years (and every year moving forward) you have access to those contributions tax and penalty-free by withdrawing from the Roth IRA instead of a pre-tax account.

Table 9.3 should be helpful here. Let's say Tanya has built up her 401(k) to $1.2 million by the time she's 50 and wants to retire when she's 55; before she has access to her Traditional 401(k). Starting five years in advance of her desired retirement, she'll roll over what she expects to live off in retirement from her 401(k) to her Roth IRA. She'll continue to do this every year until she reaches age 59½ (at which point she can continue to withdraw from her 401(k) without penalty).

Table 9.3   Tanya's Roth Ladder

Age	Roll Over to Roth	Withdraw from Roth
50	$60,000	$0
51	$60,000	$0
52	$60,000	$0
53	$60,000	$0
54	$60,000	$0
55	$0	$60,000
56	$0	$60,000
57	$0	$60,000
58	$0	$60,000
59	$0	$60,000
60	$0	$60,000

Important: Keep in mind that any conversion from a pre-tax account like a Traditional 401(k) IRA to a Roth IRA will be taxed because a Roth IRA uses post-tax contributions. You'll be taxed on any contributions and earnings to date in the year you make the conversion. Depending on how much you're rolling over, this can be a hefty amount, so prepare yourself for that – but you'll still get around the 10% early withdrawal penalty by treating it as a rollover, and your earnings can grow inside the Roth account, tax-free, from that point forward.

Lastly, if you're wondering why not transfer all of the money from your 401(k) to a Roth IRA at once, the answer is because you'd likely be hit with a big tax bill if you did it all at the same time – both in terms of the taxes you're paying, and potentially the rate at which you're taxed *if* the transfer put you in a different tax bracket. By converting the money in smaller chunks, based on what Tanya thinks she'll need to support herself for a year ($60,000), she spreads her income out over several years, keeping her tax rate low.

If you are considering retiring early or working less, the Roth ladder is a great way to gain access to your 401(k) or IRA funds without paying a penalty for early withdrawal.

Tracking Your Investments Across Multiple Accounts

For those of you who have multiple investment accounts, it can be difficult to track how they're performing and whether or not you need to rebalance any of them across all of your investments. If this sounds like you, I have two money apps (or websites) that can help: Blooom and Personal Capital. Blooom is great because it will analyze your 401(k) or IRA and tell you how you should rebalance your portfolio – it can even do it for you! The one downside is that they only work with 401(k)s and IRAs at the time of this writing. If you're working with more than that (such as a taxable brokerage account), I suggest you check out Personal Capital. My one issue with Personal Capital is that they provide a LOT of detail – some might say too much – but at least you get a high-level view of how balanced your portfolio is and how it's over time. Find both on my website at www .wealthonadime.com/resources.

Creating Generational Wealth

All right, money maker, you've come across a lot of info in this book so far, and while the vast majority of it was focused on your financial journey and potential wealth, I want to take a few pages to focus on strategies you can use to create generational wealth for your family – whether that be a child, a niece, a nephew, or other loved ones.

If you've ever wondered how millionaires and billionaires pass down wealth to their families – think, HBO's *Succession* (loved that show) –then you'll like this section. For the record, if you're at this level, I do recommend talking to a financial advisor, but it's good to have an idea of the possibilities.

While I don't have any kiddos of my own just yet, here are the two concepts I want anyone and everyone who has kids to know about creating generational wealth:

1. How the wealthy use 529 accounts to make sure their families never have to pay for educational expenses ever again.

2. What I wish my parents started for me as a kid: custodial IRAs.

Using 529s for College Savings

Ever wonder how rich people send their families to college? They're likely using something called a 529 or Qualified Tuition Program, which is a particular type of tax-advantaged investment account made specifically for educational expenses. This includes tuition, books, and so on for colleges, trade schools, and vocational schools. Similar to a Traditional 401(k) or IRA, your investments in a 529 savings plan grow tax-deferred and can be used tax-free for anything from tuition to books – but that's not the only reason they're used by the millionaires of the world. Here's the real reason:

1. You can start or contribute to a 529 for your child or any other family member, so long as they have a Social Security number. You could even do this in your name before a child is born and then update it once a child is born.

2. As the owner of the account, you can change the beneficiary at any time to a completely different family member completely tax-free. This means if the beneficiary decides not to go to college, doesn't utilize all of the funds, or passes away unexpectedly, that you can transfer the name and keep that wealth within the family without having to pay taxes on it. I cannot underscore enough how crazy and unique this is to 529s from a wealth-building perspective.

3. Ditto if the owner of 529 passes away – it can stay within the family tax free.

4. Then, the next beneficiary in the family goes to school tax-free or for free, depending on how well those investments performed over time. The process continues so long as there are remaining funds in the account and successors or subsequent beneficiaries are identified.

So not only do you get tax-deferred growth and tax-free money to spend on educational expenses, but you also get to transfer that money to another child, nephew, cousin, etc. This is WILD in the world of money, and luckily, 529s are available to the average money maker, too! Further, in addition to the tax-deferred and tax-free benefits, it may also come with a tax deduction or tax credit depending on which plan you select.

Tanya really wants to help build wealth for her family, so she encourages her sister to set up a 529 for her niece, this way, Tanya can contribute to it whenever she wants. She plans to make a contribution on her niece's next birthday.

So how do you start a 529?

1. **Pick a plan:** 529 accounts vary state by state, and you can start a 529 in any state you like, regardless of where you or the

beneficiary lives, or where the beneficiary might go to school; 529s will always provide their tax-deferred and tax-free benefits, though the donor will only be eligible for any potential state tax deduction or credit if the plan is in their state. The 529 College Savings website has a great tool to compare plans at: https://www.collegesavings.org.

2. **Set up your account:** Just like any other type of investment account, you'll need to set one up using the Social Security number of the beneficiary, or your own and switch it to the beneficiary at a later date.

3. **Pick your investments:** You're a pro at this part by now – and with a 529 you can change your investments twice a year.

4. **Spread the word:** Because anyone can contribute to 529, not just the owner of the account, spread the word so family and friends can also contribute to the beneficiary's education. There is no maximum contribution limit for a 529, so this is a great way for others to help. If you prefer, consider sharing a link on a birthday invitation or in lieu of regular gifts during the holidays.

And because I know you'll have a few questions, here are some FAQs:

- **Q:** But what if my family member decides to go to school out of state?
  - o **A:** No problem! Funds from 529s can be used for qualified educational expenses in any state, regardless of where you or the beneficiary lives.
- **Q:** What happens if they go to a trade school or vocational school?

- o **A:** You're good! Funds from a 529 savings plan can be used at any two-year (or four-year) university, trade school, or vocational school.
- **Q:** What if the beneficiary doesn't use all the funds in the account?
  - o **A:** This would likely be great for your family! Simply let it compound and change the beneficiary once another family member heads to school.

Still have questions? Get all the info you need at https://www.collegesavings.org.

Fun fact about rich people

As of 2022, every taxpayer in the United States has an annual gift limit of $16,000 they can use to give money to family members or a friend before that money is taxed. It's a thing. But instead of maxing out their individual gift limit of $16,000 per donor, the super-wealthy will *super-fund* a 529 by contributing $80,000 per donor (or $160,000 per couple), or five years' worth of contributions, all at once. This means they can make a one-time investment and let that money grow and compound over time. If they did that with $80,000 when a child was born and never contributed another dime, by the time the beneficiary is 18, that account would grow to $281,433 (a $201,217 profit) assuming a 7% rate of return – and anything that beneficiary wouldn't use, could be transferred to another family member.

How Your Child, Niece, or Nephew Can Invest from Age 1

The last thing I want to cover to help you build generational wealth is what's known as a custodial IRA. Like a regular IRA, a custodial IRA is a Traditional or Roth IRA that a custodian (usually a parent) can open in the name of a minor. The only trick here is that any contributions to the account must be made with earned income on behalf of the minor; not the parent. By now, you're probably thinking – but how is my six-year-old going to make money? Or doesn't this break some type of labor law?

Fortunately, in the name of generational wealth, the answer is no. The U.S. Department of Labor Fair Labor Standards Act that protects children under the age of 14 provides exceptions for working in businesses owned by their parents; babysitting; minor chores around a private home; and performing in radio, TV, movies, or theatrical productions. And while real earned income is a requirement, so long as there is paperwork to back it up, like a signed receipt or some other type of agreement, you and the minor will likely be in the clear.

As for the type of work a child can do, that part is up to you and the child. Many parents start businesses that then employ their children for things like envelope stuffing or being in photos for advertisements. My recommendation: get creative! In 2022, the same maximum contribution of $6,000 applies, just like a regular Traditional or Roth IRA.

Once you set up a custodial account, funds will stay in the name of the custodian (yourself) until the minor turns 18 or 21, depending on the state. At that point, the account must be transferred to the beneficiary and acts as a Traditional or Roth IRA would where tax-deferred growth and penalties apply (with the exception of educational expenses). For this reason, I recommend selecting a Roth IRA if considering a custodial account, so the beneficiary can have tax and penalty-free withdrawals before age 59½ on contributions.

Keep in mind that custodial IRAs follow the same contribution limits as adult IRAs – but given that time is on their side, that still gives your child a huge head start!

Summary

Congratulations, money maker! You officially made it through Chapters 7–9 on investing and have seriously leveled up your money game! As a quick recap, here's what you learned this chapter:

- The considerations Tanya made to accelerate her financial strategy and put herself on track to retire early.
- Why you'll want more than your 401(k) or Traditional IRA if you want to reach FIRE.
- How to pick a brokerage company and open up your own account.
- How to use a backdoor Roth IRA.
- How to use a Roth conversion ladder if you plan to retire early.
- How to create generational wealth using custodial IRAs and 529 accounts.

You should be proud! There was a lot of terminology and concepts that a ton of people wouldn't have made it through, but you stuck with it. Even if you're not in a place where you can put these strategies to use just yet, that's not indicative of where you'll be in the future. I'll be sending you good vibes in hopes that you can use them someday soon!

In the next few chapters, I'll cover the topic of homeownership as something you might consider in your financial journey as a next step or investment strategy.

Chapter 10

Confessions of a First-Time Homebuyer

Thinking about your dream home or trolling Zillow just for fun lately? In this chapter and those that follow, I'll cover the ins and outs of homeownership, what you should consider even before you start the home search, and the steps involved should you decide it's the right decision for you. But before we get there, I have a few confessions about what I may have done differently on my own homeownership journey. Now, in the following chapters, particularly where I cover the rent versus buy debate, I talk a big game about how homeownership is a very personal decision, renting is nothing to be ashamed about, and ultimately, that multiple factors be considered before making what may be the largest purchase of your entire life. Personally, I don't think that homeownership is for everyone, and yet I purchased my first home in July of 2017 – in one of the most expensive cities in the country – and plan on owning more properties in the future.

So, why did it make sense for me? In my opinion, a few reasons:

1. Mortgage rates were the lowest they'd been in the past 20 years.

2. I kept seeing rent and the price of homes rise in my area – Washington, DC – so if I wanted a home, it would make sense to move quickly.

3. Almost 30 at the time, I didn't want to live with three roommates anymore, and rents for one-bedrooms were climbing.

Based on market conditions at the time, if I could afford the down payment, it wouldn't cost that much more to own than it would be to rent.

4. I *really* wanted a home of my own.

That last one is particularly important.

I couldn't give you an exact reason as to why I was so hell-bent on buying a home ASAP other than equating it to some symbol of having "made it" at the time. While it's easy for me *now* to disagree with the idea that owning a home somehow qualifies as you as an adult – part of me wonders if I might have still felt that way, if I had never bought my own. We are all susceptible to cultural pressures, and it would be naive of me to think I'm any less susceptible than those who may feel pressured to own a home – though I do think it's important that we actively work to dispel such beliefs we consciously or subconsciously tell ourselves as we learn and grow.

Want to know something we *should* all do as we get older? Listen and learn from other people's experiences, especially if we've yet to encounter them ourselves. If you're lucky and listen carefully enough, you can dodge obstacles and maybe even build upon someone else's success. So, in this chapter I thought I'd cover what I did right and what I wish I had done differently when I first went from student debt warrior to first-time homebuyer.

Here's what I'll cover:

- My timeline and lessons learned from buying my first home.

- How being disciplined with your finances before you start saving for a home can help you in the homebuying process.

- The types of accounts you should consider when saving for a home.

Then, in Chapters 11 and 12, I'll get into all the reasons you may want to buy a home (or not) and the steps you need to take to get there, from determining how much you can afford to the day of closing, keys in hand.

So, let's take a trip down memory lane, starting from when I first paid off my student debt in 2016.

My Homeownership Journey

The scene takes place in Washington, DC. I'm single and flying solo when I decide to save up for my first home – which means I'll need a lot more money. I'm still working at the same firm at this time, though I had negotiated my salary several times by then to $72,000, not including any performance bonuses. I originally wanted to buy a two-bedroom and rent out the second bedroom to a roommate but couldn't make the numbers work – either (a) the down payment required in a competitive market was more than I could afford, or (b) with a lower down payment, the monthly mortgage payment would have been higher than I was comfortable floating in the event it took me a while to find a solid roommate. So, my hunt eventually narrows in on an "affordable" (read: nonexistent in DC) one-bedroom apartment that meets my top three requirements:

1. Must be above ground level (because I'm petrified of bugs).

2. Natural light (because I didn't want to be depressed).

3. An in-unit washer and dryer (because I never wanted to go back to the days when I had to use a laundromat).

After about two months of seriously looking at condos and co-ops, I found my future home – a condo building in my neighborhood that was being completely gutted and turned into about 20 units. I saw a model two-bedroom unit and made an offer on a one-bedroom almost immediately. Because it was new construction, I'd have the rare opportunity to back out later if I wanted, once my unit was built. The downside? There was no negotiation.

The condo was $345,000 – a 10% down payment cost $34,500 plus closing costs. Yikes.

Condo versus co-op

The major difference between a condo and a co-op (short for co-operative) is how they are owned. Similar to owning a house, a condo gives you ownership of a particular unit in a building, as well as a percentage of the common areas, which will be managed by a condo board. This means you can buy and sell a condo similar to how you would a home. A co-op, on the other hand, common in major cities like New York and Washington, DC, gives you ownership in a share of the entire building or property, and requires any buyer be approved by a co-op board before purchasing. This can make selling a co-op a bit more complicated, and depending on the type of co-op, you may be limited in what selling price you can re-list a property for. That said, co-ops are usually cheaper than condos in a given area, so you'll want to weigh the pros and condos.

As you might remember, I was able to pay off almost $45,000 worth of student debt in a little over three years using the avalanche method and cutting expenses wherever possible. A big part of my ability to do this was automating my cash flows and payments till I got really comfortable with my weekly spending cap and the exact contributions I was formerly making to pay off my debt.

Once I did pay off my student loans, it honestly felt like I was rich for a hot minute – that's what happens when all of a sudden, a few hundred or thousands of dollars you were putting toward debt gets freed up. Life was good.

I could have done a lot with that money – I could have changed my lifestyle or put it toward a luxury vacation – but instead, I decided I wanted to buy a home. It was ironic at the time because just a few years earlier, I thought I would never be able to afford a home or a family without a partner– a frustrating concept. Looking back, my decision to buy a home may have been less about the property and more about proving to myself that even if I lived in a shoebox of an apartment, I wasn't going to have to rely on anyone but myself to make that possible. That sounded great.

A major plus side? Once I decided I wanted a home, there was never a question of whether or not I could do it. I *knew* I could. I also knew *exactly* when I'd be able to buy a home because I was so consistent in paying off my debt for years. It just came down to timing. Now, depending on the type of account I would use – savings and/or investment accounts – my money may have gotten a little boost or taken a hit from the market. Ultimately, I used both (more on this in just a bit). But I knew buying a home was more than possible – it was doable – and sometimes believing you can hit a big goal like that is half the battle.

To say this a bit differently, I don't think being debt-free is what ultimately enabled me to buy a home. Of course, it's a heck of a lot easier to save for anything when you're not making debt payments every month – but even if I still had debt, I might have generated extra income somewhere. Or, the reverse, I could have had no debt but spent all my savings. What really helped me buy a home were the habits I had developed over time – not my lack of debt or my increased salary. I could have changed my lifestyle to set a whole bunch of money on fire *real* quick – do you know the vacation I could have taken?! But I already had my eyes set on another goal and was excited because even if it took a while, I knew I could do it.

> Note: This isn't to say I took no vacations. Travel has always been a non-negotiable for me and I think it's important to prioritize whatever makes you happy. But I did stick to my sinking fund and stayed within my means.

So without getting into all the details, here's a quick overview of my timeline.

1. Even as my income rose, I continued to live in the same row house with three roommates for a total of five years. I never owned a car or had a car payment. I kept my expenses as low as possible, except for my non-negotiable sinking fund for travel and holiday gifts. At the height of repaying my debt, I was making extra payments of around $1,500/month – that made for a pretty high savings rate (over $2,000 per month) once I was debt free. In other words, I had already created a gap between my income and living expenses. This made saving a breeze once I got my debt out of the way.

> Note: This applies to building wealth, too. It took me over three years to pay off my student loans, little by little. But after I bought my home and my net worth hit its first $100,000 in 2018, it really started to take off because I wasn't overwhelmed by the idea of making such a large contribution from my paycheck. I also had help from the stock market, thanks to compound interest and some years where I experience 19-22% gains.

2. In May 2016, when I was a few months out from paying off my loans and knew I wanted to buy a home, I opened a taxable brokerage account. I'm new to investing at this stage and didn't optimize my use of tax-advantaged investment accounts. More on this later.

3. I also used a high-yield savings account (HYSA) around this time, splitting contributions between my investment and savings account as soon as my loans were paid off in September 2016. I still worked side gigs and saved everything I could, including a significant work bonus.

4. In April 2017, as part of my offer on the condo, I put down a deposit of $10,350 from my savings. Writing that check was scary!... but I was ecstatic when the offer goes through.

5. Thanks to some help from the market, my taxable brokerage account grew 15% in just over a year. In July 2017, I withdrew my funds (which I'd pay taxes on at the end of the year) and covered the remaining closing costs with savings.

6. I closed on July 12, 2017, and got the keys to my new place. My new monthly payment was $1,958 consisting of a $1,482/ month mortgage, $232/month HOA, plus $244/month in property taxes and homeowners' insurance. This was almost triple my previous rent of $712 – but I knew I could handle it because I was already so used to the Money Moves System.

Here's what the above looks like over time (see Figure 10.1).

Figure 10.1   My Journey to Homeownership

Dec 2012	Sep 2016	Dec 2016	Jun 2017
Started paying student loans	Became debt free	Invested work bonus	Inspection & final walk through

May 2016	Starting Oct 2016	Apr 2017	Jul 2017
Opened taxable investment account	Reallocated former debt payments	Put down earnest deposit	Closed on home

Nothing happens overnight, money maker, but not too long after I made it a priority, I was able to purchase my first home. I decorated it exactly how I wanted and loved the location – in the same up-and-coming neighborhood where I first moved to DC, but closer to the metro, restaurants, and my office. It was perfect.

When I first closed on the home, my monthly payment was almost $2,000, including HOA fees and property taxes – a number I knew I could handle by reallocating my budget. A few years later, I would refinance my mortgage from a rate of 4.0% to 2.85%, lowering my monthly payment – all in all – to $1781/month, including my HOA and taxes. I lived in and created some great memories in that apartment over five years. I also AirBnB-ed it multiple times to pay for vacations and even sublet an apartment on the water during the pandemic – one of the best decisions I've ever made for my mental health.

In 2022, after five years in that apartment, I decided to rent the condo full-time. Even during a time when people weren't super-pumped about moving into small one-bedroom units, I still got enough rental income to cover all associated costs. It's been a #nore-grets decision the entire time.

But I did learn a few lessons along the way. Here are five things I learned over five years in my dream condo.

Lessons Learned

Ever heard the phrase "Hindsight is 20/20"? We all probably have a few things we wish we could have done differently in life and on our financial journeys. For example, I wish I had asked my parents to start a custodial IRA for me when I started working at age 16. I wish any of us even knew what that was. I also wish I had contributed more to my 401(k) in my 20s. You live and you learn, money maker.

So when it comes to buying a home, I hope you appreciate the lessons I learned the hard way.

Lesson 1: Use the Right Type of Account

Ultimately, I used a high-yield savings account and a taxable broker-age account to save for my first home. That said, there are definitely pros and cons to consider depending on your timeline, risk toler-ance, and other investments.

Wondering which accounts you might use? Here are a few recommendations.

Generally speaking, if you're on a tight timeline, I recommend using a high-yield savings account or certificate of deposit to save for your first home. Both have higher interest rates than a standard sav-ings account. I realize this might come off hypocritical as someone that also used a taxable brokerage account for my own home.

Here's why I don't recommend it.

While using an investment account can help your savings grow, had the market dipped during the period I was saving for a home, I would have been screwed. If you planned to buy a home in 2022 and had a good chunk of your savings invested, then you already know what I'm talking about because the S&P500 dropped 20% in the first six months of this year. So, if you're willing to risk a drop like that and have flexibility in your timeline to recover or save longer if needed, then an investment account might make sense. If the thought of that happening makes you anxious or you'd be extremely upset, then a savings account or higher interest CD is the way to go.

The other option would be to use an investment account in hopes of making gains you can use to pay for the home. If you do go with an investment account, consider using a taxable brokerage account, this way any investments in tax-advantaged accounts can continue to benefit from tax-deferred growth.

Lastly, while I wouldn't recommend it, you could considering using a Roth IRA to withdraw any contributions (but not earnings) without triggering the 10% penalty so long as you've had the account for five years. Specifically for your first home, you can withdraw $10,000 from a Roth IRA at any time, or $10,000 from a Traditional IRA without penalty for your first home (which the IRS defines as not having owned a home at any point in the past two years). Earnings must be used within 120 days toward the direct purchase of a home (down payment and/or closing costs) to meet this requirement.

FYI, while you can withdraw $10,000 toward your first home with a Traditional IRA and avoid the 10% penalty for early withdrawal, you'll still be taxed because of the pre-tax contributions. For this reason, I prefer the Roth IRA over a Traditional IRA for a down payment, though generally speaking, it's advised to save for your home and let your investments grow long term.

Using a 401(k) to save for your home

You might be wondering if you can use money from your 401(k) to buy your first home. While the answer is yes, I don't recommend it for a few reasons. First, if you withdraw funds from your 401(k) for your first home, you can't avoid the 10% penalty (like you can with an IRA up to $10,000) and will be taxed. The other option is to take out a loan against your 401(k) where you pay yourself back. While this may sound okay because the money goes from yourself to yourself, it comes with an interest rate, meaning you'll be required to make larger than usual contributions to your 401(k) to pay that loan back. This isn't necessarily a bad thing – it could make for more in your 401(k) – but it's worth noting that contributions to meet your 401(k) loan don't benefit from an employer match. Overall, I think you're better off using a high-yield savings account or Roth IRA, CD, or taxable brokerage account.

Lesson 2: Don't Spread Yourself Too Thin

The second lesson I want to pass down from my home buying experience is not to spread yourself too thin when coming up with the down payment and closing costs. One of the easiest ways to avoid this is to give yourself a little extra time to build up your savings till you're sure it will cover your needs. Your down payment will be a percentage of the final negotiated price and depends on the type of mortgage you apply for (although I generally recommend putting down at least 10%) and closing costs can run about 3 to 6% of the total mortgage.

I also don't want you to dip into your emergency fund. The reason for this is twofold: first, you want to save this for truly unexpected emergencies, which may or may not be related to your home purchase – like a dental emergency – and second, you'll likely encounter an unexpected repair, if not several, after you close on the home. In the event that repair isn't covered by insurance or you're required to pay the costs upfront, you'll want to have this cash on hand to avoid taking on any debt.

To be totally honest, I almost bit off a bit more than I could chew here. I used the majority of my emergency savings to cover my home purchase – far more than what I would recommend to anyone else. At the time of my loan application in April 2017, I reported exactly $44,474.32 in liquid assets. While I would have a few thousand dollars more in savings by the time I actually closed on my home in July, I would ultimately pay a total of $43,932.74, including the Earnest Money Deposit (EMD) and closing costs. In fact, I sank my savings so low that I actually borrowed money from my parents so I could furnish the apartment and have a buffer in my emergency fund. While I paid them back that year, I acknowledge that this was an immense risk (and a privilege), so don't be like me in this regard!

The bottom line here: don't risk your emergency savings. Instead, consider pushing your timeline out a bit further to keep the rest of your finances intact.

Lesson 3: Be Prepared for the Unexpected

Closely related to Lesson 2, Lesson 3 is to be prepared for the unexpected – and for the unexpected to always be pricey. I know plenty of money makers that have learned this the hard way.

If and when you buy your first home, it'll be based on certain expectations. You'll have an inspection done, know about any HOA fees in advance, and have a ballpark figure for anything you'd like to repair or improve – but all of these are likely to change over time.

For example, not long after buying my condo, our building realized that the ceilings of the fourth-floor apartments were leaking – we needed a new roof, which was super expensive. This triggered a *special assessment*, or an added fee, where in addition to our HOA fees, each tenant would be required to pay somewhere between $1,000 and $2,000 extra in just a few months. Many of the tenants were upset about this, likely feeling or actually being a bit house-poor after spending so much money on their down payment and closing (the building was new, so everyone moved into their new units around the same time). Most owners had not prepared for the unexpected.

You don't want to be like that person going into your new home.

Another example of this is the fact that despite moving into a new unit, the washing machine in the unit above mine broke – on two separate occasions – turning my kitchen into a waterfall display. The first time, my insurance company determined that it was of no fault to the tenant above mine and I would be responsible. Luckily the tenant was willing to cover the cost of repairs. The second time, my insurance reimbursed me, but only after I fronted the cash to the contractor to fix my entire ceiling, which incurred significant damage. It had to be dried out and mitigated for mold, new sheetrock, paint, and so forth. Had I not built back up my emergency fund, I would have risked a mold issue and might have had to live with that hole in my ceiling for a while.

Other surprises that occurred after I bought my home:

- The monthly HOA fee increased.
- The building had to replace all the fire doors because they weren't up to code.
- The condo board hit us with two other "special assessments" of over around $2,000 each.
- My ceiling had to be repaired. Again.

And this was in a *tiny* one-bedroom apartment. A lot more can go wrong when you're talking about an entire home with a foundation, landscaping, and so on.

Lesson learned, in my experience, repairs on your new home will be inevitable so make sure you're prepared to react when you need to.

Lesson 4: Move on Your Own Timeline

One important takeaway I hope you get from this book is that your timeline should make sense for you and your finances, not the expectation you feel the world may have set for you. In a world where "adulting" is now a verb, it can be easy to get wrapped up in someone else's timeline, but depending on your savings rate, other priorities, and the housing market, it may be in your best interest to speed things up or delay the process a bit depending on your circumstances.

Pick a speed that works for you, and go with that.

Lesson 5: Nothing Is Forever: Don't Freak Yourself Out

The last lesson I want to touch on is that nothing is permanent, including – in a good way – your first home. In my experience, there was this moment of totality, of feeling like the check I wrote marked an irreversible decision that I would never be able to take back, even though I knew I wouldn't be spending the rest of my life in a one-bedroom apartment . . . though I did love that apartment as much as Carrie from *Sex in the City* loved hers.

My point here is don't freak yourself out! Remember, you're in control of your finances and this decision is yours to make.

Even though your first home will likely be your most expensive purchase to date, that doesn't mean it's permanent. The likelihood that the value of your home will go up over time, and you may want to sell at some point, is very high. Also, life changes pretty quickly. Almost five years after buying my apartment, I decided to move in with my boyfriend and put it up for rent. Things change, life moves fast, and while it is a big financial decision, it's not one that you're stuck with forever – so move at your own pace for what feels right for you.

I hope these tips have been helpful and that you will learn from my experience when considering your first home.

Now that you know some of the things I learned the hard way, in Chapter 11. I'll go over some of the other considerations you might want to make when deciding to rent or buy, before diving into the homebuying process in Chapter 12.

Chapter 11

The Rent Versus Buy Debate

I should buy something soon, obviously.

—An actual friend of mine over text

There's this really screwed-up idea in America that buying a home is something we all need to do – not dissimilar to the idea that becoming an adult requires getting married or starting a family. The quote above is from an actual friend of mine, in real life, who was considering buying a home, even though the market was crazy, and he didn't know whether or not he would stay in that particular area. To be clear, the fact that he was considering buying a home wasn't what got me. A home can be a great investment and provide a great source of stability for people. It was the "obviously" part of that sentence, like he either (a) had to do it or (b) was a no-brainer – both of which are not true for most money makers.

Also, what if you just like renting? ::shrugs shoulders::

The idea of buying a home can be a bit overwhelming at times. For starters, there are so many things to consider, from finding the right home to getting a mortgage you can actually afford. Then, aside from the process of finding a home you actually like, you'll have to cough up a ton of cash – for many, the largest check they'll ever write – and that's before closing costs. Combine that with rising home prices and interest rates, and no wonder there's a never-ending debate about whether it makes sense to rent or buy a home across

America. For many, it will be one of the biggest and most expensive decisions they'll ever make.

And that's even before we get to saving for a down payment, which can be difficult on its own, especially for younger generations and single individuals.

So, in this chapter, we're going to cover the rent vs. buy debate from all sides, including:

- Why buying a home can be difficult
- The pros and cons of homeownership
- Four questions to ask yourself before buying a home

Let's dive into it.

Why Buying a House Can Be Difficult

If the idea of homeownership sounds like a far-fetched dream to you, you're not alone. There are many reasons why homeownership for younger generations in particular is becoming more difficult year after year, especially (but not exclusively) in the years following the pandemic. More and more, depending on interest rates, and especially in cities with a high cost of living, it may make more sense to rent than buy.

Reason No. 1: The Student Debt Crisis

One of the main reasons why it's so hard for millennials and Gen Z to afford homes is that they face a student debt crisis, unlike anything their parents or previous generations experienced. As I mentioned earlier in the book, over 45 million Americans owe $1.7 trillion in student debt — an average of around $37,000 per person. Given this financial burden, many millennials and younger generations can't save up for a home, and even those who do may have other financial priorities by the time they get there, like starting a family or saving for retirement. Keep in mind that many Americans, even if they have repayment plans designed to help them, are paying student loans for the first 20 to 25 years of their adult lives.

Reason No. 2: Some Housing Markets Are Crazy

According to the U.S. Department of Housing and Urban Development, the median home price in Q2 of 2022 was $440,300.[1] That's a pretty high number – with some home prices being easily double that in major cities like Boston, New York, Washington, DC, and LA – don't even get me started on San Francisco! Even if home prices went back to where they were before the pandemic, the median home would still cost around $329,000.

Factor in the total cost of owning a home after you pay off the mortgage, and it may make more sense to rent in some markets depending on the interest rate you're able to get approved for. For example, let's look at the total cost of purchasing a home worth $440,300, the median home price in Q2Q2 of 2022, assuming a 10% down payment (see Table 11.1).

Table 11.1   Total Cost of a Mortgage Over Time

Cost of Home	10% Down Payment	Loan Amount	Interest Rate	Monthly Mortgage Payment	Interest Paid Over Time	Total Mortgage Cost	Total Cost of Home
$440,300	$44,030	$396,270	4%	$1,892	$284,797	$681,067	$725,097
$440,300	$44,030	$396,270	5%	$2,127	$369,545	$765,815	$809,845
$440,300	$44,030	$396,270	6%	$2,376	$459,032	$855,302	$899,332

Note: The above shows the monthly payment and total cost with interest for the mortgage only, not including property taxes or any applicable HOA fees.

Based on Table 11.1, you see quickly the total cost of a home can escalate. At an interest rate of 5.5%, the total cost of a home on a 30-year fixed mortgage almost doubles from the price you bought it for, and it would take several years to build up any significant *equity* –the difference between what your home is worth and what you owe on your mortgage. Keep in mind that the monthly payment shown does not include additional costs, such as property taxes or HOA fees.

Now, if your resulting payment might be comparable to whatever your rent would be, or you're confident you could refinance for a lower mortgage rate down the road, then buying might make sense. It did for me. But if the resulting monthly payment would be significantly higher than your rent, and you're otherwise fine with renting, then you may be better off doing that and investing the difference in the stock market. Either way, you'll want to run the numbers, factoring in both your monthly payment and the total cost of the home over time.

Reason No. 3: Mortgage Rates Are Climbing Right Now

In response to the increased price of goods and services in 2022 – whaddup, inflation! – the Federal Reserve increased what's known as the *benchmark interest rate*, which in turn, increases all other interest rates on savings accounts, credit cards, mortgages, and so forth. The idea here is that by making it more expensive to borrow money, people will spend and borrow less, which will force the price of goods and services to drop and bring inflation down. This is great for savings accounts and certain types of savings bonds. Unfortunately, it sucks for anyone who needs to borrow any type of money and anything else that interest rates touch, including mortgages.

See that little uptick in 2022 shown in Figure 11.1?

Figure 11.1 Historical Mortgage Rates

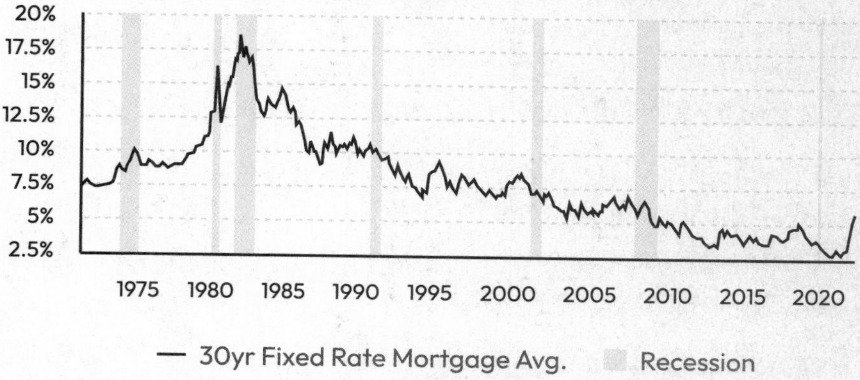

— 30yr Fixed Rate Mortgage Avg.   ▨ Recession

Source: https://fred.stlouisfed.org/series/MORTGAGE30US. Federal Reserve Economic Data. Original source: Freddie Mac.

From January to September 2022 alone, mortgage rates increased on average from 3.22% to 5.66% as of September 1, 2022.[2] Compared to when mortgage rates were closer to 3%, this is a huge jump for most Americans – especially for younger homebuyers who may not remember when mortgage rates were upwards of 7.5%.

Remember when I told you even a 1% difference matters on a loan or investment? This is another example of that.

Let's take a 30-year, fixed, $300,000 mortgage. With a 4% interest rate, that home would cost $1,432 per month, not including other costs like homeowner's insurance or property taxes. Compared to a rate of 5% and that same home would cost $1,610, or $178 more per month. Looking at the total cost of the home over 30 years, that's a $64,159 difference in interest. That's enough to make some people – a lot of people – reconsider or at least wait a bit on their dream home. Whether or not the recent rate increases keep you from buying likely depends on the selling price of the home – but it is something to keep in mind when shopping around for mortgages. Even a fraction of a percent can make a big difference. Luckily, many economists and the Mortgage Bankers Association estimate that interest rates will drop back down to around 4.4% by 2024 – so fingers crossed, money makers!

The Pros and Cons of Homeownership

As I mentioned earlier, just because I bought a home myself doesn't mean I think it's right for everybody. Below are some pros and cons of homeownership to help determine if homeownership is right for you.

Pros of Homeownership

- **A fixed mortgage is stable.** This is beneficial when trying to build wealth over time. Having one of your largest monthly expenses be constant can be really valuable. It enables you to take more risks, plan out investment contributions, and so on, knowing it won't change.

- **It can be a good investment.** Depending on the housing market and whether or not you make improvements to the home, you could turn your property into a rental or sell it for a profit and use it to reinvest or buy another property. Keep in mind selling a home usually costs 5–6% in seller closing fees, and you'll likely need the sale to pay down any remaining balance on your mortgage. I'll get into some advanced strategies for selling and investing in real estate in Chapter 12.

- **You can build equity.** This means you own a larger and larger portion of your home's value over time. That said, the equity is only valuable if and when you either (a) sell your home, assuming a profit or (b) borrow against the equity you've built up, usually cheaper than taking out a personal loan, using what's called a home equity line of credit (HELOC) or a home equity loan.

HELOC versus home equity loan

A HELOC and a home equity loan are two ways a homeowner can borrow against the equity they have built up in their home. A HELOC is a line of credit, similar to a credit card that you use to borrow against your home with a variable interest rate. A home equity loan is more like a regular loan, paid back in fixed installments with a fixed interest rate. A HELOC is often preferred over a home equity loan for its flexibility in that you can borrow as you go, up to your approved credit limit. While many people think a HELOC or home equity loan must be used for home improvements, they can really be used for anything – and usually have lower interest rates than a personal loan. This makes borrowing against your home a solid option for repairs or an unexpected emergency.

- **You can make the place your own.** Another big benefit of homeownership is making the place your own! Want to paint the walls, open up the ceiling, do some crazy landscaping – the choice is yours! While you may be subject to HOA laws depending on your type of home, they generally only restrict common areas as opposed to inside the four walls of your unit.

Cons of Homeownership

- **You are your own landlord.** While the idea of being able to do whatever you want to do to your own place may sound exciting, it can also be expensive! As your own landlord, you'll be responsible for purchasing and making any necessary repairs, which may include buying new appliances and paying for the cost of labor to get a plumber, painter, and so on as needed. If you plan on buying a rental property, separate from your principal residence, this may also involve paying a property management fee (usually around 8–12% of the monthly rent) to handle some of these logistics for you. The time and money involved in keeping up your property are important reasons why one may prefer to rent instead of buy.

- **It doesn't always lower your costs.** As mentioned earlier, while a fixed mortgage essentially freezes your monthly housing payment and may be less expensive than renting over time, it's never guaranteed, especially when you factor in the cost of maintenance. Depending on the housing market and the price of your home, it may actually be cheaper to rent than purchase a home once interest is accounted for. Not sure how much your home will cost you in total? Find my favorite calculator at www.wealthonadime.com/resources.

Given these pros and cons, the rent versus buy debate is worth considering carefully. That said, if you've considered the above and still think you're interested in buying a home, below are a few final questions to ask yourself before making the jump.

Questions to Ask Yourself Before Buying a Home

Now that you understand the pros and cons of homeownership, below are a few questions to consider before starting the search.

1. **How long do you plan to stay in the home or area?** If you're only planning to live in a certain area for the next few years, it may make more sense to rent than to buy, unless you plan on turning that purchase into a rental property to generate passive income – and you're confident that the rental

income would cover the cost of your mortgage and associated fees. This is actually what I did after living in my first home for almost five years. It's become a great little passive income-producing property!

2. **Can you afford the cost, and is it worth it over time?** In addition to the down payment, there are several other costs you should be prepared to pay when buying and maintaining a home. Additional costs include things like closing costs, title insurance, private mortgage insurance (PMI), homeowner's insurance, and any other fees such as HOA fees. You'll also be responsible for any repairs, property taxes, landscaping, and so on.

3. **What are your long-term money goals?** Owning a home can be a great investment, but it's not right for everyone. If you're not sure about the home, what the value of it might be in a few years, and/or don't love the idea of renting it out, then you might be better off living in a rental property.

4. **Do you want to be a landlord?** One benefit of renting is that there's usually a landlord or property management company to take care of the cost and time involved in repairs, upkeep, and so on. If you value that convenience and aren't willing to do the repairs yourself or hire someone to do it for you, then you may want to reconsider whether buying is the right move.

While everyone's answers will be different, these questions should help you decide whether homeownership is right for you. Keep in mind there's no right or wrong answer! There is no shame in being a renter for life who prioritizes other aspects of your life or investments. Ultimately, the best decision is the one that makes sense for you and your money goals.

Summary

I hope this chapter was helpful in understanding why homeowner-ship may not be the obvious choice for every money maker. To be clear, it's not that I'm against homeownership, but rather, that it's a decision to be made on an individual basis, depending on market conditions, your priorities, and how important owning a home is to you.

As a recap, here are some considerations you learned about this chapter:

- The total cost of owning a home
- The differences between a HELOC and home equity loan
- The pros and cons of owning a home
- The three main questions to ask yourself when considering a home

If you've considered the above and still want homeownership in your future, I'll cover all the steps of the home-buying process in Chapter 12.

So, are you thinking about your new crib yet?

I love that for you.

Notes

1. https://fred.stlouisfed.org/series/MSPUS, Federal Reserve Economic Data.
2. https://fred.stlouisfed.org/series/MORTGAGE30US, Federal Reserve Economic Data; original source: Freddie Mac.

Chapter 12

Nine Steps to Homeownership

A ll right, money maker . . . If you've made it this far and you're still thinking about your dream home, then this chapter should give you a quick rundown on all the steps. Unlike myself, who was in "go with the flow" mode, I want you to feel as prepared as possible going into this process. No one needs a surprise on top of a down payment, so I'll cover the nine main steps you'll encounter so you can feel like a pro before you even start the search.

Want a little cheat sheet? Here's what I'll cover:

1. Determine how much you can afford to spend on your down payment and monthly mortgage – pssttt, we'll cover first-time homebuyer programs here, too.

2. Find your home – we'll cover the differences between a realtor, real estate agent, and broker in just a bit.

3. Shop around for a mortgage.

4. Make an offer with an earnest money deposit (EMD).

5. Finalize your mortgage with the lender.

6. Get your inspection (in most cases you pay for this, not the seller).

7. Get homeowner's insurance.

8. Final walkthrough – fingers crossed!

9. Close on the home and CELEBRATE!

After we've gone through these steps, I'll also cover a few advanced strategies you'll want to know as you continue to build wealth and consider real estate as part of your wealth strategy, including house hacking and how to use a 1031 exchange if you're considering buying multiple properties.

In breaking down each step, I hope you'll be much more prepared to buy your first home! But before we get there, let's go over some quick real estate lingo.

Real Estate Lingo

When I first started my home search, I only knew the basics. I knew I wanted a real estate agent, but I didn't realize the seller *usually* pays the fee or that having an agent was optional. I had no clue about the difference between a realtor or a real estate agent – but luckily, I ended up with a fantastic realtor at the recommendation of a friend. I knew what a mortgage was and how interest worked, but not much beyond that in terms of upfront costs. So, before we get to the steps on buying a home, I thought a quick lingo lesson could be helpful.

Here are some terms you'll want to know:

- **Down payment:** The amount you put down on a mortgage to purchase your home. This also reduces the total amount you borrow, and thus how much interest you'll pay over time. How much you put down will be different for everyone, depending on the type of loan and your preference. I'll cover this later in the chapter.

- **Earnest money deposit (EMD):** Also known as an *earnest deposit*, this is a check you'll write as part of your initial offer to indicate you're serious about purchasing the home. It's usually the first time you'll have to get out your checkbook, before and separate from your down payment – and it usually runs between 5% and 10% of your total offer – so take a deep breath! In the event that your offer is accepted, this contributes to your down payment or closing costs at the time of closing. In the event the deal doesn't go through because the inspection fails (unless you wave the inspection) or some other type of contingency goes into effect, you'll get the money back. You'll also get it back if the seller declines your offer.

- **Escrow account:** At a basic level, an escrow account means the money is being held by a third party – in this instance, not the buyer or the seller. Your EMD will be held in an escrow account, for example. When you buy a home, however, an escrow account may also be used by your mortgage company to hold funds and pay for expenses that are separate from your mortgage – like homeowner's insurance. If this is the case, those costs will be included in your monthly mortgage payment and you'll be made aware in advance.

- **Homeowners insurance:** Protects you in the event of damage, though the extent of what it covers depends on the type of insurance you get – similar to how you can have different types of healthcare coverage depending on your plan and health insurance premium. At a bare minimum, homeowners insurance will likely protect you from damage in case of a fire and theft, just like renters insurance. You can also get personal liability coverage, which protects you in the event someone is hurt in your home – slips and falls, for example – and tries to hold you liable (read: sues you).

- **Private mortgage insurance (PMI):** An insurance you're required to get if you don't put at least 20% down on a *conventional* mortgage loan, one of the most common types of mortgages. Because you're putting less than 20% down, PMI protects the lender (not you) in the event you default on your loan. The cost of PMI can vary from .5% to 1.9% the cost of the mortgage per year and usually adds a few extra hundred bucks a month to your monthly payment. For example, if you take out a $300,000 mortgage, the cost might be an extra $125 to $475 per month. PMI will either be paid by you (borrower PMI: BPMI or lender PMI: LPMI) in exchange for a higher interest rate on your mortgage. If you pay BPMI, you can request to have PMI removed once you have 20% equity, or refinance to remove LPMI when you have 20% equity or if the value of your home increases (thereby increasing your estimated equity).

- **Settlement company:** A company that handles the crazy amount of paperwork you'll be required to sign at the time of closing. They'll also hold your EMD and provide title insurance. You can choose whichever settlement or title company you like, not just the one your lender recommends, so feel free to shop around for who has the best rates.

- **Title insurance:** Title insurance is annoying because it's something that you'll very rarely ever need . . . but then again, that's the joy of insurance. Title insurance protects you in the event a lien or other claim is made against the home, which you now own, for something that occurred before you owned it. For example, if a state came after you for unpaid property taxes from a previous owner, your title insurance would protect you from financial loss.

Realtor versus real estate agent versus broker

Why make life simple when you can have three similar names for people that do very similar jobs? There are many titles for the person who might help you through the homebuying process, but the differences are important – here's what you need to know:

- Real estate agent: can help you buy or sell your home, and while they are required to have a real estate license, they cannot be considered a Realtor unless they have joined the National Association of Realtors (NAR).

- Realtor: a real estate agent who has passed licensing and joins the NAR, which requires committing to a code of ethics that they put their buyer's interest before their own. Ideally, you want a real estate agent, but if you know of a realtor you like and trust, they can help you too.

- Real estate broker: can do everything a real estate agent can do, but usually manages their own company or team of real estate agents. Unless your real estate agent has their broker's license, they probably report to a broker.

Okay, now that you're speaking the right language, let's dive into the steps for buying a home. This is where things get exciting, even though you'll likely be writing the biggest check of your life . . . but all in the spirit of good things!

Step 1: Find Out How Much You Can Afford

Determining how much you're able and willing to pay for your home is one of the most important things you'll do in the entire homebuying process. Not only should your home align with your financial goals, but you also want to make sure the resulting monthly mortgage won't put too much of a strain on your budget. Lastly, you'll want to take advantage of any potential programs or mortgage loans you can get approved for.

What's a Comfortable Down Payment?

How much you can afford for a down payment usually impacts how high the cost of a home you'll be able to afford. Now, in a competitive housing market like we've seen in recent years in the United States, you might need more than the standard 20% down – but in many cases, you can get away with less. For example, I only put down 10% on my first home. Many government-backed programs also allow as low as 0–3.5% down – particularly helpful if you make a low income or are planning to rent or flip a property, in which case, you'll want to minimize your upfront investment as much as possible. All that said, remember that the lower the down payment, the more the home will cost you in interest over time (that's why most people recommend 20% as opposed to a lower down payment, if possible).

For starters, determine how high or low you're willing to go on your down payment, keeping in mind that the higher the down payment, the lower your monthly mortgage will be. On the flip side, the lower your down payment, the higher your mortgage payment will be, costing you more in interest over time.

Once you have an idea of what you'd like to put down, there are a few more considerations to make:

- Keep in mind the additional closing costs you'll be required to pay, right before you get handed the keys to your new home. Closing costs are usually 5–6% the total amount of the mortgage.

- If your down payment is less than 20%, you'll be required to pay PMI, which can add a few extra hundred dollars to your monthly payment. NerdWallet has a great calculator you can use to figure out what your PMI might be. Find it on my resources page at www.wealthonadime.com/resources.

- If you're considering renting out your property in the future, you'll want any rental income to cover the cost of the mortgage. The higher the down payment, the lower your mortgage will be, and the easier it will be to cover that cost.

All this said, only you will know what you're comfortable with for a down payment and the resulting monthly payment. Once you have an idea of what you'd like to pay, you can then start to narrow in on your loan options.

Which Mortgage Loans Are You Eligible For?

Which mortgage loans you're eligible for also impacts how much of a down payment you'll need. Most money makers will use a conventional or Federal Housing Administration (FHA) loan, though there are others to choose from depending on your circumstances and the area you're looking to buy a home in. Figure 12.1 provides a quick glance comparison – although you can always go with a higher down payment if you'd like.

Figure 12.1   Mortgage Loan Types

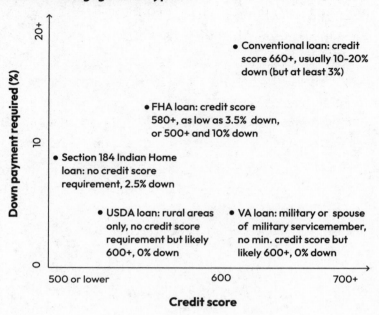

Conventional Loans

Conventional loans are best for those who are able to put 10–20% down and are shopping around to get the best interest rate on their mortgage. Most conventional loans require 10–20% down but can go as low as 3% and are intended for those with credit scores of 660 or above. Because they are offered by private lenders, including mortgage companies and banks, they often have the most flexibility to lower interest rates, so don't be afraid to talk to multiple lenders about what you may qualify for.

FHA Loans

An FHA loan is backed by the U.S. Federal Housing Administration and provides buyers the opportunity to put as low as 3.5% down so long as you have a credit score above 580 (or as low as 10% if your credit score is between 500 and 580). Personally, I wouldn't recommend such a low down payment if you're a first-time home buyer (unless you're planning to flip the property) because it will increase the cost of your monthly payments and the total cost of the home over time. That said, they are great for those who might have a lower credit score (and, therefore, can't qualify for a conventional loan) or if you're looking to lower the cost of your initial down payment.

> Note: All government-backed loans require that you intend to use the home as your primary residence for at least one year.

USDA Loans

Like rural areas? A USDA loan is backed by the U.S. Department of Agriculture (USDA) and can be particularly useful to those who have a credit score below 580 as it does not carry a credit score requirement – though you'll get approved more easily if you have a score of 640 or above. USDA loans come in two forms with different eligibility requirements and repayment terms, though both are intended for low- to medium-income money makers. For example, the Single Family Housing Direct Loan requires that the borrower be unable to get any other type of home loan, and lack "decent, safe, and sanitary housing" while the USDA Guarantee Loan has less strict requirements.

If you're not sure whether you'd qualify for a USDA loan, you can always ask your mortgage lender. They'll be able to walk you through the qualifications to see if you're eligible.

VA Loan

If you or your spouse have at least six months' worth of active service in the military, reserves, or national guard, you may be eligible for a Veterans Administration (VA) loan with as little as 0% down – pretty crazy! Also, thank you for your service! A major benefit of VA loans is that unlike the other types of loans, they come with 0% PMI, but do have a VA funding fee that can be paid upfront or rolled into your monthly payment. If you put $0 down, the VA funding fee is 2.3% of the total cost of the loan in 2022, although you can lower it to 1.65% by putting at least 5% down. Also, if you have a low credit score or have experienced a major financial setback, like bankruptcy, it's usually easier to qualify for this loan than for a conventional or FHA loan. That said, it's important to know you can't waive any contingencies with a VA loan that might make your offer more attractive to a seller. You'll learn all about this in Step 4. Make a Strong Offer.

Indian Home Loan Guarantee

The Indian Home Loan Gaurantee Program lesser-known program reserved for American Indian or Alaska Native families, including Alaska villages, tribes, or tribally designated housing entities. While buyers must be considered creditworthy, there is no hard-and-fast credit score requirement, and the loan requires a minimum down payment of 2.5%. You can learn more about this program, also known as Section 184, at https://www.hud.gov/program_offices/public_indian_housing/ih/homeownership/184.

> Note: You may be able to get multiple offers for the same type of loan – so make sure to shop around for the best rate!

Will Your Monthly Payment Work with Your Budget?

Need help figuring out whether the monthly payment from your mortgage will work with your budget? I like Rocket Mortgage's calculator because it estimates your total monthly payment, including your mortgage plus any estimated taxes and insurance. Find it on my resources page at www.wealthonadime.com/resources.

If you're not sure you'll be able to float the new monthly payment, or you're on the fence, one other thing you could do is test out the payment with a new budget for a few months to make sure it feels comfortable. If the monthly payment would be larger than your current rent, simply deduct the difference and transfer it to a savings account for the time being. If you can handle that for a few months and it still feels good while meeting your other money goals, then you should be good to go.

How Much Can You Get Approved For?

Remember your DTI ratio from Chapter 6? Your DTI ratio measures your anticipated monthly debt versus your income – which is important for lenders who decide what you can get approved for but should also be important to you. If factoring in your estimated mortgage payment brings your DTI higher than 36%, it may be a red flag that your budget will be stretched too thin if you move ahead with the property. If that's the case, consider waiting till you can afford a higher down payment, to reduce your monthly mortgage payment and lessen the burden on your budget.

> Reminder: If your DTI is over 43%, it's less likely you'll be approved for a qualified mortgage.

First-Time Homebuyer Programs

In addition to the different types of loans that might be available to you (e.g., conventional, FHA, etc.), your state may offer a special program, tax credit, or tax deduction for first-time homebuyers. Unlike government-backed loans, these are usually open to a larger set of money makers, regardless of income or credit score. If offered, they'll likely provide some type of financial assistance toward your down payment, a tax credit (which reduces the amount of taxes you owe), or a tax deduction (which reduces the amount of your income that is taxed). The specific types of programs and down-payment assistance offered varies by state, and you can find links to all of them (organized by state) through the U.S. Department of Housing and Urban Development here: https://www.hud.gov/topics/rental_assistance/local.

Public Housing Assistance for First-Time Homebuyers

At the national level, the only other major type of assistance is reserved for those who benefit from public housing assistance, called the Homeowner Voucher Program. Essentially, the program provides vouchers that can be used for meeting monthly payments. To apply to the program, you must be a first-time homebuyer and will need to contact your local public housing agency.

Other Ways to Bring Down Your Costs

After you've decided the type of loan you might be eligible for, there are still a few other areas where you might be able to save throughout the homebuying process. While your real estate agent or mortgage lender may recommend certain companies to provide the services shown in Table 12.1, remember that you can still shop around for the best rates/companies. Some of them may only save you a little bit – while others, like title insurance, can save you hundreds. While a few hundred bucks might not sound like a lot now, it can be helpful to set aside for a future home repair, or fixing something up after you move in.

Table 12.1   Homeownership Costs You Can Shop For

Service/Item	Average Cost	How Much You Can Save
Mortgage	Depends on the home	Thousands to tens of thousands over the life of the loan
Title Insurance	$500–$2,000	$500–$1,000
Homeowner's Insurance	Varies by state, with an average in 2022 of $1,383 for a $250,000 home across the United States	Lower your costs by changing your deductible, bundling with other types of insurance, or getting certain upgrades like a home security system.
Inspection	$350–500	$100–200

Step 2: Shop Around for Lenders

I recommend shopping for lenders the second you're really serious about purchasing a home. The reason is that if you're pre-qualified or pre-approved, you can make an offer ASAP as soon as you find the house you want. Especially in a competitive market where homes are flying off the market in a matter of hours or days, you want to be able to move quicker than the next money maker. Getting pre-qualified or pre-approved can help.

What's the difference? Getting *pre-qualified* usually involves a "soft credit inquiry" and will give you a good idea of what mortgage you're likely to get approved for – but that could always change. I recommend getting pre-qualified before starting the search for your home. Getting *pre-approved,* on the other hand, requires a lender to run a *hard credit pull,* which will impact your credit score (you don't want too many of those while home shopping), but gives you an extra level of confidence you'll be able to deliver on an offer quickly.

Reminder: if you're worried about your credit, check out my Quick Guide to Improving Your Credit in Appendix A.

Other things you want to consider in shopping for lenders:

- **What interest rate are they offering?** Getting a lower interest rate is usually the main factor to consider when shopping for mortgages. The lower the interest rate, the more money you're going to save over time. Keep in mind that even a fraction of a percentage can cost you hundreds of thousands of dollars over time, depending on the total cost of the home.

- **Do you want a fixed or adjustable mortgage?** Using an adjustable rate *mortgage* (ARM) means your lender has the right to change the interest rate and monthly payment on your mortgage over time. Instead, I strongly recommend choosing a fixed mortgage so there are no surprises. Keep in mind if rates drop later, you can likely refinance at that time. While an ARM may be lower than a fixed rate initially, there's nothing stopping the lender from increasing the rate down the road. I strongly caution against this and would not recommend an adjustable mortgage to a friend.

- **Consider using "points"?** Mortgage points or "origination points" allow a lender to reduce the interest rate from what you'd normally get approved for on a loan. Every point reduces your mortgage by 0.25% – which makes a big difference – but will also cost you 1% of the total mortgage price. For example, if you're taking out a mortgage of $275,000, then one mortgage point, or a 0.25% reduction in your interest rate, would cost $2,750 (or 1% of $275,000). Keep in mind this is an upfront cost to be paid at the time of closing. Your lender may also allow you to buy a fraction of a point or more than one point, depending on how far you'd like to go.

Once you have your down payment saved and an idea of what you'll get approved for, it's time for the fun part – finding your dream home!

Step 3: Find Your Home

Note: for the purpose of this section, we'll refer to a realtor, real estate agent, or broker as a "real estate agent" throughout.

While there are several places you can start the search for your home, like Zillow or Rocket Homes, eventually you'll want a realtor to help you with the process. Why? Because they're in the best position to structure your offer, as well as catch things you might not notice when touring homes or items you'll want the inspector to pay extra attention to, such as differences in the type of heat and their cost over time.

My two cents? While you don't actually *need* a realtor to buy a home – it's not a requirement – you want to have one, especially since the seller pays their fee (not you). This is definitely a situation where you want someone on your side who's an expert in this area – and that's what a realtor does. It's their job to know the market, do their best to make sure that offer goes through, and get the home you're looking for as smoothly as possible.

In my case, I was already working with a realtor when I came across the listing for the condo in my neighborhood. That said, my realtor was still extremely helpful in guiding me through the ins and outs of the homebuying process. With her help, I was able to weigh all the pros and cons of the unit, its costs, and be super-confident when I finally made my offer. Five years later, even though I now rent out that property, it's still the largest purchase I've made to date, and I wouldn't have been as comfortable with it if I hadn't had a realtor that I trusted to answer my questions along the way.

Long story short: Find a realtor you trust, who isn't pushy, and is willing to answer every question under the sun. The right one will have your best interest at heart to make the process go as smoothly as possible.

Step 4: Make a Strong Offer

Making an offer is undoubtedly the most suspenseful part of the entire homebuying process. Think of it like an auction. You're safer aiming high than aiming low, but obviously you want a number you're comfortable with, and you don't want to pay more than you have to. This is also when you'll write a check for your EMD – for many, the largest check they'll ever write, prior to the full down payment on closing day.

This is also where your realtor really comes in handy. They're likely to be a lot more familiar with the local housing market than you are, and this is a scenario where surrounding yourself with people more knowledgeable than you (or me) in a specific area can really pay off.

Something I didn't realize before I bought my home is that making a strong offer involves many other factors than just the price. Are you waiving any *contingencies,* or requirements that are generally agreed to as part of the offer, like an appraisal or inspection contingency? Are you pre-approved so you can close quickly? All of these things come into play, and your realtor is in the best position to help you structure it. Of course, nothing happens without your say-so, and just because an offer is accepted doesn't mean you'll end up closing on the home (though it is likely).

One trick you might have up your sleeve when making an offer is what's called an *escalation clause*. If you're really serious about a home, an escalation clause can increase the chances that your offer will get accepted. It does this by automatically increasing the price of your offer by whatever amount you specify, for example, $2,500 or $5,000. Worried about your price going too high? You can also set a limit for what you want your offer to increase up to, and the escalation clause only goes into effect if there is another offer.

For example, if you wanted a house being sold for $300,000, but were worried about competing offers, you might put in an offer starting at $300,000 with an escalation clause in increments of $5,000 up to $340,000. In this example, if another offer went up to $325,000, your escalation clause would go into effect $5,000 increments at a time, to $330,000 (the minimum escalation needed to beat the other offer).

Once you put your offer in, escalation clause or not, the ball is in the seller's court. Usually, you'll hear a response in a day or two, though it can take longer in some cases.

Lastly, depending on the state you live in, if the seller hasn't already provided their *real estate disclosures*, you should ask for these now, though they'll be required to do so at least three days before closing. Some states even require them before you make an offer. Disclosures will document what appliances are included, if there's anything they need to disclose about structural units, like the roof for example, as well as whether there's been any other major issues with the property – like a pest control issue.

Step 5: Finalize Your Mortgage

Once your offer has been accepted, you'll need to finalize the terms of your mortgage with the lender of your choice. This is why it's always better if you start your search for a lender early, ideally getting pre-approved in advance. That said, you can change your lender after pre-approval if all of a sudden you get a bad vibe or are offered a better deal.

Finalizing this process will involve a full mortgage application, a hard credit check, including a slew of paperwork you'll need to submit, ranging from pay stubs to bank statements. Once your application is submitted, your lender will provide what's called an official *loan estimate* – this has all the details of what's estimated to be included in your mortgage and future monthly payment. It also includes any fees, points, and/or credits that may be extended. You'll see something similar called a *closing disclosure* later in the process, that will confirm these costs or note any changes on closing day.

Step 6: Get Your Inspection

Repeat after me: Get an inspection on your future home *no matter what*. Even if you waive an *inspection contingency*, meaning your offer could go through regardless of whether something comes up in the inspection (which may make your offer more attractive to the seller), an inspection is still worth it just so you know what you're getting into. You can still get an inspection even if you waive the inspection contingency, you just can't use the results to renegotiate the offer. Worst-case scenario, if something was terribly wrong or super expensive to fix, you could still back out by forfeiting your earnest deposit.

An inspection is paid for by you, the buyer, and usually costs anywhere between $200 and $500 depending on the size of the home. While it sucks to have another thing to pay for, it's worth it to catch anything your buyer may not have disclosed. Once completed, the inspector will provide you with a full report. Depending on your offer, the seller may be required to fix any identified issues prior to selling the property, or it may be something for you to fix if you waived the inspection contingency.

Again, waiving an inspection contingency doesn't stop you from getting an inspection, it simply means you can't use it to renegotiate or withdraw your offer without losing your deposit.

Step 7: Get Homeowners Insurance

In some cases, your homeowners insurance may be wrapped up with your mortgage as part of your monthly payment. In others, you'll pay it directly, but that doesn't mean you can't shop around for it.

You'll need to have your homeowner's insurance in place at least three days before your closing.

Step 8: Final Walk-Through

Before closing on the property, you'll have a final walk-through regardless of the inspection or whether the seller was required to fix anything. This is your chance to make sure everything is still intact (e.g., appliances, light fixtures) and the home as not been damaged, for example, by the seller moving out. If the seller was required to fix anything, know that it might not be done to your satisfaction – some may only do the bare minimum to continue with the sale – but hopefully that's not the case!

Step 9: Closing Day!

It's time to celebrate!

Closing day is when you actually get the keys to your home. You'll likely have to sign a bunch of paperwork on the day of closing, including a closing disclosure, which is basically the final form of your loan estimate that details the final terms of your loan, final closing costs, and so on. If anything has changed from your original loan estimate, it will be included in that disclosure.

Once the paperwork is all done, you'll get your keys, and you're all set! So, get ready to pop your favorite bottle, plan a housewarming party, and enjoy!

Building Wealth with Real Estate

Up until now, we've covered all the basics of buying a home as your primary residence – but what if you're looking to real estate as a strategy to build wealth? In this section, we'll cover three strategies you might use – nothing too crazy, but very useful if you're looking to invest more in real estate over time. They include:

- **House hacking:** when you live in one part of the home and rent out the others to cover your costs; either through room-mates or by purchasing a multi-family unit.

- **Flipping a home:** this is one way to make some quick money on a house, but it's not without its risks, which we'll cover in just a bit.

- **Using a 1031 exchange:** real estate investors use this to avoid paying capital gains tax on the sale of one investment property, so long as the profits from that home are used to buy another one.

House Hacking

House hacking is the process by which you rent out a portion of your home, using that rental income to pay your mortgage. If you're don't mind roommates or managing a multifamily unit – like a home with an apartment in it, or a duplex – it can be a great way for you to build wealth by letting rental income pay a portion (if not all of) your mortgage loan. That said, as landlord of the unit, it's not without its caveats. Here's what you can expect if you plan to house-hack.

- Be prepared to cover and handle any and all repairs not covered by homeowners or renters insurance.

- If renting fully furnished, make sure you account for those costs too.

- Expect that finding a good tenant can take time, and that you may lose a month or two of rent in finding new tenants when a previous tenant leaves. FYI, services like Zillow rental manager and MySmartMove can help you screen tenants for criminal history, credit, and so on, though you will need the prospective tenant's permission to do so

- In most states, you'll need a business license to rent out a portion of your home.

An alternative way to invest in real estate

In addition to directly buying or flipping a real estate property, real estate investment trusts (REITs) are one way that you can invest in real estate without having to buy a piece of land or property outright. In most cases, to invest in a REIT means you're investing in a company that buys, sells, and/or manages multiple investment properties using money pooled from investors like you (see Figure 12.2). As the company generates profits from that investment, the investors receive a portion of that profit in the form of a dividend. Unlike regular stocks, these are considered "non-qualified" dividends and taxed as ordinary income.

Figure 12.2   Real Estate Investment Trusts (REITs)

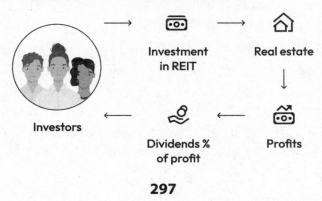

Investors

Investment in REIT

Real estate

Dividends % of profit

Profits

Flipping a Home

If you've ever seen an HGTV episode, then there's a solid chance you are already familiar with the concept of flipping a home: you buy a home, invest a certain amount of money in repairs or a rebuild, and then sell it at a profit. What you may not know is the best way to go about doing that.

For starters, if you know you might be interested in flipping a home from the get-go, you should consider bringing in a contractor before putting an offer on a home to give you an estimate of how much time and money it might take to get the job done. That estimate may also inform how much you're willing to put down on the home.

Homes usually increase in value in one of two ways – they might *appreciate,* growing in value over time, which would be a "buy and hold" strategy, or you can make *capital improvements* that increase the value of the home through repairs and/or upgrades. This section focuses on capital improvements, which hopefully result in a profit after it's sold! If you plan to make capital improvements, you can use what's called the *70% rule* to guide what price you may be willing to pay for an investment property.

The 70% Rule

If you plan to make improvements from the get-go, one rule of thumb to determine how much you want to offer on a home is called the *70% rule.* This means you'd offer no more than 70% of what you expect the home to be worth *after* any improvements, minus the cost of those repairs. While it's not a requirement of any kind, the rule is intended to make sure you don't go totally crazy on the offer. It also helps reduce your risk. For example, if you expect that you might spend $40,000 on repairs and sell a home for $300,000, then you wouldn't spend more than $170,000 on that home. The selling price is also known as *the after-repair value* (ARV).

Purchase price = (70% × expected sale price) – repair costs
Example: (70% × $300,000) – $40,000 = $170,000

Of course, this is just one rule of thumb. Only you will know how confident you are in your ability to flip a property given current market conditions, the conditions of the home, and how much money you have to put into that home.

Lastly, in calculating your potential profit on a home, make sure to account for the cost of holding the property while you're improving it. For every month that goes by, you'll be on the hook for that mortgage, utilities, HOA, etc., which makes time just as important as the cost of repairs here. This is known as the *cost of holding* a property. Remember that you'll also be required to pay capital gains tax on any profit from the sale.

If selling the property immediately after repairs wouldn't get you the profit you're looking for, consider renting a few years to pay down the mortgage and build more equity in the home.

Want an easy way to estimate your profit from flipping a home? I include a simple calculator at www.wealthonadime.com/resources. Below are the calculations you'd need to run the numbers yourself.

Calculating the Return on Your Real Estate Investment

1. Total investment = Down payment + Cost of repairs + Cost of holding the property

2. Gross profit = Sale price – Seller's closing costs (between 3 and 10% of the sale price) – Total investment – Remaining mortgage balance

3. Total net profit = Gross profit – Capital gains tax on sale

Funding Your Repairs

Thinking about making some improvements on your home? While I wouldn't recommend this for a property you plan to flip and sell quickly, if you plan to use it as a rental property or want to improve your current home prior to selling, you might consider using a HELOC or home equity loan (covered in the previous chapter) to fund the improvements – the idea being that when you sell the home, you make your money back. That said, keep in mind either option will put you on the hook for a higher set of monthly expenses, and may take some time for the money to come through. It also requires you to have equity in a home, which you may not have if you went with a small down payment or haven't already been paying your mortgage for several years. It can take about 45 days to get access to a HELOC and anywhere from two weeks to two months for a home equity loan, depending on the lender. You'll also want to make sure there is no prepayment penalty on the HELOC or home equity loan, so you can pay it back ASAP after the sale to save money in interest – most of them don't have prepayment penalties, but it never hurts to check!

> Reminder: Just like your mortgage or a credit card, you'll want to shop around for the best rate on a HELOC or home equity loan.

Using a 1031 Exchange

If you've ever read *Rich Dad, Poor Dad* by Robert Kiyopsaki, you probably already know about this tactic for real estate investors interested in owning investment properties. Here's how a 1031 exchange works. Let's say you have one rental or investment property. You bought it for $300,000 and sell it for $350,000. Normally you would have to pay capital gains tax (which we learned about in Chapter 8) on that $50,000 profit. But with a 1031 exchange, you can legally use that $350,000 sale to go toward another investment property without paying those taxes. This means, assuming the value of your properties continues to increase, you can continue to level up without paying capital gains. The big caveat is that a 1031 exchange cannot be used for a primary residence – although you may have had a primary residence that turned into a rental or real estate investment property, which would be okay. It's definitely an advanced strategy, but one that's good to know of if you end up buying investment property down the line.

To check whether the 1031 exchange would work for the property you're considering, use what's called *the napkin test*. This is an easy way to check that the new property you're buying is of equal or increased value, and requires you hold equal or increased equity as the home you "exchange" it for.

Figure 12.3 is an example of what that might look like.

If for any reason you were to fail the napkin test, for example, the

Figure 12.3 The Napkin Test

Category	Property A	Property B
Value	$200,000	$300,000
Equity (down payment)	$50,000	$75,000
Mortgage	$150,000	$225,000

value of property B is less than the value of property A, then you'd be taxed on that portion – known as *the boot*.

There is no limit on how many times you can use a 1031 exchange, and the exchange can be used in any state and across states as part of the federal tax code. While it must involve "like-kind" property, it includes single-family and multi-family units, vacation properties, commercial property, and land so long as it's used for business or investment purposes.

Lastly, here are some frequently asked questions (FAQs) about 1031 exchanges – though if you're seriously considering one, I highly recommend you speak to a tax professional.

- **Q:** Can I do a 1031 exchange if I've already sold my property?
    - o Yes, you have 45 days from the time of closing to identify a new property (if you haven't already) and 180 days in total from the date of closing on Property A to closing on Property B .
- **Q:** I'm not comfortable with the idea of selling one property before I've bought the other. What can I do?
    - o You can use a "Reverse 1031," which is where you buy Property B first, then have the same number of days to close the sale on Property A. Obviously this requires more upfront cash or financing to purchase Property B before you have the proceeds of Property A, but it is possible.

I hope this chapter was helpful in leveling up what you know about the homebuying process, and maybe even teaching you a strategy or two you can use as you build your empire moving forward.

Summary

So that's it, money maker! Another chapter down, only one to go! Here's a quick recap of what you learned this chapter:

- The nine steps to buying a home.
- What to consider when selecting your lender or reviewing a mortgage offer.

- The items and services you can shop around for during the homebuying process.

- The 70% rule for estimating how much to spend on a home you intend to flip.

- How you might avoid paying capital gains tax on an investment property using a 1031 exchange.

Still have questions? I'd love to hear them! Shoot me a message at hello@beworthfinance.com.

Closing

Wow WoW WoW!

CONGRATULATIONS, money maker!

::airhorn:: airhorn:: airhorn::

Can you believe you made it through 12 chapters worth of learning how to level up your money?

How ya feeling?!

Hopefully, financial freedom is just around the corner for you. My biggest dream for you isn't that you become super-wealthy overnight (though that would be amazing), but rather that you understand and feel confident about the steps you can take to get there over time.

You made a lot of strides in this book, money maker! You learned how to build a budget, automate your finances using the Money Moves System, accelerate your debt payoff plan, and a bunch of tactics you can use while investing. I can't wait to see you put those money gems and million dollar habits to work!

You also learned a few lessons from other money makers like Claire, Julia, Eric, and Tanya. We saw how Claire readjusted her spending to get ahead of her credit card debt while keeping her non-negotiables like a gym membership intact. We felt for Julia as she dealt with some tough emotions in relation to her family and money, but was eventually able to set some boundaries so she could continue to help them while also contributing to her own goals. We followed Eric as he implemented the Money Moves System and realized that managing his money didn't have to be as complicated as he thought – he's pretty pumped about that trip to Banff next year! And lastly, we saw Tanya level up her money game, making huge strides with her investments to be the first millionaire in her family.

And now, it's your turn to take control of your financial future.

Have you learned something that can help you take one step forward when it comes to your money? A way to plan for your money goals beyond the immediate future? A new strategy when it comes to investing?

To be honest, I knew you'd do it all along.

In the first chapter of this book, I asked you what financial freedom meant to you, and if you followed the steps in this book, you wrote an answer as part of your Chapter 1 worksheet. Now, I want to ask whether you feel any closer to your own version of financial freedom, or maybe your definition of what that means has changed.

Don't tell me . . . I want you to define it for yourself. You can't get closer to something if you don't know what it is, so let me know your definition here:

_____

_____

_____

Nice!

Now, if you haven't already, take a few minutes to be proud of yourself because not everyone would have (a) made the decision to face a topic like personal finance head-on, and (b) have stuck with it through all 12 chapters. You're officially a money-making rockstar, and I can't wait to see what moves you make next!

To ensure that you keep this ball rolling, I want you to take a few minutes to outline your most important takeaways from the book and your next or most important steps, even if they're for a goal that's off in the distance.

Most Important Takeaways

1. _____
   _____
   _____

2. _____
   _____
   _____

3. _____
   _____
   _____

4. _____
   _____
   _____

5. _____
   _____
   _____

Your Next Money Moves

1. _____
   _____
   _____

2. _____
   _____
   _____

3. _____

_____

_____

4. _____

_____

_____

5. _____

_____

_____

Money maker, I am so proud of you!! And I can't wait to see what you do next.

When I first started Beworth Finance, my goal was to teach a few other women like me the basics about how they could improve their money. Writing a book like this to reach thousands of other money makers *like you* has been an absolute privilege, and I only hope you learned something that you can pass along to your inner circle.

Thank you for bringing me along for the ride.

Wishing you good fortune, in all ways,

Kimberly Hamilton

Founder, Beworth Finance

Appendix

Improve Your Credit Score Guide

As I mentioned earlier in the book, I'm not against the use of credit cards by any means and am happy for any money maker to use them so long as you do so responsibly. Instead of thinking of credit as a bad thing, I consider it a tool – just like your money – to live your best financial life. And to use that tool, you're going to want a solid credit score.

Why Having a Credit Score Is Important

Your credit score is a measure of how likely you are to pay back a given debt, such as a credit card or personal loan, based on several factors taken from your credit history. It's used by lenders to determine how likely you are to pay back a loan or credit card; they also use it to decide the terms of your offer, such as what interest rate is attached to your credit card or loan. If you've used a credit card, took out a loan, or were affiliated with someone else's credit before (for example, you were an authorized user on a credit card), then you already have a credit score. If you've never used credit, you might not have one yet – and you'll likely want to change that so you can be eligible for credit offers moving forward.

Having a high credit score is great because you are more likely to get approved and receive a better interest rate. If you have a poor credit score, or no credit history at all, you'll want to improve it – not just for financial reasons, but also for other areas of your life where credit can be important. For example, a landlord may run a credit check when you're applying for an apartment, or a potential employer may run a credit check when you're applying for a job (in both cases, they are required to inform you before doing so).

Your Credit Score Versus Credit Report

Your credit score is calculated based on the information tracked and reported by three major credit reporting agencies: Equifax, Experian, and TransUnion. Credit reports do just as they say: they report on a bunch of details related to your credit history, going back seven years. Your report will also show any accounts you had open in the past seven years, as well as any mistakes you may have made, like a missed payment or debt that went to collections. While credit scores use the same type of information, your exact score will vary depending on the scoring model.

The two most popular models included a FICO score and a Vantage score. While the exact makeup of any credit score is unknown, we do know the basic factors. The percentages below are for a FICO score, though it's important to note that your payment history is most important regardless of the scoring model.

- Payment history (35%): Do you make payments on time?
- Amounts owed (30%): How much did you owe at the end of your last billing cycle, and what percentage of your available credit limit are you actually using? Ideally, you want both numbers to be low.
- New credit (10%): The goal here is to NOT apply for a bunch of credit cards or loans at the same time. Space them out to get a higher score.
- Length of credit history (15%): How long have you used credit for?
- Credit mix (10%): Do you have a mix of different credit (credit cards, loans, mortgage, etc.)?

Where to Find Your Credit Score

There are three main institutions that provide individual credit reports: Equifax, Experian, and TransUnion. Your report may look slightly different across the three agencies – I recommend Experian's because I think their layout is easiest to read. You can also download your credit report once a year, free of charge (and weekly during the pandemic) at www.annualcreditreport.com.

Got your credit score? Below are some general guidelines to see where you stack up.

Credit Score Rating	FICO Model	Vantage Score Model
Exceptional/Excellent	800–850	781–850
Very Good/Good	740–799	661–780
Good/Fair	670–739	601–660
Fair/Poor	580–669	500–600
Poor / Very Poor	300–579	300–499

If you're on the higher end of that scale, congratulations! Lenders will love you. If you're on the lower end, you'll want to work on improving your score to ensure you can get approved and get a good interest rate on your next line of credit or loan.

How to Improve Your Credit Score

Based on the credit score factors above, there are a few things you can do to improve your credit score ASAP, and then in the long run over time. This is helpful to know so you don't focus your efforts on areas that might not have a big impact, or are very difficult to change (for example, length of credit history).

Here are some things you can do in the short term to improve your credit score ASAP.

If You're Starting from Scratch (No Credit History)

- **Still need to build credit? Try a secured card:** A secured card requires you to provide funding up front, which acts similar to a security deposit to protect the lender in event of non-payment. This way, the lender takes less of a risk and can still extend you a card you can use to build or improve your credit so long as it's paid off regularly.

- **Get yourself added as an authorized user:** If you're just starting to build your credit, getting yourself added as an authorized user can help build your credit quickly. That said, the opposite is true – if someone has a bad score and adds you as an authorized user, you can take on components of their score, so make sure it's someone you trust who makes their payments on time.

If You Already Have Some Credit History

- **Strive to meet your payments:** As the no. 1 credit-scoring factor regardless of the scoring model, you should strive to do this immediately and moving forward to improve your credit in the long run.

- **Make more frequent payments to keep your utilization low:** Credit utilization, or the percentage of your total available credit limit you use, has a 30% impact on your credit score. By making more frequent payments instead of one monthly payment, you help keep this number low, helping your credit score.

- **Report your rent and utilities:** Rent, utilities, and phone bill payments made via check, Venmo, or your checking account aren't included in your credit score because they don't involve a debt. That said, companies like Level Credit are making it possible to report these payments for a reasonable fee (like $5–6/month) to help improve your credit. Some companies will even go back to report more than one year of history, which is awesome (so long as you're making those payments on time). Personally, I love this idea because it's a great way to build credit using things you already and consistently pay for, as opposed to putting yourself at further risk with a new credit card.

To view my top recommendations for secured cards, rent reporting companies, and debt consolidation apps, visit www. wealthonadime.com/resources.

- **Double-check your credit report:** If you see any discrepancies in your credit report – for example, a credit card marked delinquent you know you paid on time – having it corrected could help improve your credit history and score. On the flip side, if there is fraudulent activity, like a bank account you don't recognize, you definitely want to be aware of it. You can report discrepancies by visiting the website of each credit reporting agency (it's a pain, but you'll need to contact them all separately since not all may have the discrepancy on their respective report) . If you believe you may be a victim of identity theft, you can report it at https://www.identitytheft.gov/.

- **Call your lender(s):** Your lender may be willing to work with you to lower your monthly payment, anything that might help you improve your payment history moving forward. Changing your payment due date to be closer to after you paid may also be helpful here, making it a bit easier to make your payment.

Lastly, while there's an argument that taking out additional lines of credit can help improve your score, I don't recommend it. Payment history and credit utilization will have a larger impact, so I recommend focusing on those factors first.

Fintech Apps That Can Help

Finance apps like Rocket Money can help you monitor your credit score and report, to help you keep tabs on your score and provide insights on where to focus your efforts. You may have also heard of companies like Tally that can help you pay down your credit card debt, hopefully improving your score in the process. Most of these are essentially technology-focused consolidation companies, aiming to get you a lower interest rate and/or monthly payment, and will involve a small fee (this is normal) to handle that process. While they won't eliminate your debt, consolidation can help you keep up with payments and make it less expensive for you over time.

A Word on Credit Card Points

Full disclaimer, I'm a big fan of using credit card points and rewards in exchange for travel. I've funded entire trips, I love airport lounge access, and there are other perks like no foreign transaction fees depending on the card (I'm obsessed with my Chase Sapphire card). All that said, the points are definitely NOT worth it if you're unable to pay any credit card in full – in which case, you're making interest payments that outweigh the benefit of any possible points scenario. So don't do it for the points, but enjoy the perks so long as you're on top of it.

If You Need Some Serious Assistance

If you're having major trouble keeping up with your debt payments, I highly recommend contacting the National Foundation for Credit Counseling (NFCC). The NFCC is an incredible resource to help those with debt in collections or otherwise struggling to meet their minimum payments. Through the NFCC you can connect with a nonprofit credit counseling agency that will help you in considering a debt management plan, different from the debt settlement plans you may have heard about (and have a reputation for scams). Through a free or low-cost debt management plan, the credit agency will work with lenders to try and get you a lower interest rate, paused payments, and so on to help pay down your debt. They'll be able to walk you through the details to determine if a debt management plan is right for you.

Institutions and policies to protect you

- The Fair Credit Reporting Act protects money makers against unfair use and reporting of your credit-related information. As part of the act, companies that report your credit information have specific obligations and the duty to investigate any disputed information. It also means you have the right to know what's in your credit file and the right to dispute any information that is inaccurate or incomplete.

- The Equal Credit Opportunity Act prohibits lenders from discriminating against applicants on the basis of race, color, religion, national origin, sex, marital status, or age. If you believe you or someone you know has been discriminated against, you can report it online at https://civilrights.justice.gov/

- The Consumer Financial Protection Bureau (CFPB) was established in 2011 by the Obama Administration to protect money makers like you. It's intended to make sure consumers are treated fairly by not just lenders, but by banks and other financial institutions as well – extending past your credit. If you want to submit a complaint about a financial product or service, need help with your finances during the pandemic, or have some other inquiry, you can learn more on the CFPB website at https://www.consumerfinance.gov/.

Acknowledgments

To my parents, thank you for teaching me the value of a dollar and demonstrating a strong work ethic, at work and at home – I couldn't have written this book without either. Thank you for supporting me on every path I've chosen, for always encouraging my thirst for knowledge, no matter how many questions I asked as a kid, and your endless, unwavering support.

To Ross, thank you for constantly reminding me that starting this book was an accomplishment in and of itself, for surprising me with peanut butter cups when I was writing for hours on end, and for seamlessly switching roles between partner and design consultant at a moment's notice. You've cheered me on every step of the way. I am so proud to stand behind the cover you designed and fortunate to have you as a partner.

To my Beworth family, from former students and coaching clients to anyone who has ever liked, followed, learned from, or shared my content. I wrote this book for all of you. Thank you for supporting and being part of this growing community.

To friends and family who have supported me since I started Beworth in 2019. You've been cheerleaders, photographers, focus group participants, market research leads, soundboards, reviewers, copyeditors, branding consultants, and more. I can't thank you enough.

To my editor, Julie Kerr, thank you for reviewing countless drafts, your valuable feedback, and your many votes of confidence that I would eventually complete a book I was proud to stand behind. We did it.

Lastly, to the team at John Wiley & Sons for giving me this opportunity. There can never be enough female minority authors in this space, and I am thrilled to count myself as one amongst a growing cadre. This opportunity was wildly unexpected and has challenged me in the best of ways. It's been a privilege to write and I can only hope I pay it forward through the copy. Thank you.

About the Author

Kimberly Hamilton is a former student debt warrior turned financial educator, coach, and speaker. In 2012, with little savings and a newly minted master's degree, Kimberly struggled with almost $45,000 worth of student debt, making $15 an hour. Working for a consulting firm in Washington, DC – one of the top 10 most expensive cities in the United States – she had no clue how to manage her finances but became obsessed with learning how. During this time, she realized that a path to financial freedom and wealth was possible for her, even if she had little savings to work with. Starting small but moving quickly, she was able to pay off her student debt in a little over three years, double her income in four, and buy her first home in five, just before her 30th birthday. If she continues building wealth at the same speed, she'll have the option to retire by age 45.

As a Latina and the first woman on her mother's side to finish college, Kimberly understands the pressure of wanting to be the first in your family to "make it" – and the learning curve that comes with it. Having learned from her own financial struggles and success, Kimberly founded the company Beworth Finance to help others make smart money moves in a way that's relatable to the average money maker. She's led workshops with partners like Capital One Cafe and Ladies Get Paid, and has been seen in *Forbes, Business Insider, Markets Insider, Apartment Therapy, Health* magazine, and other major media outlets. In 2021, she left the field of international development to provide financial education full-time at a major fintech company.

Professionally, Kimberly is a Certified Financial Educational Instructor and holds a master's degree in International Affairs with a concentration in economic development. Personally, she loves a good book (surprise) and a spicy margarita.

To learn more about Kimberly and her work, follow her on social media @BeworthFinance or visit www.BeworthFinance.com.

Index